Week 1/Day 1
Read:
2Th. 1:3 We ought always to thank God for you, brothers, and rightly so, because your faith is growing more and more, and the love every one of you has for each other is increasing.

Reflect:
What I "ought" to do is often not what I actually do. How many "oughts" have you neglected this past week? We are used to seeing "oughts" as oppressive reminders of our constant failing. "Oughts" are a relentless pressure to do better, be better, do more, and be more. I ought always to thank God for you, but I don't always. I may judge or critique or ignore or need or want you. I don't "always" thank God for you, but I ought to. Is this an oppressive, "shame on me" *ought to*? Or is this an invitational, "you really ought to get in on this!"? This *ought* is an invitation to grow in love for God and others. It is an opportunity to enjoy and to appreciate and to love others well. It is my opportunity to experience God more fully and more consistently. God's "oughts" are an invitation to his joy. What God says "ought" to be true for me is the same as what I would want to be true for me if I only saw my life as clearly as he does. Oh, to always want to do what I always ought to do! Do you have a vision for what "ought" to be true of your life being exactly what I want to be true of your life? How would you like to want and to experience exactly what God wants you to want and to experience? This is no pipe dream. This is not only for the super spiritual. This is a possibility that God is holding out to you.   God is all for this, he stands ready to empower you as you move toward him. Will you consistently and intentionally move toward him? Closing the gap on faith and love is a life long process of moving toward God and others. All large movements begin with and are comprised of, single moments. Take this single moment, give it to God as him to make it part of the larger movement of closing the gap.

Day 2
Read:
2Th. 1:3 We ought always to thank God for you, brothers, and rightly so, because your faith is growing more and more, and the love every one of you has for each other is increasing.

Reflect:
Who is the "you" that we ought to always give thanks for? It is our brothers. In the New Testament the plural form of "brothers" regularly refers to both men and women. We ought to give thanks for all of those in our family of faith. Not just the ones I like, respect, prefer. Not just the ones who don't annoy me or don't disagree with me. Not just the ones who think like me, vote like me, and "like" me.

2

We ought to always thank God for all of the ones he has put in our family. You choose your friends, but you don't choose your family. God chooses who will be your biological and spiritual brothers and sisters...your choice is to love them and always thank God for them. Give thanks for those who annoy you. Give thanks for those who have spoken ill of you or have been unkind to you. Give thanks...get a thankful heart...become a thankful person. You cannot love God if you do not love the people God has placed around you. Many want a deeper experience with God, they want his peace and power but they do not want his process. A large part of that process is to learn to love in real and practical ways the people God has given you to love. Not the ones you find it easy to love but all God has given you to love. Close the gap today in love and gratitude for all the ones God has put in your family. Think and act in practical ways. If you want to know God better in "theory" then go love others in theory. If you want to know God in the actual practice of your life, then go love people in actual practice as well.

Day 3
Read:
2Th. 1:3 We ought always to thank God for you, brothers, and rightly so, because your faith is growing more and more, and the love every one of you has for each other is increasing.

Reflect:
Faith is confidence. Who do I trust? Do I have faith in my government, my friends, my job, my intellect, my talents? Relatively speaking it's good to be able to have some confidence, some faith in these things. But in an absolute sense, only God is worthy of our final and complete confidence. He alone is incapable of failure. He alone is able to "hold" our complete faith because no one and nothing can stop him from being faithful. Faith is like a plant: it is a growing thing, or it is a dying thing. It cannot be a static thing. How do I learn to put my ultimate confidence in God? The key words are "growing" and "more and more." Movement, decisions, choices, time, repentance, time...these are the descriptions of "growing." "More and more" is a description of closing the gap day-by-day. If I have arrived, then there is no "more." But in this life we will always be arriving, so our focus must be "more and more." When you feel anxious, look for misplaced confidence. Putting your faith in God will not always remove anxious feelings, but it will help you get at what is often the root cause. Don't worry that progress seems slow; plants grow slowly, but they do grow. If you want to grow in faith, you will. You and God are the only ones who can stop it. He is all for it, so he won't stop it. That leaves only you...what will you choose? Close the gap today by continually transferring trust from self (or anyone or anything else) to God.

3

Day 4
Read:
2Th. 1:3 We ought always to thank God for you, brothers, and rightly so, because your faith is growing more and more, and the love every one of you has for each other is increasing.

Reflect:
Do you really think that every single one of the believers in the church Paul was addressing felt love for each other? Not likely. As best we can tell, it was a good church and love was evident there, but it was not perfect there. What is likely is that they were acting in love for one another even when (especially when?) they did not feel loving or the other was not acting in a lovable way. If you are a Christian, then God dwells in you through the Holy Spirit. If the Holy Spirit dwells in you, then you have the ability to love others and the "desire" to love others on "tap." However, you must truly and continually "tap" into that love source that is available to you. You have at your disposal not just the ability to love people, but the opportunity to grow in your desire to love people. You can actually grow in your Christlike "wanting." Your desires can more and more match his. This is an exciting possibility...to love what I ought! This love Paul is speaking of here is part vision-casting: he sees the seeds budding and is calling the buds to become full-grown trees. Do you love everyone God has put in your sphere of influence? If the Holy Spirit indwells you, then you are at least moving that direction. Do not mistake "like" for "love." You can love someone and be annoyed by them at the same time. But you cannot "act" with love towards someone and continually "act" like they are annoying you. How can you learn to not *act* and also not *be* annoyed by others? How can you learn to feel and express love to others? Christ in you is your hope, your opportunity, your power. This is possible, this is necessary...what will you do today to close the gap?

Day 5
Read:
2Th. 1:3 We ought always to thank God for you, brothers, and rightly so, because your faith is growing more and more, and the love every one of you has for each other is increasing.

Reflect:
Here we see that their love was not yet perfect. It is "increasing," so it had room to grow. God does not grow. He does not increase or improve. Why not? Because he is perfect. He does not change because any change would be a step down from perfection. He does not need to get better at love; his love is perfect. He does not need to understand me better. His understanding of me and everything else is complete.

4

Some have implied that God is petty to number every hair on my head and track sparrows when there are so many other big issues to which he could be paying attention. This is a misunderstanding of the nature of God. His knowledge is immediate and complete. Immediate means he does not have to go get it, read, learn, or collect data; he has all knowledge. Complete means that there is no knowledge that he does not have. So he doesn't "count" hairs on heads or "track sparrows falling"...he knows it all, it is simple to him. We, on the other hand, need to grow in every way possible. We need to always be "increasing." In knowledge, in spiritual fervor, in faith, and, of course, in love. We need to settle this fact in our minds...we are growing in faith and love, or our faith and love are dying, drying up. You are not now and never will be a static being. You are moving in a direction. Move in the direction of faith in your interactions with God and love in your interactions with others.

Week 2/Day 1
Read:
Heb. 11:1 Now faith is being sure of what we hope for and certain of what we do not see. 2 This is what the ancients were commended for.

Reflect:
Some see faith as being in opposition to knowledge or facts. This is incorrect. Faith is confidence. We can be confident of something that is factually true or of something that is factually false. Everyone has faith, all the time. Not everyone has faith in what is *true* all the time. Faith has also been compared to a "blind leap" or a "leap in the dark." Leaping into dark, unknown places is folly, not faith. And if you are blind and must leap, you need someone who can see to tell you where you will land, or you should not leap. But what of trusting God when you cannot see what is ahead? Well then trust God, but that is far from a leap into the dark. That is a wise and rational decision to walk with someone who is never in the dark, who sees everything as it is and will be. Have you ever trusted someone to the point that if they tell you something is true, you don't doubt them? They may be wrong at some point, but their track record is so good you have no reason to doubt them. So acting on the information they give you is never a "leap in the dark"; it is a wise choice based on past experience. This is why it is important to get to know God better and better, both through his word and through personal life experience. Unlike other people, we have learned to trust that he will never be wrong. To put our confidence in him to the point of "taking a leap" is never a blind choice or even a leap into the "unknown." How can it be unknown if we know *him*? How can it be blind when *he* sees everything so clearly? To close the gap on our faith in him we must close the gap on our relationship with him. What will you do and think today in order to close the gap on relationship with God and confidence in God?

5

Day 2
Read:
Heb. 11:1 Now faith is being sure of what we hope for and certain of what we do not see. 2 This is what the ancients were commended for.

Reflect:
What do you hope for? We hope for certain kinds of weather, health, election outcomes, sports scores. These hopes are normal and part of being human. But what do you ultimately hope for? What is the one hope that supersedes all other hopes? Do you know? Do you give it consistent thought? Do you talk much about it to others? What we hope for shapes who we are. Because we live out of our hopes, we could, if we were attentive enough, be able to tell what a person is hoping for by listening to their words and watching their actions. What do you hope for? Is it enough to hold through this life and beyond? We can be sure of what we hope for as long as our hope is well-placed. When our hopes are misplaced, then our confidence will be misguided, or more likely we will consistently live with insecurity rather than confidence. Hope for health, hope for good weather on a day off, hope for a raise, hope for any number of normal things. But above all else guard your heart, and make sure your ultimate hope—the one hope that keeps all other hopes tethered to what is real—is in the gospel. Hope for eternal life. Hope for peace with God. Hope that you will be accepted into the beloved when this life is over. Hope that what you do, when done for Christ, will matter forever. Hope that he will never leave you or forsake. Think about, talk about, and live out of the gospel hope. This is hope of which you can be sure. Close the gap on your faith today...think about and talk about your ultimate hope.

Day 3
Read:
Heb. 11:1 Now faith is being sure of what we hope for and certain of what we do not see. 2 This is what the ancients were commended for.

Reflect:
Certainty in the current age is a sign of arrogance. We are not supposed to be certain of things because it means we think we "know." If we "know" something that someone else does not believe to be true, then we are labeled unkind and judgmental. The overall cultural trend is towards a worldview where the only certainty is what I feel (who can debate that?) and what humans can discover. These trends are moving away from a God who reveals what is certain. A contributing factor in this movement is a history of people misusing "certainty."

How many people have done great harm by claiming to have a "word from God"? This kind of certainty is a kind of final "trump" card. Who can debate "certainty" that comes out of a word from God himself? This person welds great power. Institutions and individuals have misused the power of "certainty" and have caused many to be suspicious of anyone who claims a "certainty" from God. But is certainty arrogance? Can it not be confidence? How can we live well without certainty? Should I be certain about what I am giving my life for? Should I not have certainty about what happens when this life is over? Does God want me to live with certainty in the areas that form the foundations for who I am and what I do with my days? Of course he does! Do not pretend to be certain about things you are not. If you do not know something, admit it. But do not hesitate to be certain about things God has revealed to us. It is not arrogant to have received a gift of certainty. Thank God today that you can be certain. Close the gap today on your certainty...be humble regarding the things you don't know for sure, and be confident regarding the things you do. Confident, grateful, humble.

Day 4
Read:
Heb. 11:1 Now faith is being sure of what we hope for and certain of what we do not see. 2 This is what the ancients were commended for.

Reflect:
What are you certain of that you do not right now see? The list is quite long: events in your history, people in your past, your own heart and brain, gravity, air. We sometimes try to make our faith yield to proof that is not required elsewhere. "God, show me!" "Unless I see I will not believe!" Jesus said those who have not seen and believed are blessed. What makes them so? It is because what is most vital is currently unavailable to the human eye. We do not see God, yet everything depends on him. We do not see God, yet our purpose comes from him. Those who have placed their confidence in God even though they have not seen him are blessed precisely because they are living their lives in line with what ultimately matters the most. To believe without seeing is not irrational; it is to realize that what is seen is ultimately temporary. What is unseen is eternal. What is irrational is to only believe what you see. To do this means you doubt most of what is real because most of what is real is currently not available for you to see. C. S. Lewis said that he believes in God like he believes in the sun. Not because he sees it, but because of it he sees everything else. To not see and yet believe is to be positioned to see everything as it actually is. Close the gap today on believing what you are not seeing and not being over impressed with what you are currently seeing.

7

Day 5
Read:

Heb. 11:1 Now faith is being sure of what we hope for and certain of what we do not see. 2 This is what the ancients were commended for.

Reflect:

The "ancients"...an impressive word. It means ancestors, those who have gone before us. Since what matters most at the end matters most now, then a great place to learn about what matters now is from those who have come to an end. God commended the ancients for their faith. Their journey is finished, the final chapter written, and what did God write on their "tombstones"? "Here lies the ancients, I commend them for their faith." So of all he could have said about them, "They worked hard", "They endured much", "They made an impact", God commended them for their faith. Why? It was their faith that led to all the other commendable aspects of their lives. Their work was prompted by faith, as was their endurance and their love. All the many commendable aspects of those in our spiritual lineage are "sub-aspects" of their faith. They believed God and from that belief flowed acts of faith. What if you decided that "faith" was the most commendable quality you could have? What if you made it your ambition to be a man or woman who actually "believed God"? Not for some miracle, but rather you believed God by actually loving people around you: forgiving them, serving them, refusing to see them as roadblocks to your own interests but rather as your main interest. Faith is not a detached, otherworldly demeanor. Faith is impressive to God, commendable to him...because it causes us to live as if he really exists. It results in actionable love for others. Our faith in him shows up in the way we act towards others. Close the gap today on "the commendation of God"...live with faith, revealed in love.

Week 3/Day 1
Read:

Heb.11:3 By faith we understand that the universe was formed at God's command, so that what is seen was not made out of what was visible.

Reflect:

"In the beginning God..." This is how the Bible begins. It begins with ultimate reality, the one who has always been and will always be. It does not start with man or earth or the universe but with God. All of our thinking must begin at the same place. This is not weir, or unreasonable; it is critical to coming to right conclusions about our lives and the world in which we live. All thinking processes and conclusions have a starting point, a beginning. If the starting point is me, or mankind, or math, or finances, or gravity, then the chain of thought will follow from there. So how do you begin a thinking process with God?

How can I do math problems or spreadsheets beginning with God? That seems silly. It simply means that in all of our thinking and living and believing, we begin with the reality of God. He has always been, he will always be. Therefore, I must look at myself, my studies, my work, the physical world, and the interactions of humanity with the reality of God as the starting point. A certain governor was known to write the word "Jesus" at the top of every agenda sheet he was given before a meeting. Why did he do this? To remind him that as he dealt with budgets and taxes and prisons and school systems and laws, that the starting point for thinking clearly about anything is Jesus. Close the gap today on your faith...put Christ at the beginning of every thought, word, action.

Day 2
Read:
Heb.11:3 By faith we understand that the universe was formed at God's command, so that what is seen was not made out of what was visible.

Reflect:
Is the Bible less than scientific? No, it is more not less than science. Science requires human interaction: experimentation and observation. God has given us what humans cannot observe or discover.
He has told us what has always been here (himself) and how the universe came to be (he made it). The world of space and time had a beginning. All physical things have a cause. You cannot have an uncaused chain of events. A line of dominos falling must have a first domino. To get to today you must have crossed through all the days that came before this one. If there were an infinite number of days before you got to this day, how would you ever get to this day? You could not. You cannot travel an infinite number of days and get to today. God alone is infinite. He exists outside of space and time. He alone is uncaused. God is Spirit, he made what is seen (and finite) because he is unseen (infinite); he is Spirit. Do not be scared of science or of the grand claims of those who have been given certain kinds of minds as gifts from God. Science cannot tell us what has always been, where everything came from, why anything exists at all, or what happens when this life is over. It can speculate, but mere speculation is not really the place of true science. What we really need to know in order to live well in the ultimate sense—with purpose—only God can tell us. No human can; we can only guess. Yet on the whole we tend to be terrible guessers. Don't guess. Instead understand that the universe was made by God, and therefore everything in it, including you, exists for him. Close the gap on confidence in God: think clearly about the fact that we what we most need to know only God can tell us.

Day 3
Read:
Heb.11:3 By faith we understand that the universe was formed at God's command, so that what is seen was not made out of what was visible.

Reflect:
What about evolution? What about it? Even if evolution on a large scale were true, it would explain very little. Evolution is not an explanation; it requires one. It presupposes an order and a design, a very elaborate design. Do not be put off by the attempted use of the word "evolution" as an automatic dismissal of God as creator. Evolution (even if it were a fact as commonly believed) would not explain the universe. It would not explain itself. It would not explain you, your real need, and your real solution. Everyone lives by faith; not everyone's faith is well-placed. We understand (know) by faith (of course, since we were not there) that the universe was formed at God's command. Everything exists because God wanted it to. It continues to exist because he still wants it to. There is enormous practical application of this reality. If everything exists because he wanted it to and continues to exist only because it pleases him that it does...then what does this say about ultimate human purpose? What are the applications and implications for your day-to-day life to live in a world and in a body that were made by him, for his pleasure? There are multiple problems with evolution on a macro scale but possibly the largest problem, practically speaking, is the attempted use of it as a principle to replace God. This, of course, is nonsense. Evolution would require design...it does not supply or explain it. Close the gap on your faith...quit being tricked by grand claims of culture that do not explain what they say they do. God is the designer and therefore he is the owner...the rightful king of our lives.

Day 4
Read:
Heb.11:3 By faith we understand that the universe was formed at God's command, so that what is seen was not made out of what was visible.

Reflect:
Why is there something rather than nothing? Some say everything is the result of chance. But what are the "chances" of everything that exists coming into existence from nothing? Zero. The chances are zero. So I ask again: why is there something rather than nothing? Because God spoke, and at his command the universe was formed. He did not gather raw materials and build a universe; he spoke all that is into existence. What does it even mean that he "spoke"? He doesn't have lungs, or vocal cords, and he doesn't live in air. When God "spoke" and said "Let there be!" it is a way of saying he "willed it to be so," and then by his power (ability) he made it so.

I can "will" my fingers to move, and they do. I can will that words form on this computer, and they do. I am creating words, but my "will" operates from what exists. He is able to will things into existence that did not exist before. All that is seen was not made out of existing things but rather from the will and power of God. This is incredible to consider, but it is no more incredible than to consider the possibility that all that exists suddenly "sprung" into existence from nothing. In fact, it is much more reasonable to believe that things that look to be designed came from a mind. We do not believe that, in the physical universe, things "pop" into existence on their own. We believe ("we" being scientists as well as "lay" people) that things are not uncaused, that if something now exists, it is because something caused it to happen. So this being true, why would people believe that the universe itself—the biggest of all existing things—would be able to be "uncaused"? As you walk through God's world today and you think about what you see, do not be fooled; all that you see is "caused." The streets were planned and built by a "mind." The same with your lunch and the buildings you walk into. These did not "just happen." They were planned, caused. The same is true about the universe. The same is true about you. The same is true about your co-worker and neighbor. Close the gap on your faith and love today. See all things and all people as products of the mind and will of God.

Day 5
Read:
Heb.11:3 By faith we understand that the universe was formed at God's command, so that what is seen was not made out of what was visible.

Reflect:
The universe is not God or a part of God. This may seem obvious to you, but it is not for many. For many, God is the universe or the universe is God. When this is thought to be true, then the universe or parts of it are worshipped. The sun, the stars, the earth, people...any number of created things can take the place of the creator in a person's heart, mind, and will. Imagine that from your skill and creativity you handmade a gift for a friend. Then when you presented the gift to your friend, they took the gift and began to thank it for being made. They turned from you and spoke to the gift as if it had made itself for them. You watched as they showed others the gift you had made and extolled the beauty and virtue of the gift without acknowledging you as the one who had made it. Perhaps it would make you angry, but more likely it would make you sad. Besides being a very strange thing—making much of a gift and nothing of the giver—it is a tragic thing. It's tragic because the gift is given to demonstrate love and relationship. The gift is not the point, the relationship is. So when the giver is disregarded and the gift becomes the focus, then the relationship that might have been will not be. Life, existence, and the physical universe are all gifts. When we marvel at

some part of this gift, it should cause us to reflect on the giver of the gift. His power, beauty, extravagance, creativity, and many other features of personality come to mind. When we see a hummingbird hover over a flower, we should consider his attention to detail. When a thunderstorm rages over the ocean, we should be humbled at his might. What we see from our little corner of the universe is impressive. What do you think it will be like when we can see the fuller extent of what he has made and done? As humans launch satellites into space and they transmit data back of the wonders that we have only just began to understand, our opportunity for awe increases. It is impressive indeed that a human can make a satellite and launch it into space. However, it seems strange to be overly impressed with a human launching satellites or even with the unfolding wonders of the universe and miss the one who made it all.

Week 4/Day 1
Read:
Heb.11:4-6 By faith Abel offered God a better sacrifice than Cain did. By faith he was commended as a righteous man, when God spoke well of his offerings. And by faith he still speaks, even though he is dead. By faith Enoch was taken from this life, so that he did not experience death; he could not be found, because God had taken him away. For before he was taken, he was commended as one who pleased God. And without faith it is impossible to please God, because anyone who comes to him must believe that he exists and that he rewards those who earnestly seek him.

Reflect:
Is God so petty that he cared about the kind of sacrifice one brother offered over another? Then, was it because of God's rejection of Cain that he turned against his brother in hate? No, God rejected Cain's "offering" because it was not worship. Cain's heart was already turned against God and his brother. Cain's offering was not given in faith. How could it be when his heart was so filled with self and with rage? Abel offered a better sacrifice than his brother because Abel came to God in faith, in desire for relationship. Cain's heart was seen in his response. God even gave him a chance to see when he asked him, "Why are you so angry, why are you feeling sorry for yourself?" Cain had the opportunity to repent of what was in his heart and to allow God to heal it. Instead he took his anger out on his brother. What is most amazing about the story is that God still showed Cain grace. He received undeserved mercy. But what of Abel, how does he still "speak" even though he is dead? They are in fact both dead, and they both speak. One speaks a warning and the other, a vision. The warning is evident: our hearts can turn dark and take us to dark places. The vision that Abel's life speaks to us is that a heart that is given to God and a life of offering given to God are not a waste even if (when) that life is over.

12

Both are dead, but the story of Cain's life is waste; the story of Abel's (shorter life) is God's glory. It's likely no one will write the story of your life so that others will read it years after you are gone. But it is still your opportunity to have a life that continues to "speak" long after you are gone. How so? The same way Abel's life "speaks": it is because God "spoke well" of him. God said to him, "Well done!" You have the same opportunity. You have before you, for as many days as you are given, to live in a way that will result in God himself "speaking well" of you. What is this path of "well done"? It is the path of faith. It is to live towards God and others as if God is alive and worthy of our very lives. Faith is living for the glory of God and the good of others. It is to offer our lives to him as a "better sacrifice" in order to hear from him "well done!" Close the gap today; live for the "well done" of God.

Day 2
Read:
Heb.11:4-6 By faith Abel offered God a better sacrifice than Cain did. By faith he was commended as a righteous man, when God spoke well of his offerings. And by faith he still speaks, even though he is dead. By faith Enoch was taken from this life, so that he did not experience death; he could not be found, because God had taken him away. For before he was taken, he was commended as one who pleased God. And without faith it is impossible to please God, because anyone who comes to him must believe that he exists and that he rewards those who earnestly seek him.

Reflect:
We don't know much about Enoch, but we know enough. He walked with God. It is interesting that he was able to escape the curse of Adam in that he skipped the dying process. But what is most important is the reason that happened. Adam walked with God in the Garden (or God walked with him), then he walked away from God and, in so doing, brought death. Enoch walked with God and, in so doing, escaped death. Clearly this is not God's plan for very many people; most will go to God through death's door. But Enoch's life instructs us on how to live reversing the curse. We do so by walking with God. Notice God commended him, too. So we know three things about Enoch: he walked with God, he escaped the dying process, and God commended him. We don't know whether he was famous, handsome, athletic, had a lot of possessions, or was really smart. Walking with God is another way of saying "walk by faith." To walk with God means to live in line with his will and his ways for your life. It will require making choices that indicate you trust him and believe that he alive and able to accomplish his purposes. It requires actions and attitudes that demonstrate your confidence that his ways are the best ways and life with him is the best possible life. Enoch walked with God, but it is unlikely his walk was perfect. It is more likely his walk was authentic.

In his heart and then on the whole in his life he walked God's ways. Why did he get to escape death? Was he that much better than everyone else? Maybe…we can't say. But his great escape was caused by the fact that he earned God's commendation by the fact that he walked with God. You will likely not get to skip the dying process, but if you walk in faith by believing the gospel, you will get to skip the curse of death.

That which is so fearful for much of humanity—death—has lost its sting for you if you are his child. What matters most at the end, matters most now. What will matter most at the end will be relationship with God, revealed in the relationships you have with others. Since that will matter most at the end, it matters most now. Right now, today. Walk with God in faith, by walking alongside others in love. You will probably still have to pass through death's door someday, but death has already lost in your life. And death will not have the final word in your death; life will. Close the gap, live by faith today with the end in mind.

Day 3
Read:
Heb. 11:4-6 By faith Abel offered God a better sacrifice than Cain did. By faith he was commended as a righteous man, when God spoke well of his offerings. And by faith he still speaks, even though he is dead. By faith Enoch was taken from this life, so that he did not experience death; he could not be found, because God had taken him away. For before he was taken, he was commended as one who pleased God. And without faith it is impossible to please God, because anyone who comes to him must believe that he exists and that he rewards those who earnestly seek him.

Reflect:
All things are possible for God. Does this mean God can do anything? Yes and no. God's power, sometimes called his omnipotence, means he can do anything that can be done. He can make the universe, raise the dead, and become incarnate in Christ. He cannot, however, do what is self-contradictory to do. He cannot make a rock too big for him to pick up. This is not a real thing to be done; it is merely clever words tied together in a sentence. If someone presses you on a question like this and he refuses to listen to the fact that it is an irrational sentence, then simply tell them, "yes, he can." Then if they say, "Well then he can't pick up the rock!" You can reply, "Oh yes, he can do that as well." It's okay to answer nonsense with nonsense. Now, let's go back to the larger issue of what God can actually do and what he cannot. He cannot ever stop being God. He cannot, not be love, or powerful, or eternal. Furthermore, it is impossible for us to please God apart from faith. Why is this? Why is he making such a demand on us? Let's think about it. What is faith? It is confidence. Who is God? He is ultimate reality, from whom all things came into existence and for whom all things exist.

14

So faith is confidence in and compliance with the one we belong to and exist for. So how would it be possible to live as beings made by him for his pleasure in a way that resists him and his will and at the same time bring him pleasure? This is another statement of nonsense. It could be worded like this to get the full meaning. "Without pleasing God it is impossible to please God." Well of course that is true; so what is the point? The point is that a life of confidence in God(faith) is the same thing as a life that pleases God. It is not complex; it's just difficult. We really only have to do two things...actually one because the second flows from the first. We have to trust God. When we trust God, it will show up in love for others. Love God with all of who you are, and love others as you love yourself. This is very simple and enormously difficult. But in this, all things are possible because God is all for this, and he will help you live this way. Close the gap on a life of faith. Look to God to do what would be impossible for you by yourself. Look to him to help you trust him completely and to love others authentically.

Day 4
Read:
Heb. 11:-6 By faith Abel offered God a better sacrifice than Cain did. By faith he was commended as a righteous man, when God spoke well of his offerings. And by faith he still speaks, even though he is dead. By faith Enoch was taken from this life, so that he did not experience death; he could not be found, because God had taken him away. For before he was taken, he was commended as one who pleased God. And without faith it is impossible to please God, because anyone who comes to him must believe that he exists and that he rewards those who earnestly seek him.

Reflect:
Atheists believe that God does not exist. Agnostics believe that they do not or cannot know whether God exists. Some believe it is irrational to claim he exists. Others believe it is arrogant to claim to have knowledge of his existence. But it is neither irrational nor arrogant to have this knowledge. We have knowledge of his existence because he has made himself known. We did not discover him; he revealed himself. He has done so in the world he has made, like art made by an artist. He has done so in the conscience he has placed inside each of us. He has done so in human history as recorded in Scriptures. He has done so in Jesus Christ, God incarnate. To believe is to be persuaded, to have come to a conclusion. Clearly we can have real knowledge of his existence and then have rational belief that he exists. Why is this important? Because before anyone will come to him (approach him for help, salvation, direction), they must believe he exists. It's not a condition that is arbitrary like "In basketball you must not lift your pivot foot, or you will lose possession of the ball." Why is this so—why are you not able to pivot with both feet?

Is this a condition of reality, like the laws of gravity? No, it is merely a rule made up by the inventor of basketball because it is what he chose; it could have been otherwise. The reality of God and the "laws" of human interaction with him are never arbitrary. God, never just makes up the "rules of the game" because he feels like it, and it could just as easily have been another way. What he tells us and commands us is tied to the way he has designed life to be, and it is connected to the nature of who he is. Why can't God just give us a break and whether we believe him or in him or not, just go ahead and be a "good sport" and give everyone the same things. Because this is not a game, and he is not making it up as he goes. If a person does not actually believe God, that God exists, he will not come to him in a way that leads to actual relationship with God. If you go to him as a peer, or a demigod, or a large reflection of yourself, you are not going to him at all. You are going to a figment of your imagination. Figments of your imagination cannot save you, they have no power to change things in the real world. Believe in the God who actually exists. Then when you "come to him" you are actually coming to a God who can save you, and help you, and have relationship with you. Close the gap today: come to Him as he actually is, not as you might be imagining him to be.

Day 5
Read:
Heb. 11:4-6 By faith Abel offered God a better sacrifice than Cain did. By faith he was commended as a righteous man, when God spoke well of his offerings. And by faith he still speaks, even though he is dead. By faith Enoch was taken from this life, so that he did not experience death; he could not be found, because God had taken him away. For before he was taken, he was commended as one who pleased God. And without faith it is impossible to please God, because anyone who comes to him must believe that he exists and that he rewards those who earnestly seek him.

Reflect:
Many seek God for a reward and they do so earnestly, yet they do not get what they seek. Doesn't this mean God does not keep his promises? No, it means they do not understand what God promised. What exactly is the promise here? The answer is found in the question, "what" or better yet "who" is object of the seeking? Let's reword this: "Those who truly seek God will be rewarded by finding him." God told Jeremiah, "When you seek me with all your heart, you will find me." And he told Abraham, "I am your very great reward." God is the reward of this promise. Those who seek him will find him. To some this is like hearing they won the lottery and finding that the prize is "only" relationship with God and being disappointed. They are missing the perspective necessary to understand the scope of this great promise. This highlights an important fact about faith.

It is impossible to please God without it; it is also impossible to "be pleased with God" without it. When we have learned to trust God, our eyes are open more and more to who he actually is and what relationship with him is "worth." Then he becomes the prime object of our seeking. Or maybe we find that what we were seeking after and never finding contentment in was all the time just a poor substitution for what our hearts truly desired. Of course, we seek meaningful human relationships. We seek meaningful vocations and vacations. We seek health and happiness. But there is no promise in scripture that we will always or ever get these things. Though most often, if we live as God has designed us, we will find these things to be true about our lives. But when it is true, it will be because we are seeking God as our highest God. And when we seek him, we find relationship with him and satisfaction in him. When we are finding our greatest satisfaction in him, we are positioned to find contentment and even joy in what he brings into our lives. When we find our ultimate meaning in him, we tend to find the other aspects of our lives, whatever they are, meaningful as well. Faith pleases God and faith makes us pleased *with* God. Close the gap today on what you truly seek. Seek God. He has promised to be found when you do.

Week 5/Day 1
Read:
Heb. 11:7-10 By faith Noah, when warned about things not yet seen, in holy fear built an ark to save his family. By his faith he condemned the world and became heir of the righteousness that comes by faith. By faith Abraham, when called to go to a place he would later receive as his inheritance, obeyed and went, even though he did not know where he was going. By faith he made his home in the promised land like a stranger in a foreign country; he lived in tents, as did Isaac and Jacob, who were heirs with him of the same promise. For he was looking forward to the city with foundations, whose architect and builder is God.

Reflect:
When hurricanes form out in the ocean, officials warn coastal residents of what they believe is to come. Many pack their cars and flee inland to safety; some ignore the warnings and stay. Why do the ones who stay, do so? They do not trust the officials because they are often wrong. The location of where the storm will hit is hard to predict. The severity of what the storm will be is hard to estimate. Some people, after being warned several times and finding the warning to be false or only partially true, become jaded to the predictions. They stop believing. They have lost faith in the weatherman. Noah was given a storm warning. A flood unlike anyone had ever seen was coming. He believed the warning and made preparations. Imagine if the weatherman giving the weather report was actually in charge of the weather.

It would not be a prediction of what might happen; it would be a description of what will happen. Why did Noah believe and others did not? Faith. He believed God while others did not. His fear was "holy" because it was not primarily fear of the water; it was awe of God. His fear would not be called "holy" if it were a fear of drowning. He knew that when God said he was going to bring judgment, it was a decided fact. So in "holy fear" he set out to make preparations to escape the coming judgment. God still speaks of a coming judgment. Some believe, others do not. The preparations are not to build a boat but to believe the gospel. Jesus rescues from the coming flood. This rescue is ultimately a future reality. It is fully experienced when we die. But it is also present in its application. As we believe God now by living in line with his loving "warning," we experience the "undoing" of Adam's judgment in our lives. Our lives are changed for the better when we live believing God when he warns us that to live apart from him is to experience emptiness. To live to know and love him and to make his love known is to experience increasing fullness. Close the gap today. Learn to live in "holy fear." Our only fear need be a heart that does not love and obey God.

Day 2
Read:
Heb. 11:7-10 By faith Noah, when warned about things not yet seen, in holy fear built an ark to save his family. By his faith he condemned the world and became heir of the righteousness that comes by faith. By faith Abraham, when called to go to a place he would later receive as his inheritance, obeyed and went, even though he did not know where he was going. By faith he made his home in the promised land like a stranger in a foreign country; he lived in tents, as did Isaac and Jacob, who were heirs with him of the same promise. For he was looking forward to the city with foundations, whose architect and builder is God.

Reflect:
Everyone is proving God true. How is this so? Those who live apart from him, refusing to live by faith in him, are proving him true in the ways their lives unfold externally, internally, and ultimately...eternally. Those who live by faith in him are proving him true as well. Who they are becoming on the inside, the ways their lives are changing on the outside, and the ways their lives end up ultimately are proof of God's promises. This is how Noah's faith "condemned the world." He showed that without faith it is impossible to please God, but he also showed that it is possible to have faith and therefore to please God. What makes his faith a "condemnation" is that he was not special. His faith was not a singularity; only someone as great as Noah could pull it off. Noah was a normal man. His faith was a gift from God. All can receive the same gift if they choose.

When people refuse to respond to God and they live the results of life apart from God, they cannot in the end blame God. Faith in God was not beyond them. This is how Noah's life becomes a condemnation. But his life is also a commendation. He commends righteousness to us. He, through faith, became an heir to the family fortune, the great riches of righteousness. Righteousness is right standing with God. His faith brought him an escape from a death by drowning, but that was a temporary escape. He eventually died. What was more important was that his faith brought him into the family inheritance. He became an heir to right relationship with God. This transcends this life and is a fortune that you "can take with you." When you see the human devastation of sin, let it break your heart. But keep this in mind: "this too is proving God true." Now, demonstrate the blessing of faith in your life. Do not merely be a sign of condemnation for the world; be a person of commendation. A person whose life receives God's commendation by faith and a person whose life can commend God to others. Close the gap today; see how your life can commend God to others. This is your responsibility, and this is your opportunity.

Day 3
Read:
Heb. 11:7-10 By faith Noah, when warned about things not yet seen, in holy fear built an ark to save his family. By his faith he condemned the world and became heir of the righteousness that comes by faith. By faith Abraham, when called to go to a place he would later receive as his inheritance, obeyed and went, even though he did not know where he was going. By faith he made his home in the promised land like a stranger in a foreign country; he lived in tents, as did Isaac and Jacob, who were heirs with him of the same promise. For he was looking forward to the city with foundations, whose architect and builder is God.

Reflect:
God told Abraham, "Go the place I will show you." This is curious, how do you "go" (present tense) to the place "I will show you" (future tense)? Clearly God knew where he wanted Abraham to end up; why didn't he just tell him? How was it that Abraham obeyed and "went" even though he did not know where he was going? He knew the direction; he just didn't yet know the final destination. Faith requires action. It is not a feeling. It is confidence in God and in his will and ways. How much faith is necessary? Just enough to move your feet in his direction. The steps can be slow, they can be faltering, they will often be two forward and one backward, but steps of faith will move you in a direction towards his will and ways for your life. Very often, perhaps most often, you will not get the "next after the next" steps. You will get the next steps. Then when you take those, you will again get the next steps. God does not want you to trust a series of directions; he wants you to trust him.

The reason Abraham did not get the "full map" is that he would then no longer have to seek God. He could simply consult his map. God was not just interested in Abraham going places and getting "stuff done." He was interested in building his faith and deepening his relationship. So he told him "Go to the place I will show you." Abraham went, looking to God to show him, step-by-step, where he was to go. Be careful to not wait for the full plan to unfold before you obey with next steps. If you do, you will likely stay stuck and not experience what God has for you. It is likely the next steps are not exciting, and look rather mundane, even tiresome. Take the next steps, close the gap. The next steps today will surely include looking to God in faith and loving others around you in practical ways.

Day 4
Read: Heb. 11:7-10 By faith Noah, when warned about things not yet seen, in holy fear built an ark to save his family. By his faith he condemned the world and became heir of the righteousness that comes by faith. By faith Abraham, when called to go to a place he would later receive as his inheritance, obeyed and went, even though he did not know where he was going. By faith he made his home in the promised land like a stranger in a foreign country; he lived in tents, as did Isaac and Jacob, who were heirs with him of the same promise. For he was looking forward to the city with foundations, whose architect and builder is God.

Reflect:
When Abraham got to the land of promise, he did not establish a permanent home there. He went to the place God had called him to, but he lived an "unsettled" life there. Does that strike you as strange? There are a number of people who proclaim what is called a "prosperity gospel." *Gospel* is a word that means "good news." This theological framework believes that the "good news" is that in addition to eternal life, God wants you healthy and wealthy in this life as well. This theology would not work well in many parts of the world where people are suffering for their faith. It doesn't work well anywhere, for long. Abraham went to the land of promise and did prosper there, but he lived the life of a migrant, like a stranger in a foreign land. This was the land of promise for him and his heirs, but the fulfillment of the promise was "already, but not yet." He experienced partial peace, partial blessing, partial prosperity, but it was all tentative, migratory, and transitory. Full peace, full blessing, full prosperity, full heath and joy are not found in this life. The physical promised land was a sort of "down payment" on the actual promised land. He entered the land of ultimate promise when he went to God's full presence after his death. If you look to this life to give you more than it is capable of giving, you will live with ongoing disappointment. In addition, you will tend to make decisions that are not driven by faith but rather by frustration.

20

Faith endures much now because it knows this is not all there is, or even most of what is for the Christian. Frustration is the engine that drives the life not lived by faith. Frustration that even when something is obtained—a relationship, a promotion, an experience, a purchase—it does not bring lasting fulfillment. This life cannot give what we often demand it give. It cannot because in this life we see as through a glass darkly; in the life to come we will see God face-to-face. Then our fulfillment will be complete, and our frustration will be eradicated. It has been said that some people are "so heavenly-minded they are no earthly good." This is a catchy collection of words but totally devoid of factual content. It's not possible to be too "heavenly- minded." It is certainly possible to be too "earthly-minded." The more we navigate our lives with an eternal orientation, the more we are positioned to make a lasting impact now. If we know this life is not the place of full promise fulfillment, then we are much more likely to experience the most out of this life. Close the gap on your faith: see this life as "already but not yet" in terms of the full experience of the promises of God. Your faith will become increasingly resilient, and your joy will become increasingly independent of your circumstances if you do.

Day 5
Read:
Heb. 11:7-10 By faith Noah, when warned about things not yet seen, in holy fear built an ark to save his family. By his faith he condemned the world and became heir of the righteousness that comes by faith. By faith Abraham, when called to go to a place he would later receive as his inheritance, obeyed and went, even though he did not know where he was going. By faith he made his home in the promised land like a stranger in a foreign country; he lived in tents, as did Isaac and Jacob, who were heirs with him of the same promise. For he was looking forward to the city with foundations, whose architect and builder is God.

Reflect:
Abraham lived as a migrant in the land of promise. He didn't get to spend his life in cities like you do. He didn't have ready access to food or grocery stores. He didn't have central heat and air. He spent a lot of time being hot and cold. He didn't travel paved highways. He didn't have access to medical care. No malls, no movies, no recorded music. His life was very, very basic. He was a "prince" among his people, but if you were to suddenly find yourself living his life, you would likely consider your life very, very difficult. But in at least one important way Abraham had a distinct advantage over you. He was less able to be distracted. He had no illusion that he was living in a "heaven on earth." You may not think your life is a heaven on earth either, but you certainly have many opportunities to be distracted from eternity. The cities we live in offer constant mental and physical stimulation.

We need never experience silence if we choose not to. We do not need to look forward to a city whose architect and builder is God because our cities offer so much. There is so much to do, eat, see, experience...it takes a death bed for most people to see that their "city" did not have foundations. The cities we inhabit and all the things that divert our attention from eternity are built without foundations. Of course, they have physical footings: tall buildings have concrete deep underground, often going all the way to bedrock. But in eternal terms, they still lack a foundation. They are not built to last. Our city of final destination is built by God to last. It cannot be shaken or taken by the elements of war or entropy. Eye has not seen, ear has not heard, mind cannot conceive what God has prepared for those who love him. Do not wait for a deathbed (even if you have the opportunity to die on a bed as many do not) to see this. Tonight, as you lay in your "life bed" look forward to the City of God, where he is the builder, the foundation, and the main attraction. Think of all that is wonderful in this life, and then consider that what is to come far surpasses all of it. No human mind can even conceive of the "city" the dwelling place God has prepared for his children. You can close the gap on your faith by learning to choose carefully what you look forward to. Look forward to the city designed and inhabited by God; learn day-by-day to set your hopes there.

Week 6/Day 1
Read:
Heb. 11:11-12 By faith Abraham, even though he was past age — and Sarah herself was barren — was enabled to become a father because he considered him faithful who had made the promise. And so from this one man, and he as good as dead, came descendants as numerous as the stars in the sky and as countless as the sand on the seashore.

Reflect:
Many believe that miracles are impossible (though this often doesn't keep them from asking for one when they are in desperate situations). They believe the universe is a closed system, meaning it is all that exists. Since all is "natural," by default there can be no "supernatural." There is no "scientific" reason to believe that everything that exists is natural. Science cannot tell us this; it can only tell us some things about the natural realm. Miracles are logically possible since the universe is not a "closed system." It is not self-creating. It was created by a supernatural "mind." So it is entirely possible that this creator also continues to involve himself actively in what he has made. Normally, he allows things to happen normally. But occasionally when it fits his overall purposes, he acts in a way that bypasses or speeds up normal processes. This is a miracle. It is intervention by God into the normal processes of the physical world. If you leave food on the countertop, it will begin to degrade.

22

If you intervene by putting in the refrigerator, you will slow the process of the food spoiling. If you inject a certain medicine into a sick person (who would have died without the injection), you have interrupted the "normal" process. God superseded the normal process for giving birth to a child in Abraham and Sarah. They were both past normal child-bearing age, but God intervened and Sarah was able to bear a child. Why did God do this? There is one answer but two sides to that answer. She bore a son because God willed and caused it. She bore a child because Abraham believed God when he said he would give him a son. These two facts are not in opposition; they are in collaboration. Of course, Abraham's faith could have been misplaced. He could have thought God promised a son, but he didn't. He could have believed that if he could muster enough faith then God would be compelled to do what Abraham wanted. But in reality, Abraham had faith in what God had actually promised. Faith must be based on fact, on what God has actually said. Faith must lead to action. Abraham had to take steps in order to experience the promise of God. Close the gap on your faith today by taking action on what God has promised. Do you know what he has promised? Make sure that it is in fact a promise to you. Be sure you are reading the Scriptures correctly. Most of his promises will include challenge, difficulty, and seeing him prove faithful in the midst of them. Most of his promises will lead to you loving and serving others and experiencing his love in the midst of your sacrifice.

Day 2
Read:
Heb. 11:11-12 By faith Abraham, even though he was past age — and Sarah herself was barren — was enabled to become a father because he considered him faithful who had made the promise. And so from this one man, and he as good as dead, came descendants as numerous as the stars in the sky and as countless as the sand on the seashore.

Reflect:
"Where is my miracle?" This is the question some have asked, even demanded of God. The answer is always, "You have no miracle, only God does." Miracles are signs of God's faithfulness much more than they are signs of our faith. By faith Abraham considered God faithful. Abraham's faith would mean nothing if God were not faithful. Some believe in the power of the human spirit, mind, and will to accomplish miracles. This is not true. There is no "secret" power in the universe waiting to be tapped by human potential. There is a universe (all that has been created) and there is a creator. We are part of the creation, and we are made in the image of our creator. We have potential, but we are not divine. We relate "up" to God in our image-bearing features; we relate "down" to creation in our finite, limited features. Our faith must be in his faithfulness, never in our potential.

It has been said that a lot of faith in a weak bridge will get you wet, while a little faith in a strong bridge will keep you dry. The amount of your faith is not the point (a tiny mustard seed will do); the object of your faith is the point. Our faith must be firmly in God's faithfulness. All miracles are from him and about him. They point to something much bigger than me and my current circumstances. All physical miracles have expiration dates stamped on them. A physical healing does not last forever. Provision of a car, a spouse, a job, a sum of money—even if given in ways that clearly demonstrate God's intervention—does not last. What lasts indefinitely is the glory of God revealed in his actions in and among us. His miracles point me and others to him. Is he able to do what you ask? Yes, of course he is. Then why doesn't he? Because he doesn't want to; it is not best for him and his purposes. But what of you and your purposes, what if it's best for you? In the end, what is best for his glory is best for you. Close the gap today on your faith. Ask him for what you want and do this with faith. Then trust him for what he gives and do this with faith.

Day 3
Read:
Heb. 11:11-12 By faith Abraham, even though he was past age — and Sarah herself was barren — was enabled to become a father because he considered him faithful who had made the promise. And so from this one man, and he as good as dead, came descendants as numerous as the stars in the sky and as countless as the sand on the seashore.

Reflect:
You have never seen a road sign that says "road sign here." Signs do not point to themselves; they point to something greater than themselves. If you see a sign that says "Mt. Rainer," you do not turn your back to the mountain, take pictures of the sign and drive on. You fix your gaze on the mountain and turn your back to the sign. That is the purpose of the sign: to set your attention elsewhere. You might take a picture of your family in front of the sign to remember it, but you remember the sign because of what it pointed to...a majestic mountain. In the same way, miracles are signs that point to God. We remember them and draw strength from remembering them because of whom they direct our attention to. When people fixate on signs (miracles), they lose sight of God. Satan has been known to give counterfeit miracles. They may actually be "real" in terms of accomplishing supernatural things, but they are "fake" in that they do not do what a real miracle is supposed to do and that is to turn attention and affection to God. God loved Abraham and Sarah, but he did not provide a miracle son simply for that reason. This son was a sign that would speak of God's greatness and his faithfulness through the ages.

If you read of what God did for Abraham and immediately wonder, "what great thing will he do for me?" you are missing the point. When you read of what God did, marvel at God. Beyond that, reflect on the great thing God has already done for you. It was through the lineage of Abraham that God brought Jesus the Messiah into the world and into your life. He can do no greater thing for you than this. Will you set your heart and mind to believing this? It is in fact true; it remains for you to close the gap on personally believing it more and more.

Day 4
Read:
Heb. 11:11-12 By faith Abraham, even though he was past age — and Sarah herself was barren — was enabled to become a father because he considered him faithful who had made the promise. And so from this one man, and he as good as dead, came descendants as numerous as the stars in the sky and as countless as the sand on the seashore.

Reflect:
Abraham had faith in the faithfulness of God. He believed that God would keep the promise he had made. What was the content of the promise? It was that Abraham would be the father of a nation with descendants so numerous they would be virtually uncountable. The problem was that in order to have multiple descendants you have to start with a single descendant. The promise was epic in nature, but the fulfillment of the promise was very mundane: a baby had to be born. Sarah, an older woman, had to become pregnant and bear a child. Before you move on from that fact think about not just her joy at getting pregnant after so long but what it would be like to live at that time, be that age, and go through pregnancy. The promise was epic; the days of gestation were certainly not. If you are a Christian, then God has given you an epic promise: eternal life in Christ. You will see him face-to-face someday and will become like Christ in character. He has promised believers will experience eternal life, which is not merely a large quantity of life but an entirely different quality of life. However, in the meantime, the days will often not feel epic. They will "tick" by in mundane movements of the clock and calendar. There will be times for many of us that will not just be mundane but will involve pain. Pain that is physical, pain that is emotional and mental. However, even in the mundane and in the pain, we do have to wait to the end to experience some of the "epic" nature of the promise of God. What makes the promise so spectacular is that it means we will have a fuller experience with God someday. We can know him in fuller and fuller ways right now, during the days of pain and the days of mundane. This is where and how the epic breaks into the mundane: to move through your days looking to know and love God and to make God's love known.
Whether you are sitting at a desk fighting to stay engaged with your work, or

lying in a sick bed fighting to stay alive, you have the opportunity today to encounter God. You can see where God is moving in your life now and join him. This is the intersection of the epic and the mundane. Close the gap today: see the epic in the mundane.

Day 5.
Read:
Heb. 11:11-12 By faith Abraham, even though he was past age — and Sarah herself was barren — was enabled to become a father because he considered him faithful who had made the promise. And so from this one man, and he as good as dead, came descendants as numerous as the stars in the sky and as countless as the sand on the seashore.

Reflect:
Many are concerned with legacy. How will they be remembered? What will happen to their life's work? King Solomon was concerned with this as well. He feared that all he worked for might be left to a son who proved to be a fool. Solomon's fears were well-founded: his son did prove to be a fool and split the kingdom in two. Legacy is the name of a national obituary service. You can read about people from around the nation who have died. You can read their life story in a couple of paragraphs. You can see what they thought to be important. Or at least you can see what others thought they thought was important. Why would anyone care about legacy? They will be gone, what difference does it make? Certainly, some do not care, but most do. Humans care for legacy because God designed them for impact. People know that if what they accomplish does not outlive them, then ultimately it has no lasting meaning. This is why some who do not have a gospel faith give their lives to "saving the planet" or worry about the "survival of the human race." To save a planet seems like something worth giving a single life for. To save an entire race from extinction, well, that is worth something. But what if the planet is not destined to survive? Or what if it does and the planet is just a rock hanging in space, not designed...a pale blue dot in space, a product of mere chance? What difference does it make whether it is saved or not? Meaning comes from God. The universe, the planet, the human race have been made by God for God. The legacy that matters is to hear from him about your life, "Well done, good and faithful servant." Abraham looked to a legacy that extended far beyond his own earthly life. He would only live to see the very beginning of the fulfillment of the promise. The rest he could see by faith alone. Be concerned with legacy, one that extends beyond your own life to the ends of the earth to the end of time...and beyond. But that legacy is not about you; it is about God. Live faithfully today, trusting in the faithful God to bring himself glory and others good from your life. Close the gap on faith and love today. Live for the glory of God and for the good of others. Pursue a legacy that is about him.

26

Week 7/Day 1
Read:

Heb. 11:13-16 All these people were still living by faith when they died. They did not receive the things promised; they only saw them and welcomed them from a distance. And they admitted that they were aliens and strangers on earth. People who say such things show that they are looking for a country of their own. If they had been thinking of the country they had left, they would have had opportunity to return. Instead, they were longing for a better country — a heavenly one. Therefore, God is not ashamed to be called their God, for he has prepared a city for them.

Reflect:

Imagine you are promised a gift and live expectantly with faith that you will in fact receive the gift because the who has promised is faithful. Then one day as promised the gift arrives. You open the package and there it is just as you knew it would be. As you held the gift and saw it with your eyes, your faith disappeared. Why? It was because it was no longer necessary. Faith had served its purpose. Faith keeps your hope fixed on what is to come until sight takes over. The reason these men of God died still living by faith is because if they had experienced the fullness of God's promise, then faith would be unnecessary. That's why those who have not seen and yet believe are blessed. Because what is seen is temporary, and what is unseen is eternal. To believe now what is not yet seen is not to live in delusion but to live in the fullness of reality. What we have now is valuable, meaningful, wonderful, but it is a partial not full experience. Right now, we get to run our fingers through the icing and get a taste; then we will get the cake itself. So of course, the ancients were living by faith when they died, and of course they had not received the things promised. If they had experienced it in full, then faith would not be required. But the fact that they died without having fully experienced the promise does not mean they died empty or frustrated. The opposite is true. What they experienced of God in this life became a "memory of the future" for them. They died with full hope. There are stories of the last words of men and women who lived their lives far from God. Some of these stories tell of the fear, the terror, the disillusionment in that final moment of realization. "It really does end...my life really is over." We will all die in faith. Some will die with misplaced faith: where they put their confidence will not prove to be a secure place. Some will die with well-placed faith. Their confidence in God will prove to be the only secure place. Close the gap today. See what God has done, see what God is doing, be confident in what he will do. Let that confidence impact what concerns you most today.

Day 2
Read:

Heb. 11:13-16 All these people were still living by faith when they died. They did not receive the things promised; they only saw them and welcomed them from a distance. And they admitted that they were aliens and strangers on earth. People who say such things show that they are looking for a country of their own. If they had been thinking of the country they had left, they would have had opportunity to return. Instead, they were longing for a better country — a heavenly one. Therefore, God is not ashamed to be called their God, for he has prepared a city for them.

Reflect:

You do not have to travel to a different country to experience a different culture. You can live in the same city you were born in and still be a stranger there. On the other hand, you can travel to a different country, where the language is not the same, the food and smells are different. Yet you can feel like you are home, like the people there are your people. How can this be? It is because Christians are citizens of the same country. They serve a common King and live with a common purpose. They speak the same heart language: the gospel. When Christians encounter other Christians even though they have nothing external in common—no common language, no common culture—they find they are brothers and sisters. They find that they are both strangers and aliens on earth. To admit that you are a stranger and alien on earth does not imply that you do not love your country or the earth. The opposite is true: those who have been made citizens of heaven through the gospel make the best citizens of their temporary countries. They do not have to desperately get everything from this life because this life is not everything to them. If you fail to see yourself as a stranger here on earth, you are not seeing yourself correctly. If you have "settled in" and made yourself completely at home, you are "settling" for far less than you are an heir to. You are an heir to a "far country." This is not your home. Because of your eternal citizenship, you do not have to despair that your temporary home does not fully satisfy. "Meanwhile," Paul wrote, we "groan" longing for our heavenly home. Even in the best of times here, our hearts long for more. Not more money, or more friends, or more pleasure, or more of anything this country offers, though we are often fooled into believing those things are what will satisfy. We long for more of what we were made for: the fullness of God's presence. Close the gap today on seeing more clearly where your citizenship truly lies. Reflect on what has not satisfied you. Reflect on what has.

Day 3
Read:

Heb. 11:13-16 All these people were still living by faith when they died. They did not receive the things promised; they only saw them and welcomed them from a distance. And they admitted that they were aliens and strangers on earth. People who say such things show that they are looking for a country of their own. If they had been thinking of the country they had left, they would have had opportunity to return. Instead, they were longing for a better country — a heavenly one. Therefore, God is not ashamed to be called their God, for he has prepared a city for them.

Reflect:

Peter urged his friends to live as aliens and strangers in this world by turning against the sinful desires that would war against their souls. These desires are not just the "big sins," the things that are overt in the destruction they bring. These desires can be subtle, more covert. In fact, they most often are. They can be the desire for more, for better, or just for other than what I have. The drive of the sensual to control and direct our lives causes us to live for pleasure rather than for larger, longer-lasting "good." We can trade what we know for what we feel and become slaves to our own desires. The desires of the flesh make us petty in our relationships, easily offended, easily angered...quick to write people off and throw relationships away. There is no neutral space. No neutral thought, song, movie, book, day, or experience. All that happens in, to, and around us is shaping us into certain kinds of people. There is enormous shaping pressure coming from the culture we live in and the sinful desires that live in us. These pressures are waging "war" against our souls. They attempt to misshape us into their broken image while God intends for us to be shaped into the image of Christ. For many Christians the focus of the "war" is centered on cultural forces arrayed against them. Externals become the most important battle space. Media, sexual trends, the courts, the schools, the shifts in family structures all look to be the "real fight." But if we miss the fact that the most important war is internal not external, then we will surely lose the war against our souls. "Above all else guard your heart," says the Proverb, "because out of it flow all the issues of your life." To live as a stranger and alien here is not primarily about a "culture war"; it is about a "soul war." You must continually pay attention to what you are allowing to shape you on the inside. This has a negative component ("avoid" certain things that misshape you) and a positive component ("pursue" things the shape you). Close the gap today regarding your perspective on your "alien status." See the war for your soul as being winnable. It is a fight that will continue until you die, but it is a fight you can become more skilled at if you only will give yourself to that task.

Day 4
Read:

Heb. 11:13-16 All these people were still living by faith when they died. They did not receive the things promised; they only saw them and welcomed them from a distance. And they admitted that they were aliens and strangers on earth. People who say such things show that they are looking for a country of their own. If they had been thinking of the country they had left, they would have had opportunity to return. Instead, they were longing for a better country — a heavenly one. Therefore, God is not ashamed to be called their God, for he has prepared a city for them.

Reflect:

Moses was given a vision of his people living in liberty in a land of promise. He was also given a commission to lead his people out of the land of slavery to that promised place. He did not believe he was up to the task, and in many ways, he was not. However, God intended to reveal himself through Moses' insecurity and inabilities. As Moses took on the task God set before him, he encountered difficulty after difficulty. He was challenged by his enemies as well as his own people. He poured his life out for others, and very often they questioned his leadership and his motives. He took his people to the threshold of the Promised Land only to have to turn back into the wilderness because of their unbelief. Finally, after decades of living off of God's faithfulness, the people were able to enter the land God had promised. Yet, Moses could not go in. He was only able to see it from a distance. He died in the wilderness, looking into the land of God's promise. Did God cheat Moses? Is the final chapter of Moses' life disappointment, emptiness, and futility? Did he give his life for a goal that was never accomplished? I will give you one sentence from the book of Exodus that will give you the answer to all of these questions. "The LORD would speak to Moses face to face, as a man speaks with his friend." So, what is your answer? Was his life one of futility or of fullness? Did God cheat him or bless him beyond all measure? How you answer these questions will help you evaluate your own perspective regarding your status as an "alien and a stranger" here and now. Moses received the greater promise. He did not walk on a certain piece of ground in the Middle East, but he did get to the place of promise. In addition, as he walked in the wilderness, far from the land of promise, he walked with God as his friend. Wherever we walk with God as a friend, that place becomes the place of promise for us. Close the gap on your friendship with God. Friendship with God is tied most closely to absolute obedience to him. He is not looking for a junior partner; he is looking for one whose heart is fully surrendered to him.

Day 5
Read:

Heb. 11:13-16 All these people were still living by faith when they died. They did not receive the things promised; they only saw them and welcomed them from a distance. And they admitted that they were aliens and strangers on earth. People who say such things show that they are looking for a country of their own. If they had been thinking of the country they had left, they would have had opportunity to return. Instead, they were longing for a better country — a heavenly one. Therefore, God is not ashamed to be called their God, for he has prepared a city for them.

Reflect:

Can a father be ashamed of his child and still love that child? Of course he can. When a child lives in a way that is counter to the values of the father, then the father is ashamed. But the opposite is true as well. When a child lives their father's values, then the father is proud. The men whose lives are described here were not perfect men. In fact, Moses did not miss the Promised Land because of the sin of his people; he missed it because of his own sin. Yet even though those men were not perfect in every action, they were perfect in their overall life-orientation. They lived, over the course of their lives, headed towards the will and ways of God. They may have taken two steps forward and one step backwards, or even sometimes two steps backwards, but the trajectory of their lives was pointed towards God. Because this was true, God was not ashamed to be called their God. In fact, for generations to come God would call himself "the God of Abraham, Isaac, and Jacob." He was very proud to own these flawed sons. He was happy to be known as their father. Their individual actions were not always in line with God's family values, but their life-direction was. When they got off track, they got back on. Most of your life as a follower of Christ will be spent getting back on track. This doesn't mean you will or should get way off into terrible situations and stay there for long periods of time. It does mean, ideally, that you will make day-by-day course corrections. It may mean occasionally those corrections will be large in nature, but often it will mean we must adjust a degree here or there. These course corrections are immensely important because to be off a single degree on a compass heading over a long period of time, means you are eventually going the exact opposite direction from where you should be going. "Closing the gap" is simply a way of saying make small and immediate course corrections that keep you on track over the long haul. It is also a way of saying make the small and immediate obedience choices that will propel you forward in your journey. Making God "proud" is a good and appropriate life objective. This doesn't require detailed perfection, but it does require a settled direction. It is a life pointed his way over the long haul. It has been called a "long obedience in a single direction." Today is a single step in that journey.

WEEK 8/Day 1
Read:

Heb. 11:17-19 By faith Abraham, when God tested him, offered Isaac as a sacrifice. He who had received the promises was about to sacrifice his one and only son, even though God had said to him, "It is through Isaac that your offspring will be reckoned." Abraham reasoned that God could raise the dead, and figuratively speaking, he did receive Isaac back from death.

Reflect:

What is the reward for passing a test? Often it is a more challenging test. In learning math, the tests become more and more difficult. The same is true in learning piano or perfecting your skill at a sport. Faith grows like a muscle or a skill. It must be pushed beyond its current level in order to go the next level. This faith development is painful, just as muscle development is. When you push a muscle, lactic acid builds up making the muscle painful to use; it can take a couple of days to recover from a difficult workout. But the saying "no pain, no gain" is certainly true in muscle development. It is also true, for the most part, in faith development. When we feel pain, we tend to automatically believe something is wrong. This can be true: pain can indicate an injury and be a sign to "stop!" But it can also be the side effect of going to a new level and be a sign to "press on!" When our faith gets pressed, it means we are in "water over our heads." It seems like what we are being asked to endure or to choose is beyond our ability, and it probably is. But when we respond to God in faith to the current situation, we are becoming spiritually resilient for what is ahead. If we try to evade or avoid the current challenge, we find ourselves increasingly unprepared for future challenges. Abraham's greatest test of faith was built on his prior experience with God. When God told him to "go to the place I will show you," Abraham went. When God told Abraham he would have a son, Abraham chose to believe him. Those are a couple of the big items we know about; no doubt there where hundreds of smaller choices Abraham made to learn to trust in God's faithfulness. Now when this next test came—the biggest test of all—it was no doubt a great stretch, but it was not totally beyond him. It was just "a bit more." All the days of saying "yes" before this prepared Abraham for this day of a very large "yes." Close the gap today on your faith. There are going to be opportunities to trust him today, to say "yes" to him. Take those opportunities; they are your preparation today for what God has next.

Day 2
Read:

Heb. 11:17-19 By faith Abraham, when God tested him, offered Isaac as a sacrifice. He who had received the promises was about to sacrifice his one and only son, even though God had said to him, "It is through Isaac that your offspring will be reckoned."

32

Abraham reasoned that God could raise the dead, and figuratively speaking, he did receive Isaac back from death.

Reflect:
What if pain avoidance is of higher value to me than faith development? If growing in faith is so painful should we opt out of growth? There is certainly a way to opt out of growth, but there isn't a way to opt out of pain. "No pain, no gain" is true in many cases. But what is also true, and often not taken into account in our choices, is there can be "Pain, with no gain." Abraham could have refused to offer his son as a sacrifice because he was afraid of the pain. Abraham could have said "no" and he would have escaped the pain of that terrible and wonderful day. But he likely would have lived for many days (as many parents do) in fear of losing his son. He may very well have believed that it was his responsibility to "help God" keep his promise. He could have lived a controlling, unhappy, fretful life and passed that fear on to his son. You can sometimes decide to forgo some of the pain of trusting God. The pain of asking someone to forgive you. The pain of dying to pride. The pain of putting someone first who you don't even like or the pain of blessing someone who is cursing you. You can forgo all this pain by simply doing life in your own way, on your own terms. But what pain will you experience in your life as you live this way? What gain will you miss out on? When you go to measure the potential costs of radical obedience to God, do not fail to measure the costs of disobedience and the vast benefits of obedience. Remember Jesus, who for the joy set before him endured the cross, scorning it shame. Close the gap today. What faith choice is in front of you right now? What are the potential costs involved in making that choice? What are the costs of not making it? What is God offering you by giving you this faith choice to make? Do you see his invitation to gain through this pain? Will you take his invitation?

Day 3
Read: Heb. 11:20-31 By faith Isaac blessed Jacob and Esau in regard to their future. By faith Jacob, when he was dying, blessed each of Joseph's sons, and worshiped as he leaned on the top of his staff. By faith Joseph, when his end was near, spoke about the exodus of the Israelites from Egypt and gave instructions about his bones. By faith Moses' parents hid him for three months after he was born, because they saw he was no ordinary child, and they were not afraid of the king's edict. By faith Moses, when he had grown up, refused to be known as the son of Pharaoh's daughter. He chose to be mistreated along with the people of God rather than to enjoy the pleasures of sin for a short time. He regarded disgrace for the sake of Christ as of greater value than the treasures of Egypt, because he was looking ahead to his reward. By faith he left Egypt, not fearing the king's anger; he persevered because he saw him who is invisible.

By faith he kept the Passover and the sprinkling of blood, so that the destroyer of the firstborn would not touch the firstborn of Israel. By faith the people passed through the Red Sea as on dry land; but when the Egyptians tried to do so, they were drowned. By faith the walls of Jericho fell, after the people had marched around them for seven days. By faith the prostitute Rahab, because she welcomed the spies, was not killed with those who were disobedient.

Reflect:
Some of these acts of faith are epic: an entire nation narrowly escaping destruction by passing through a sea on dry land, or the walls of an enemy city falling down without any human help. But some of this feels normal, mundane. A father blessing his sons. Another giving burial instructions for his remains. Some seem shocking: a woman putting her child in a woven basket into a river, and a prostitute being used to accomplish God's purposes. But the overall picture you get from this passage is that faith is woven into real life. There are times when faith is expressed in ways that defy human explanation and imagination; in those times what God is doing is obvious. There are other times when it takes the eyes of faith to see what God is doing. Faith is confidence in God. Confidence in God is expressed in distinct actions. You don't have to feel confident to take faith steps. Faith is acting in a way that demonstrates you believe God is alive and that he is involved. Our faith demonstrates God's faithfulness. We believe him and that "acted on" belief reveals God to others, and to ourselves. You may have the opportunity to demonstrate God's faithfulness in some epic fashion. If you do, it will probably mean you are going through epic difficulty or suffering. Look again at the passage; there is a principle there. The more amazing the intervention of God in our lives, the more desperate the need was. Do not assume you will have epic intervention minus the epic struggle. However, it is more likely you will have many opportunities to demonstrate God's faithfulness in multiple mundane ways. It will be the collective testimony of many days of faithfulness when God's work in our lives will take faith to see because it will not be immediately obvious. Close the gap today: look for God, see what faith sees in the circumstances of your life today. If the struggle is great, look for what he might do in the midst of it to make his greatness known.

Day 4
Read:
Heb. 11:32-34 And what more shall I say? I do not have time to tell about Gideon, Barak, Samson, Jephthah, David, Samuel and the prophets, who through faith conquered kingdoms, administered justice, and gained what was promised; who shut the mouths of lions, quenched the fury of the flames, and escaped the edge of the sword; whose weakness was turned to strength; and who became powerful in battle and routed foreign armies.

Reflect:

How do you explain the list of people in this chapter that has been called the "hall of faith"? Gideon was faithless, so God had to prove himself several times. Barak was a coward. Samson was a carnal, brutal man. Jepththah was a rash and foolish man. David was a murderous adulterer. In fact, there is no one in the Bible, apart from Jesus, who was consistently "heroic." This chapter has been misnamed; it should be the "hall of faithless people who saw God be faithful." It's not that their lives did not contain demonstrations of faith; it's that their lives demonstrated inconsistent faith, but God demonstrated consistent faithfulness. It is "through faith" they experienced the legendary things we read about all these years later. But the point of this passage, of the Bible, of life itself is God. He is the faithful one. The point is never the greatness of a person's faith but the greatness of God, the one who makes human faith more than wishful thinking. Be encouraged by the failure of the people God used. Their failures are not our excuse to continue to live in failure. But their failure removes our excuse that because of our failure God cannot use us. Failure is not fatal for you. Do not have faith in faith. That often means we try to "feel" like we believe. Do not have faith in yourself. That often means we believe that outcomes depend mostly or entirely on "how much faith we can muster up." Your faith is to be in the faithful God. Because it is about him and not you, a very small amount of genuine faith is plenty. Do not accept sin in your life. But do not believe that God cannot use you because of your failure. He does not delight in our sin. But he does delight in showing his greatness in our weakness. Close the gap on where you are now and where God wants you to be. Sure, he gets glory from using broken vessels. But he gets great delight in seeing his broken vessels becoming increasingly whole and more fully his.

Day 5
Read:

Heb. 11:35-40 Women received back their dead, raised to life again. Others were tortured and refused to be released, so that they might gain a better resurrection. Some faced jeers and flogging, while still others were chained and put in prison. They were stoned; they were sawed in two; they were put to death by the sword. They went about in sheepskins and goatskins, destitute, persecuted and mistreated —the world was not worthy of them.
They wandered in deserts and mountains, and in caves and holes in the ground. These were all commended for their faith, yet none of them received what had been promised. God had planned something better for us so that only together with us would they be made perfect.

Reflect:

The gospel is your only hope. To have the faith to see dead, loved ones raised to life is not enough.

To have the faith to endure terrible suffering and torture is not enough. To have the faith to be killed in horrible, terrible fashion is not enough. To live in unbelievable circumstances in order to be faithful is not enough. What is enough if these things are not? The sacrifice of Jesus is. The "better" thing that God had planned for us and for those who died before the coming of the Christ is just that: the coming of the Savior to the world. Those who died prior to the incarnation were saved by faith that trusted God alone for salvation. They were not saved because their faith took them through terrible circumstances; they were saved because their faith took them to God for salvation. It is by God's grace that all are saved through faith. This has always been the case. Some people have been able to endure much because they had faith in themselves, or in a certain hoped-for outcome. But although this faith may have given them extra human stamina and strength in the short term, it is not the faith that can ultimately save. Some people have been able to endure much because of their faith in a certain god, or idol, or even a demon. Their faith increased their resiliency and allowed them to overcome much, but that faith is not enough to ultimately save them. Have you ever been confused by people who do have faith in the gospel but are able to live with great endurance and hope in the face of great difficulty? You need not be. Faith and hope are powerful factors in human lives. Even if the object of faith is not real, the presence of faith can make a difference in outcomes. Faith is not what is most important. What is most important is that our faith is well-placed in the one true God. Some will have overcoming faith that is misplaced in their own ability. This faith can do much, but it will in the end fail them. You can have a stumbling, faltering faith that is placed in God. Though you may fail along the way, he will not fail you in the end. By all means close the gap: seek to grow in your faith. But grow in your faith in God, not in some kind of faith that tries to exist in isolation from him. The gospel is your only hope, hope in Christ alone.

WEEK 9/Day 1
Read:
Heb. 12:1-7 Therefore, since we are surrounded by such a great cloud of witnesses, let us throw off everything that hinders and the sin that so easily entangles, and let us run with perseverance the race marked out for us. Let us fix our eyes on Jesus, the author and perfecter of our faith, who for the joy set before him endured the cross, scorning its shame, and sat down at the right hand of the throne of God. Consider him who endured such opposition from sinful men, so that you will not grow weary and lose heart. In your struggle against sin, you have not yet resisted to the point of shedding your blood. And you have forgotten that word of encouragement that addresses you as sons: "My son, do not make light of the Lord's discipline, and do not lose heart when he rebukes you, because the Lord disciplines those he loves, and he punishes everyone he accepts as a son."

Endure hardship as discipline; God is treating you as sons. For what son is not disciplined by his father?

Reflect:

Imagine preparing to run a race by loading your pockets with stones and then tying a rope around your legs to impede your movement. Of course, this is foolish. No one who wanted to run their best race would do this. The race marked out for us is a life of faith. The ones who have gone before have shown us how to run. They have also shown us not to run. They did not all run equally well, but they have all finished their race. We have learned from their success and from their failure that God is the faithful one. Now it is your turn to run. This is not a short race; it requires perseverance to finish well. Even if your life proves to be short in terms of years that God gives you, you must have endurance to finish well. The sin that so easily entangles does its nasty work in our lives, first by redirecting our perspective. We believe the race is too hard, and a life of obedience is not really possible or maybe not even desirable. We begin to see the very things that hinder the best life possible as being the best life possible. Sin turns our perspective upside down. The obedience God is calling you to is entirely for your benefit. Of course, it is for his glory, but his glory in your life is always for your ultimate benefit. The good news is that you can throw off the things that hinder your life of faith. It may feel like throwing away the things that hinder and entangle you in this life of faith are a part of you. Perhaps you have become so accustomed to them that you think they are an actual part of you now. You can't imagine living life without that deed, that attitude, that perspective, that anger, or lust, or pride. But if you are a Christian, they are not a part of you; they are stones you have picked up from the ground. You can, if you will, cast them back to the ground. Christ offers you that kind of freedom to run this race marked out for you. Close the gap today. Consider your perspective on sinful attitudes and actions. Do you really see them as they are? Will you look honestly at them today? Will you throw them off? Are you convinced that you can? Son or Daughter of God, you can.

Day 2
Read:

Heb. 12:1-7 Therefore, since we are surrounded by such a great cloud of witnesses, let us throw off everything that hinders and the sin that so easily entangles, and let us run with perseverance the race marked out for us. Let us fix our eyes on Jesus, the author and perfecter of our faith, who for the joy set before him endured the cross, scorning its shame, and sat down at the right hand of the throne of God. Consider him who endured such opposition from sinful men, so that you will not grow weary and lose heart. In your struggle against sin, you have not yet resisted to the point of shedding your blood.

And you have forgotten that word of encouragement that addresses you as sons: "My son, do not make light of the Lord's discipline, and do not lose heart when he rebukes you, because the Lord disciplines those he loves, and he punishes everyone he accepts as a son." Endure hardship as discipline; God is treating you as sons. For what son is not disciplined by his father?

Reflect:
The great cloud of witnesses, the men and women who have gone before us, have demonstrated that a life of direction does not have to be a life of perfection in order to finish well. Their examples are instructive, helpful, and important, but they are not near enough. For one thing, since their examples are imperfect, we cannot make their lives the focus of our lives. The same is true for living "heroes." There are men and woman alive today who can teach us much about a life of faith. The work of God in their lives encourages, challenges, and motivates us. But we cannot make their lives the focus of our lives. If you lived for a period of time with any "great Christian" past or present, it is very likely you would be surprised and possibly disappointed. But only if you think someone out there is living a life of faith perfectly. It is not necessary or advisable to become cynical about the possibility of learning from men and women who have experience with God. Their imperfection does not mean they don't have much to teach us. So we must not become hero worshippers or cynics, but we do need a focal point for this life of faith. That focal point is Jesus. We are to be aware of the cloud of witnesses, but we are to fix our gaze fully on Jesus. We are to learn from others, but we are to make Jesus the focus of our lives. He is the author and perfecter of our faith. From beginning to end, he remains our point of focus. He did not fail or falter. He endured great suffering because he had great perspective. He is not a dead example; he is a living, active, involved example. We do not have to just look to the written gospels to learn from him, as vitally important as that is. We can look to him day-to-day because he is alive. Close the gap on your faith today by looking at your circumstances through the eyes of Jesus. How would he act if he were you? How does he want you to act? He is with you.

Day 3
Read:
Heb. 12:1-7 Therefore, since we are surrounded by such a great cloud of witnesses, let us throw off everything that hinders and the sin that so easily entangles, and let us run with perseverance the race marked out for us. Let us fix our eyes on Jesus, the author and perfecter of our faith, who for the joy set before him endured the cross, scorning its shame, and sat down at the right hand of the throne of God. Consider him who endured such opposition from sinful men, so that you will not grow weary and lose heart.

In your struggle against sin, you have not yet resisted to the point of shedding your blood. And you have forgotten that word of encouragement that addresses you as sons: "My son, do not make light of the Lord's discipline, and do not lose heart when he rebukes you, because the Lord disciplines those he loves, and he punishes everyone he accepts as a son." Endure hardship as discipline; God is treating you as sons. For what son is not disciplined by his father?

Reflect:

How do we really learn anything from someone who is perfect other than we are not? How does considering Jesus and his triumphant victory on the cross help us not grow weary and lose heart? We are not Jesus, we are not perfect. We do grow weary, and we do lose heart. Some have resisted sin to the point of losing their lives. But those who are yet alive have not. Is all this encouragement only available for martyrs and Jesus? What about normal, average, weary, and disheartened believers? Is this a rebuke without encouragement? It seems to be written to encourage, but how can it be? Consider Jesus, fix your eyes on him. What do you see when you see him? You see a man who was tempted in every way just as we are, yet without sin. You see a man who wept over a dead friend. You see a man who begged his Father for another way, yet yielded to his Father's best way. You see a man so stressed by coming events that he sweat blood and longed for the encouragement of his friends. Jesus is perfect, but he was tempted just like you are. The reason you are to consider him in your own struggle is that his victory over sin can be yours. There is no reason why you must give in to sin. There is no reason why you cannot experience his strength and be of stout heart. The whole point of him being tempted in every way as we are yet without sin is to reveal to us that we do not have to give in. Adam and Eve did not have to sin; they chose to. You do not have to sin. You may think this is make-believe talk. You may believe that sin is so strong that it cannot be beaten. This would be true except for the gospel. You must begin to believe more and more each day that you do not have to sin. Because you do not have to sin. I am not suggesting you will reach sinless perfection in this life. You will not. I am suggesting that you can close the gap each and every day. You do not have to move backward, ever. You can, if you will, move forward. Consider him, today, now.

Day 4
Read:

Heb. 12:11 No discipline seems pleasant at the time, but painful. Later on, however, it produces a harvest of righteousness and peace for those who have been trained by it.

39

Reflect:
How would a person "make light of the Lord's discipline?" Perhaps by seeing it as random, chance events. Perhaps by thinking God is unfair to you, or unaware, or uncaring of what is happening in your life. Maybe it is by trying to "tough it out" and to refuse to be bowed down by the discipline. How might a person "lose heart" because of the Lord's rebuke in their life? Maybe it would it be as a result of them concluding God does not really love them because if he did he would not deal with them in this way. But fathers who love their children are willing to discipline their children. Children in the moment of discipline may not feel loved by it, but if the child has a good father then his discipline is a very high form of love. Disciplining a child is hard for the father and the child. They would both prefer to enjoy "easier" expressions of love. But when discipline is needed, the loving father does not run down the easy path. Is your heart conflicted? Has God been treating you as a son or daughter through loving discipline? We are delighted when he is delighted in us. We love it when God is not ashamed to be called our God. But even when he is unhappy with our choices, he is our Father. We experience his love when we feel his pleasure and when we feel his displeasure. Not every trouble that comes into your life is because of God's displeasure. But when God does bring discipline in order to reorient us to himself, we must not hide from him. It is unlikely we will ever enjoy "being" disciplined, but if we understand what is happening and pay careful attention to the outcomes, we will know the joy of "having been" disciplined by God. Fathers want their children to learn to be disciplined because liberty is only available to those who know when and what to say "no" to and what to say "yes" to. *Disciple* and *discipline* are children of the same word family. A disciple is disciplined in order to be near the one he loves. When your Father disciplines you, it is because he wants you to share his holiness. He wants you to share his very life. Close the gap on faith and love. Endure hardship as "discipleship"; God is treating you as his beloved child.

Day 5
Read: Heb. 12:1-11 Therefore, since we are surrounded by such a great cloud of witnesses, let us throw off everything that hinders and the sin that so easily entangles, and let us run with perseverance the race marked out for us. Let us fix our eyes on Jesus, the author and perfecter of our faith, who for the joy set before him endured the cross, scorning its shame, and sat down at the right hand of the throne of God. Consider him who endured such opposition from sinful men, so that you will not grow weary and lose heart. In your struggle against sin, you have not yet resisted to the point of shedding your blood. And you have forgotten that word of encouragement that addresses you as sons: "My son, do not make light of the Lord's discipline, and do not lose heart when he rebukes you, because the Lord disciplines those he loves, and he punishes everyone he accepts as a son."

Endure hardship as discipline; God is treating you as sons. For what son is not disciplined by his father? Our fathers disciplined us for a little while as they thought best; but God disciplines us for our good, that we may share in his holiness. No discipline seems pleasant at the time, but painful. Later on, however, it produces a harvest of righteousness and peace for those who have been trained by it.

Reflect:

Delayed gratification is the ability to see in the present difficulty the long-term good. To delay gratification is to embrace discipline, or discipleship. Discipline does not despise gratification; it just has a "long view" of it. It wants the gratification that lasts a long time and leaves no bitter "after taste." Immediate gratification often causes long-term misery. Why is this? Because the long view of what will gratify or satisfy is very different than the short view. The short view wants pleasure and relief from pain. The long view wants the real good...the glory of God and the good of others. The long view leads to wise choices and a deep inner development. The short view leads to foolish choices and leaves a person with a "hollow core." Learning to value what is valuable and to refuse to give our lives to what is not is a painful process. It is not like running to the store and picking up some junk food to satisfy a feeling of hunger. It is more like plowing a field, then planting seeds, then watering, weeding, and waiting for the plants to grow. Then finally after much working and waiting, you experience the gratification of a harvest of discipline. Discipline is not just about final products. It is about the process itself. Immediate gratification wants what it wants now. The process is the enemy of desire. The process stands in the way of relief right now. On the other hand, long-term gratification has learned that the process itself is part of the benefit. The harvest of peace and righteousness is a product of the process. The process is not the enemy of gratification; the process is the path to lasting gratification. Will you see the long-term good in the short-term discipline? Will you refuse to trade what is ultimately valuable for what merely brings temporary relief? Close the gap today; see beyond right now as you make your decisions about what you will do and who you will be. See with the eyes of faith to what will matter most at the end. What will matter most then matters most now. What will matter most then will be faith expressing itself in love. That is what matters most right now.

Week 10/Day 1
Read:

Phil. 2:3-11 Do nothing out of selfish ambition or vain conceit, but in humility consider others better than yourselves. Each of you should look not only to your own interests, but also to the interests of others.

Your attitude should be the same as that of Christ Jesus: Who, being in very nature God, did not consider equality with God something to be grasped, but made himself nothing, taking the very nature of a servant, being made in human likeness. And being found in appearance as a man, he humbled himself and became obedient to death — even death on a cross! Therefore God exalted him to the highest place and gave him the name that is above every name, that at the name of Jesus every knee should bow, in heaven and on earth and under the earth, and every tongue confess that Jesus Christ is Lord, to the glory of God the Father.

Reflect:
Are we really this far off? The challenge is that nothing be done out of selfish ambition. The reality is that virtually everything is done out of it. There is no room here for "some" or even very "little." This is an absolute demand, "Do nothing out of selfish ambition." This is as unrealistic a goal as has ever been stated. First, who even wants such a goal? Should I not reserve some of my life, my wishes for myself? Second, who could possibly accomplish such a goal even if they wanted to? Who wants such a goal? We all would if we really knew our own hearts. Why do we do put ourselves first anyway? We do so in order to experience happiness; we do so because we think it is the "good life." Does this ever work well or for long? Has selfishness ever taken anyone into a life that is "good"? Certainly not and it never will. Jesus, for the joy set before him, endured the cross, scorning its shame. God incarnate showed the path to real human happiness, it was in giving his life away for others. Who would want to live a life for others first? Jesus did. We also would, if we saw as clearly as he does. But then who can live such a life, apart from Jesus? "Nothing" done from selfish ambition is unrealistic. No, "nothing" is the only reasonable goal. If we were told to do just a little, or half of what we do from selfish ambition, we would remain on the path away from God. The challenge to do nothing out of selfish ambition or vain conceit is the way of Jesus. Never mind whether you will pull that off perfectly, that is the direction to head with your life. Do not settle for anything less. When you fail, do not turn back or stay down long. Get up and close the gap. Nothing less will do.

Day 2
Read:
Phil. 2:3-11 Do nothing out of selfish ambition or vain conceit, but in humility consider others better than yourselves. Each of you should look not only to your own interests, but also to the interests of others. Your attitude should be the same as that of Christ Jesus: Who, being in very nature God, did not consider equality with God something to be grasped, but made himself nothing, taking the very nature of a servant, being made in human likeness.

And being found in appearance as a man, he humbled himself and became obedient to death — even death on a cross! Therefore God exalted him to the highest place and gave him the name that is above every name, that at the name of Jesus every knee should bow, in heaven and on earth and under the earth, and every tongue confess that Jesus Christ is Lord, to the glory of God the Father.

Reflect:

It is assumed you will look out for your own interests. This is not wrong; it's normal and it's wise. You should care for your body and your soul. You should care for your family and possessions. All of this falls under the category of stewardship. It is being faithful with what has been given to you, but the challenge here is to make the interests of others your interest as well. You are to have the attitude of Jesus in regards to others. Attitude describes our essential orientation to others. The attitude of Jesus was humility; he put the interests of others ahead of his own. So, if it is normal to look out for our own interests and we are to look to the interests of others as well, what happens when those interests come into conflict? What happens when it seems you are in a situation where it seems to be "either" their interests "or" yours? What happens when the "also" doesn't appear to be possible? Throughout history many heroic people have given their lives for someone else. They have, in an ultimate sense, chosen to put the interests of others ahead of their own. Although this scenario is possible for you, it is not probable. What is most likely is that the conflict of interests will happen in many, mundane, normal sorts of ways. Will you maneuver, moan or manipulate to get your way? Or will you put others first by refusing to act this way, even if it means you do not get your way? Will you stay seated while others serve? Or will you get up and go? Will you listen to another's words and heart when you just want to detach and be left alone? Will you rejoice with others when you are feeling down? There are so many ways where you might experience a conflict of interests, yours or theirs. In those situations it is ultimately in your own best interests to put the interests of others first. How can this be? Because when you do so, you will be following the lead of Jesus. You will maximize your joy by closing the gap between what is true about your life and what can be true about it.

Day 3
Read:

Phil. 2:6-11 Your attitude should be the same as that of Christ Jesus: Who, being in very nature God, did not consider equality with God something to be grasped, but made himself nothing, taking the very nature of a servant, being made in human likeness. And being found in appearance as a man, he humbled himself and became obedient to death — even death on a cross!

Therefore God exalted him to the highest place and gave him the name that is above every name, that at the name of Jesus every knee should bow, in heaven and on earth and under the earth, and every tongue confess that Jesus Christ is Lord, to the glory of God the Father.

Reflect:

It is impossible for humans to get their minds fully around the incarnation. This doesn't mean we should not contemplate it, meditate on it, and have growing wonder for it, because we *can* understand it, in the same way we understand other things that are real. Our knowledge of Christ being made in human likeness is accurate and adequate even though it is not exhaustive or comprehensive. In nature, there are believed to be four fundamental forces, one of which is gravity. How these forces work and how they are tied together is not fully known. The lack of full knowledge does not keep us from living on the earth, launching rockets into space and any number of other human activities related to gravity and the other three forces. Knowledge of God is real knowledge; it is not in a separate realm than knowledge of gravity. All knowledge is in the realm of what is real. If it is not real, it is not knowledge. The reason this is important is that, for many people, talk of "knowledge of God" is pushed into the realm of "religion" which is different than the realm of "reality" where things like gravity exist. This is silly, but it has impacted many people's perceptions of faith, perhaps it has impacted yours. Jesus is the eternal Son of God. He has always been, and always will be. In space and time, he was born to a virgin as an infant. This is real knowledge, though it is fantastic knowledge. The fact of God becoming man is no more impossible or implausible than the fact of the existence of the universe itself. Gravity is a subject of academic study. There are formulas written in books that describe it. But, of course, gravity exists as an actual force in the real world; it is more than theory in books. In the same way, the Incarnation is a subject of study written about in the Bible and in other books. But, like gravity, it is something that is real in the world. The implications and applications are profound for human existence. In many ways, it is more profound even than the reality of gravity. The knowledge of the Incarnation tells you how you are to live your life; that is very important knowledge to have. Jesus is the Lord of heaven and earth. His life, death, and resurrection inform everything about our lives, deaths, and eternal destinies. He took the form of a human, which is the form of a servant. This means your essential nature, as a human, is servant. You cannot completely close the gap on understanding the Incarnation, but if you will think about it, you will grow in your understanding and appreciation for it. As you do, it will change how you see things in and around you. When you are treated as a servant, instead of becoming angry, you will understand this is who God has made you to be. This is the very form God incarnate took on himself.

Day 4
Read:
Phil. 2:3-11 Do nothing out of selfish ambition or vain conceit, but in humility consider others better than yourselves. Each of you should look not only to your own interests, but also to the interests of others. Your attitude should be the same as that of Christ Jesus: Who, being in very nature God, did not consider equality with God something to be grasped, but made himself nothing, taking the very nature of a servant, being made in human likeness. And being found in appearance as a man, he humbled himself and became obedient to death — even death on a cross! Therefore God exalted him to the highest place and gave him the name that is above every name, that at the name of Jesus every knee should bow, in heaven and on earth and under the earth, and every tongue confess that Jesus Christ is Lord, to the glory of God the Father.

Reflect:
How does humility impact obedience? Surely sin is pride, so obedience is humility. Sin believes you know better than God what will lead to your own fulfillment and happiness. In order to believe you know better than God, you have to somehow, maybe subconsciously, believe you are smarter than him. Or, perhaps, if he just had all the facts, he would side with you. However, sin often isn't that well thought through. Sometimes it is just people wanting what they want in spite of the facts of the matter. But, how do we come to want what we should not want and to not want what we should want? Pride seems to be a key factor. We are used to believing ourselves. When our thoughts or emotions tell us something is real or true we are accustomed to believing it rather than subjecting it to the truth of God. Sometimes people will say "I know better...but." How is it that we "know...but?" If we know, actually know, won't we act in line with that knowledge? Sometimes another factor comes into play. We have practiced pride so long, in the form of believing ourselves implicitly, that we have trained our mind and even our will to do what seems right for us to do. What are we to do? To start with, humble yourself today. Admit your absolute need for God, to God. Absolute means total. Without him, you have and are nothing. Confess your long-held pride in all its forms. Even insecurity and feelings of inferiority are a form of pride. Confess all of it to him. Then, enter into a pattern of retraining your reflexes for humility. Confess pride every time it appears in your life. Choose the humility of obedience. Christ did not sin, but he faced temptation with the same advantages you have...a will, a set of desires, the opportunity to choose, the Holy Spirit, and the word of God. He humbled himself to obedience on the cross. This was the culmination of a life of training for the humility of obedience. Use the resources God has made available to you and close the gap in your life. Train for obedience, humble yourself before God and others.

Day 5

Read:

Phil. 2:3-11 Do nothing out of selfish ambition or vain conceit, but in humility consider others better than yourselves. Each of you should look not only to your own interests, but also to the interests of others. Your attitude should be the same as that of Christ Jesus: Who, being in very nature God, did not consider equality with God something to be grasped, but made himself nothing, taking the very nature of a servant, being made in human likeness. And being found in appearance as a man, he humbled himself and became obedient to death — even death on a cross! Therefore God exalted him to the highest place and gave him the name that is above every name, that at the name of Jesus every knee should bow, in heaven and on earth and under the earth, and every tongue confess that Jesus Christ is Lord, to the glory of God the Father.

Reflect:

Consider whose name is currently on everyone's lips? What celebrity is most famous right now? Answer quickly, because in a moment their name and their fame will be forgotten. Sometimes the famous names become infamous before their lives are complete. Their names become a "byword" even before they pass into death. The ones who die while still famous may have a name and fame that lingers like an echo for a time, but eventually the echo fades. There is a name that is currently on the lips of many as they pray, as they confess, and as they worship. The name of Jesus is famous throughout the world, but only those who follow him find his name consistently on their lips and in their hearts. When all the famous among us are "said and done," there is a single name that will be on every lip. His name will rise above all the names of the dead and formerly famous. The bowed knee of every person will acknowledge that, in the end, there is a single celebrity. The confessing tongue of every human power player will verbalize the reality that they had no power that was not delegated from above and what they believed about themselves was illusion, or delusion. Look at that beautiful person strut. Watch that talented person perform. Listen to that brilliant person persuade. Are you impressed with that powerful person's impact? Do you know that they are like dust and their glory is like a fading flower? Do you really "know" that? Does that knowledge impact how you watch, think, speak, believe, and live? Do you rejoice that you know "The Famous One?" Are you able to respect men and women without fearing them? Can you appreciate what God has given them without envying them? Will you close the gap today on time and eternity in your own life? Do now what all will do then. Bow your "heart" to Jesus and put his name on your lips today in prayer, confession, and worship. Say the name of Jesus much today. Speak it to yourself and speak it to others. When he is first on your tongue and your heart, you will be positioned to bless and not merely be impressed by others.

You will live to bless and not live trying to impress others. Jesus is the famous one, say so today.

Week 11/Day 1
Read:
John 13:1-5 It was just before the Passover Feast. Jesus knew that the time had come for him to leave this world and go to the Father. Having loved his own who were in the world, he now showed them the full extent of his love. The evening meal was being served, and the devil had already prompted Judas Iscariot, son of Simon, to betray Jesus. Jesus knew that the Father had put all things under his power, and that he had come from God and was returning to God; so he got up from the meal, took off his outer clothing, and wrapped a towel around his waist. After that, he poured water into a basin and began to wash his disciples' feet, drying them with the towel that was wrapped around him.

Reflect:
Have you been disrespected? Has someone treated you as if they were better than you? Have you been ignored, felt as if you are invisible? Has someone laughed at you, treating your ideas as a joke? Have you been cheated, and were unable to do anything about it? Have you been abandoned, disregarded, or despised? Who are you then? Are you worthless? What will you do? Fight for your rights, your self-esteem, your worth? Or will you wash the feet of the people who mistreat you? It is unlikely it would be appropriate to actually wash the feet of the people around you, especially those who think and speak ill of you. But will you forgive them? Will you ask God to bless them? Will you pray that they will live lives that bring God glory and bring them joy? Jesus had loved these men for years in practical and powerful ways. Now he was going to show them the full extent of his love by dying for them. In return, he knew they would all turn from him in fear and even betrayal. What did he do? Rise from dinner, stand above them and rebuke them for their ingratitude? No, he knelt at their feet and washed the dirt of the world from them. He would soon wash the sin from their hearts as well. What about you? How will you respond to the people God has given you to love? What if they are ungrateful? What if they are hateful? Will you wash their feet by responding to them as Jesus would? "This is too much to ask! Who can live this way?" It is not too much to ask, Jesus has already demanded you give him your entire life. This, too, is included. You can, if you will. Close the gap on your love for Jesus and others. Right now, pray for the people who are the most difficult for you to love. Pray that Jesus would give you his heart for them. Your joy will increase; your experience with God will deepen. You can do this...if you will.

Day 2
Read:
John 13:6-9 He came to Simon Peter, who said to him, "Lord, are you going to wash my feet?" Jesus replied, "You do not realize now what I am doing, but later you will understand." "No," said Peter, "you shall never wash my feet." Jesus answered, "Unless I wash you, you have no part with me." "Then, Lord," Simon Peter replied, "not just my feet but my hands and my head as well!"

Reflect:
Self-sufficiency can be a liability. Perhaps the big question in your life is whether you will ever get to the place where you have learned to not rely on your own abilities. This is counterintuitive and countercultural, but not "counter gospel." Peter did not want the master to serve him. This may look like humility in his life, but at this point Peter still knew little about that. It was his pride. In part, it was also no doubt his respect for Jesus and his position as "rabbi." But much of Peter's refusal to be served was the fact that he still did not understand the nature of the mission of Jesus, that he came to serve and not to be served. He also did not understand the true nature of his own need. In the garden Peter would try to rescue Jesus with a sword. In the dark hours after Jesus was arrested, Peter would try to rescue himself with a cowardly lie. Such is the result of self-sufficiency; it is never ultimately sufficient. Of course we should take care of ourselves, work hard, and provide for our families. But the person who believes that their own energy, gifting, skill, drive, or talent will carry them through life will end up like Peter. At the worst possible time, all they relied upon will fail them. Their self-reliance will prove to be utterly unreliable. When Jesus offers to wash your feet, let him. When others offer to wash your feet, let them. Train yourself to abide in the sufficiency of Christ. Not by being passive, or lazy, or cowardly, but by refusing to put the full weight of your confidence in yourself. The direction this "Jesus sufficiency" will take you is not into low self-esteem. In fact, it will take you to the place where you esteem him much and, as you learn that he is sufficient, you will find that his sufficiency unlike your own, does not fail. In your weakness you will find what his real and reliable strength is.

Day 3
Read:
John 13:10-17 Jesus answered, "A person who has had a bath needs only to wash his feet; his whole body is clean. And you are clean, though not every one of you." For he knew who was going to betray him, and that was why he said not every one was clean. When he had finished washing their feet, he put on his clothes and returned to his place. "Do you understand what I have done for you?" he asked them.

"You call me 'Teacher' and 'Lord,' and rightly so, for that is what I am. Now that I, your Lord and Teacher, have washed your feet, you also should wash one another's feet. I have set you an example that you should do as I have done for you. I tell you the truth, no servant is greater than his master, nor is a messenger greater than the one who sent him. Now that you know these things, you will be blessed if you do them.

Reflect:

Jesus was much more than an example. He was the savior whose death atoned for our sins. The fact that he was more than an example does not mean he was less than one. To follow in his footsteps, as Peter said we are to do, no doubt means many things, but it surely means that we must be ready to be mistreated for doing the will of God. Many are confused when they do the right thing and bad things happen to them. For some, all it takes to have a life free of challenge is to "check the boxes" on the obedience list. If we do our part, then God is obligated to do his. Our part is to do good things and avoid bad things as much as possible. His part is to respond by doing good things for us and keeping bad things from us; it is a convenient arrangement. It is also an illusion. It is a deal God never signed on to. Much of the promises of God are not for this life. In this life and beyond, the most precious of the promises is that we get to have relationship with God. There can be no doubt that living life in line with the will and ways of God maximizes human happiness and potential. God does delight in those who delight in him. Furthermore, God's ways "work" because they are in line with the way he has designed life. Yet, Jesus said that he was setting the example and we will be blessed if we follow it. What was his example? It was to serve others sacrificially. What was his blessing? He was betrayed, he was tortured, and he was crucified. His blessing was not betrayal and torture, that was his sacrifice. His blessing was the glory of his Father revealed through his obedience. His blessing was our salvation. If we follow his example, we should not be surprised if people do not appreciate us, or even reject us. Our sacrifice will not bring about anyone's salvation, but our example of patience in the face of suffering might lead someone to the Savior. But even if it does not, it will bring glory to our Father. Close the gap on your faith and love today...that anger, disappointment, resentment which you have in your heart...turn from it. Jesus has set the example, now follow it. If you will, you will be blessed, even as he was; it is likely you will feel a decrease in anxiety and an increase in peace even in this very moment. Try it and see for yourself.

Day 4
Read:

John 13:6-17 He came to Simon Peter, who said to him, "Lord, are you going to wash my feet?" Jesus replied, "You do not realize now what I am doing, but later you will understand." "No," said Peter, "you shall never wash my feet." Jesus answered, "Unless I wash you, you have no part with me." "Then, Lord," Simon Peter replied, "not just my feet but my hands and my head as well!" Jesus answered, "A person who has had a bath needs only to wash his feet; his whole body is clean. And you are clean, though not every one of you." For he knew who was going to betray him, and that was why he said not every one was clean. When he had finished washing their feet, he put on his clothes and returned to his place. "Do you understand what I have done for you?" he asked them. "You call me 'Teacher' and 'Lord,' and rightly so, for that is what I am. Now that I, your Lord and Teacher, have washed your feet, you also should wash one another's feet. I have set you an example that you should do as I have done for you. I tell you the truth, no servant is greater than his master, nor is a messenger greater than the one who sent him. Now that you know these things, you will be blessed if you do them.

Reflect:

If you have given your life to Christ, you are clean. He has washed your sins away. This is a settled fact. As you live your life as a "washed person," though you do not *have* to sin, you *will* sin. When you do sin, it is not necessary to go back and be "washed again" you need only to have your feet cleansed. One of Jesus' twelve disciples refused the cleansing of Jesus. He heard, he saw, but he did not receive. There is mystery in his rebellion, but there is also mystery in the belief of the other eleven. Eleven received the grace of his cleansing life while one refused it. What is not a mystery is that even those who are "clean" will be in need of having their feet washed by the Savior as they walk through life. Peter and the other eleven were clean, but they would still fail the Savior. They would need him to wash their feet again, and he would do so. Are you in need of having your feet washed by the Savior? Are they soiled by the places you have walked in your mind, heart, and life? Have you been putting off looking fully at him because of shame or fear? Have you been hiding from his gaze? If you have been, then you have also been sliding away from his peace. If you will look at him right now, you will not see him standing over you in judgment. You will see him with towel in hand ready to wash your feet again. The day will come when he will return as the judge of all the earth. On that day nothing will matter more than whether you have been "washed" by Jesus. But today, he is the Servant Savior...he is ready to forgive and to cleanse again. Close the gap between you and him now. Let him wash your feet. If you have "messed up", "fess up" and then get up and move on. Do not walk into another day or lie down for another night with this sin between you and the Savior.

Day 5
Read:

John 13:13-17 "You call me 'Teacher' and 'Lord,' and rightly so, for that is
what I am. Now that I, your Lord and Teacher, have washed your feet, you
also should wash one another's feet. I have set you an example that you
should do as I have done for you. I tell you the truth, no servant is greater
than his master, nor is a messenger greater than the one who sent him. Now
that you know these things, you will be blessed if you do them.

Reflect:

What kinds of gods come from the minds of men? Some are far off, aloof,
and uninvolved. Some are powerful judges, handing out prison sentences and
capital punishment. Some are just like the men who invent them, gods made
in their own image, conveniently approving of their actions and attitudes.
What kind of God actually exists? How do we know? We look at Jesus.
Imagine that the entire physical universe is like the mall. There are stores and
restaurants, and it is filled with people. In this "mall-iverse" there are a
variety of beliefs regarding ultimate reality...who or what has always been.
Some believe the mall is self-creating and self-sustaining; it is all that is or ever
has been. They believe they are the products of the mall. Others believe in
different kinds of gods and goddesses. Some worship other people who live
in the mall or who used to live in the mall, but have died. Then, imagine a
door opens into the mall. This does not sound surprising, but remember,
they believed the mall was the entire universe...there could be no door
because there is no "outside." Through the door stepped a person who
looked and sounded just like them, but he lived a life like no other human
ever had. He did things inside the mall that were impossible for anyone else
to do, then he was killed by other mall dwellers, but did not stay dead. Just as
he had said he would, he came back to life. He said this would be part of the
proof that he was not just another mall dweller, but that he had, in fact, made
the mall and everyone in it. Now people can stop guessing; they can know.
They can know who God is, what he is like. They can know who they are and
how they are to live. Think! Use your mind to consider God. Not a god
who looks somewhat like you, instead think of the God whom you look a bit
like. Have you shaped Jesus into your image? Will you close the gap between
your perception of him and the reality of him? Ask him to help you escape
your own imaginations and to see him as he really is. Look to understand him
in the Bible. Read it with fresh eyes and an open heart. Don't guess what he
wants from you, rather read and know. The details of your life may remain
mysterious, but the direction of your life is clear. You are to know and love
Jesus and to make his love known. You are to live much like he did. He will
help you unpack that today, if you will tell him that you are "all in." Are you
all in?

51

Week 12/Day 1

Read:

John 19:16-22 Finally Pilate handed him over to them to be crucified. So the soldiers took charge of Jesus. Carrying his own cross, he went out to the place of the Skull (which in Aramaic is called Golgotha). Here they crucified him, and with him two others — one on each side and Jesus in the middle. Pilate had a notice prepared and fastened to the cross. It read: JESUS OF NAZARETH, THE KING OF THE JEWS. Many of the Jews read this sign, for the place where Jesus was crucified was near the city, and the sign was written in Aramaic, Latin and Greek. The chief priests of the Jews protested to Pilate, "Do not write 'The King of the Jews,' but that this man claimed to be king of the Jews." Pilate answered, "What I have written, I have written."

Reflect:

People will die during the time you read this devotion. You may be healthy, but you are dying; everyone is. Avoidance of the reality of your death does not help you live well. To remember and reflect on your own death can make you wise. But to think of death absent the hope of the gospel often makes people fearful or foolish. When death is believed to be the loss of everything, people can live in fear. They will desperately avoid considering the reality of death, or they live with their hearts and minds imprisoned in fear. In a sense, death has already won in their lives, because it controls how they live. Others live foolishly. They recognize death is the end and, instead of living in denial or despair, they live trying to "squeeze the life out of life." This sounds like a better approach, and it can lead to certain good choices, but often it just leads to folly. Those who try to "seize the day" without gospel hope will frequently live only for the day. This doesn't lead to choices that have a long time horizon. Good life choices ask questions that are bigger and better than: "What is best for me today?" Jesus' life and death was a singularity. In all of human history there have only been four types of people. Those who are not usually wise and good, who do not claim to be God. This includes most of humanity. Those who were unusually wise and good, who did not claim to be God. This includes a limited number of "great" humans. Those who are not unusually wise and good, who claimed to be God. This includes a small number of people who were insane. Finally, there are those who were usually wise and good and also claim to be God. This includes a single human, Jesus. His life was absolutely unique. His death was absolutely unique. He did not die for his own sins; he died for the sins of others. His resurrection confirmed the gospel hope, therefore death and sin do not have the final word. As you think about what you will think about today, pay careful attention to whether gospel hope will inform those thoughts. What you think most about is what most shapes who you are.

As you think about your life today and all it various components, think some about your death as well...but think about both your life and your death in the context of the gospel hope. Choose carefully your thoughts because you are making them and they are making you. Think of life and death through the lens of the hope of the gospel.

Day 2
Read:
John 19:23-25 When the soldiers crucified Jesus, they took his clothes, dividing them into four shares, one for each of them, with the undergarment remaining. This garment was seamless, woven in one piece from top to bottom. "Let's not tear it," they said to one another. "Let's decide by lot who will get it." This happened that the scripture might be fulfilled which said, "They divided my garments among them and cast lots for my clothing." So this is what the soldiers did. Near the cross of Jesus stood his mother, his mother's sister, Mary the wife of Clopas, and Mary Magdalene.

Reflect:
Close your eyes and smell the crucifixion. Do you smell the fresh hewn lumber of the crosses, still leaking sap? Smell the sweat from the nervous guards and the anxious crowd, and from Jesus' body, heated in the throes of death. Now hear the crucifixion. The rattled breathing and the tortured final breaths of three suffering men. Hear crying, laughing, gasping, and idle banter; those are the sounds of the bystanders seeing in vastly different ways what is happening in front of them. Now, feel the crucifixion. Feel your own heart racing as an innocent man is being executed, feel the dread, the anger, and the fear in your own body. Feel the air change, as the sky grows dark and clouds roll in. Feel the earth shake under your feet. If you were there, you could have smelled it, heard it, felt it, and seen it. But unless God had given you the grace, you would not have understood it. Unless he is giving you grace right now, you are not able to understand it. This was the historical account of how God became a man to die for men and women. It is a not a "religious" story. It is a real story. It is not just a man dying in the Middle East in the first century; it is God's intersection with human history. It is not silly, nor unbelievable, nor disconnected from where you live now in your own space and time. What has happened there has real bearing on your life now. Now, read it again, but do so as if you were there and you are remembering. Read it as it is, real and true. Do you see Jesus dying and, yet, taking care of his mom? He is concerned with the sins of the world and he is concerned with what will happen to his mother. He is thirsty, with a terrible, terrible thirst. This is no two-story account of a religious fairy tale. This is an eyewitness account of the Messiah, God in human flesh, dying a real death for the real sins of the world. Close the gap today between what happened then and what is happening in your life today.

Refuse to turn the events of Jesus' life, death, and resurrection into "sort of real" things, while viewing the sights, sounds, feelings, and smells around you as "really real." It is very important that you understand this is real so that you will live in line with its truth and reality. Since this happened, and if God has allowed you to understand not just that it happened, but why it happened...then think carefully before you go into the world today. Think about the implications for your life today of the crucifixion of Jesus.

Day 3
Read:
John 19:26-29 When Jesus saw his mother there, and the disciple whom he loved standing nearby, he said to his mother, "Dear woman, here is your son," and to the disciple, "Here is your mother." From that time on, this disciple took her into his home. Later, knowing that all was now completed, and so that the Scripture would be fulfilled, Jesus said, "I am thirsty." A jar of wine vinegar was there, so they soaked a sponge in it, put the sponge on a stalk of the hyssop plant, and lifted it to Jesus' lips.

Reflect:
Why the cross? God is really smart and really powerful, so why the cross? Surely there was a better, less violent, more creative way to accomplish what needed to be done. Some theologians who do not take the Scriptures seriously have called this "cosmic child abuse." They mock the idea of a substitutionary atonement for sins. But if we start with God's wisdom and not our own, then we would conclude that since God did it this way, this is the best way. If we begin our questions with the wise, all-powerful God (and we should), then the assumption must be that if God did something a certain way, it is the best way it could be done. Why the cross? There are a number of answers and undoubtedly many more than we are even aware of, but one of those answers is the fact that there is no greater love than to give your life for another. Jesus prayed in the garden for his Father to show him another way, but there was not one. So he declared that he would obey at all costs and his will was surrendered to the will of the Father. Why the cross? Because Jesus loves you. Because you were part of the joy set before him. The cross of Christ should never lead us to think much of ourselves, but rather to think much of Jesus. When you realize Jesus went to the cross because he loved you, that is not self-centered thinking, at least not if you are thinking clearly about yourself and about him. It was while we were still sinners that Christ died for us. He did not wait until we were "better" before he loved us. He did not demand we change before he changed us. Jesus did not die for "good" people; he died for rebels, for sinners. His death for us reveals how great his heart is. What about your circumstances right now? Why are they such as they are?

Perhaps some of them are the results of your own poor choices, even so God still loves you, but he is a good Father so he will not automatically and easily remove consequences from your life. But what of the issues of your life that are not tied to your own choices? What of the difficult and even heartbreaking situations you are enduring right now, why does God allow them? Will you begin with a God who is smart, powerful, and loving? Then will you yield to him as Jesus did? Will you ask him, appropriately so, to give you another way? If he says "no", then will you say, as Jesus did, "not my will but yours?" Close the gap on your faith today. Begin your questions with thoughts of who God is. He is all-wise, all-powerful, and all-loving.

Day 4
Read:
John 19:16 Finally Pilate handed him over to them to be crucified. So the soldiers took charge of Jesus...30 When he had received the drink, Jesus said, "It is finished." With that, he bowed his head and gave up his spirit.

Reflect:
"Finally" Pilate handed Jesus over to be crucified. Pilate had tried many things to get himself out of this "Messiah mess." He tried to use a Passover loophole, but the crowds demanded that a notorious prisoner be released instead of Jesus. He sought desperately for a way to set Jesus free and at the same time protect himself, but he could not. Finally, he gave up and handed Jesus over. Finally, like "finale" and "final" indicates the end of something. In this case, it was the end of Pilate's attempts to avoid handing Jesus over to death. But this particular "finally" was not just related to Pilate, at least not in the larger sense of the Messiah. Finally, in the fullness of God's timing, Jesus went to the cross. Finally, after years of loving people, healing people, teaching people truth, and setting people free, it was time for him to show the full extent of his love. No other person in human history had much of their biography written before they were even born. Finally, Jesus was crucified as had been foretold long before he was born and as had been determined since the foundation of the world. But this finally was not the "finale." Jesus would be killed, but he would not remain dead. If he had remained dead, then there would be no gospel, no good news. He would be just another teacher of morality killed for standing against the establishment of the day. But he was not merely proclaiming a new kind of ethic; he was finally bringing the Kingdom of God directly to the hearts of men and women. Your own life will be full of "finally(s)." Finally you get that job. Finally your child graduates from school. Finally you buy a house or retire. Finally you recover from that illness. Finally this life will be over for you. Then because of the gospel, the "finally" of your death will lead to the "finally" of your entrance into eternal life. "Hope deferred makes the heart sick, but a longing fulfilled is a tree of life."

There are likely some "finally(s)" you are waiting for and it seems they may never come, and they may not. These deferred "hopes" may be making you heartsick. But there is a "finally" that is guaranteed for you by God himself. That "finally" will be a tree of eternal life. Let that sure hope encourage your heart today.

Day 5
Read:
John 19:30 When he had received the drink, Jesus said, "It is finished." With that, he bowed his head and gave up his spirit.

Reflect:
Jesus was handed over to be crucified, but only because he was willing for it to be so. He was in control of all of the outcomes of his life and death. When he had completed all that he had come to do, he declared, "It is finished." A mob had also wanted to kill Jesus at an earlier date, but he was not yet finished at that time, so he simply walked through them unscathed. Unlike every other human being who has ever lived, Jesus was in control of the exact circumstances and timing of his own death. When people attempt suicide, it is often because they feel they have lost control of important circumstances in their lives. Jesus was never in a situation where circumstances were out of his control. He did not give up on life; he willingly gave it away. His cry was not of resignation or failure; it was the sound of success. He had successfully completed what he had come to do. You are not in control of all of the circumstances of your life, but you are in control of the final outcome of it. You can determine to be found faithful in the end and no one and nothing can deter you. Faithfulness is independent of external circumstances and the impact of other people's choices. You can be found faithful whether you accumulate great amounts of money or die poor. You can be found faithful whether you are married with many children or never marry and never have children. You can be faithful if you have ongoing physical health or live with painful physical ailments. Faithfulness is your response to God in all of the circumstances of your life. This does not imply that you cannot make good choices that will impact much of what happens to you; you certainly can and must. However, no matter how many good choices you make, there will always be certain factors that are completely outside of your control. In either case, you must set your heart on faithfulness. Faithful to make the choices you have been given by God and faithful with the circumstances you did not choose but must endure. Cancer and poverty or wealth and health, nothing can stop faithfulness except you. Jesus faithfully finished his work and accomplished our salvation. Will you finish well and accomplish a life of faithfulness for the good of others and the glory of God? Close the gap. What small thing can you be found faithful in today?

Week 13/Day 1
Read:

John 20:1-2 Early on the first day of the week, while it was still dark, Mary Magdalene went to the tomb and saw that the stone had been removed from the entrance. So she came running to Simon Peter and the other disciple, the one Jesus loved, and said, "They have taken the Lord out of the tomb, and we don't know where they have put him!"

Reflect:

Confusion. What is true? What is real? What is right? What is wrong? What do I believe? What do I doubt? The word "confusion" comes from two words that mean to "mingle together." Confusion is where competing ideas, beliefs, and feelings are jumbled up inside of you. There is no clarity, there is only confusion. Confusion unnerves us, it causes us to doubt what we thought was true. When deeply held beliefs are under attack, the confusion shakes a person to their very core. When the pegs on which life was hung all fall to the ground, then life's meaning itself can fall to the floor in a jumbled mess. Jesus was not supposed to die. Certainly not like this. Not this soon. The reality and finality of his death had to be surreal to those who loved him. Perhaps Mary went to Jesus' tomb early on that Sunday, while it was still dark, because she had not been able to sleep. Confusion steals your sleep. She went to touch the tomb, to see it, to try and make it all feel real, because in her mind she just could not comprehend what had happened. Then when she arrived at the tomb, hoping to bring some order to her confused mind and heart, what she saw made things worse. Not only had they killed Jesus, now they had stolen his body. She ran. Confusion can make you feel like running away from what is in front of you. She fled to her friends and cried, "They have taken the Lord and I don't know where they have put him!" Stop, Mary. Breathe. They did not take his life; he gave it away. They could not take his body; he is not dead. Confusion makes unreality feel real. Are you confused right now? Do thoughts of some potential dark future make you feel like fighting, or fleeing? Or maybe you freeze and are unable to do anything? Take a deep breath. Do you feel the air in your lungs? It is giving you life right now. It is infusing your blood with oxygen, with life that is pumped throughout your body to your heart and brain. Most often you don't know you are breathing, even though breath is life. Has confusion come into your world? Take a breath. Do not trade what you *feel* for what is *real*. What is real? What has Jesus said? He has sustained you even when you were not aware he was there – like those life-giving breaths that you took for granted. He will sustain you now, when you are desperately aware of your need for him. Breathe deeply of air and of his peace. Air is life, Jesus is life. Confusion can make us acutely aware of what we have been taking for granted.

Day 2
Read:
John 20:3-7 So Peter and the other disciple started for the tomb. Both were running, but the other disciple outran Peter and reached the tomb first. He bent over and looked in at the strips of linen lying there but did not go in. Then Simon Peter, who was behind him, arrived and went into the tomb. He saw the strips of linen lying there, as well as the burial cloth that had been around Jesus' head. The cloth was folded up by itself, separate from the linen.

Reflect:
The tomb was empty, except for the burial clothes of Jesus. There was nothing in there, no body. Many have set out to prove that the resurrection is a hoax. This will continue to be true, some people will believe that they will be the first to do what has not and cannot be done – which is prove that the resurrection of Jesus did not happen. A number of those who set out to prove the resurrection of Jesus did not happen, instead, became followers of Christ in the process. The compelling fact of the resurrection of Jesus changed the course of their lives. Often these men did not begin their quest with neutrality about the Jesus. Often they had already decided what was real and they went looking for evidence to confirm what they believed. This fact makes their conversion even more compelling. God did not just have to take them from being *neutral* to being positive about Jesus, he had to take them from *negative* to positive. The disciples themselves went from cowardly, hiding, and self-protective men to bold, public, and life-sacrificing men. How can you explain this change? If the resurrection had not happened and these friends knew it, then they would surely not have given their lives for a lie. But the fact that all of them would be killed because of their faith in what happened on that Sunday is conclusive evidence that Jesus has risen from the dead. The tomb was empty and not because someone stole Jesus' body but because Jesus rose from the dead. The evidence is compelling. What evidence? The fact of "nothing." No other grave or tomb in human history was empty and remains empty. Empty not because of human intrigue, but because of divine power. Close the gap today on your confidence in God. The evidence of nothing is life-changing. When John looked into the tomb of Jesus on that first Easter morning, he saw nothing and he eventually believed. He would believe because he would encounter the resurrected Lord. Reflect on the empty tomb today. Reflect on how Jesus has revealed himself to you. What has he used to make himself known to you personally? Friends, Family, the Bible, the Holy Spirit, experiences...remember all these things and be grateful.

Day 3
Read:

John 20:8-17 Finally the other disciple, who had reached the tomb first, also went inside. He saw and believed. (They still did not understand from Scripture that Jesus had to rise from the dead.) Then the disciples went back to their homes, but Mary stood outside the tomb crying. As she wept, she bent over to look into the tomb and saw two angels in white, seated where Jesus' body had been, one at the head and the other at the foot. They asked her, "Woman, why are you crying?" "They have taken my Lord away," she said, "and I don't know where they have put him." At this, she turned around and saw Jesus standing there, but she did not realize that it was Jesus. "Woman," he said, "why are you crying? Who is it you are looking for?" Thinking he was the gardener, she said, "Sir, if you have carried him away, tell me where you have put him, and I will get him." Jesus said to her, "Mary." She turned toward him and cried out in Aramaic, "Rabboni!" (which means Teacher). Jesus said, "Do not hold on to me, for I have not yet returned to the Father. Go instead to my brothers and tell them, 'I am returning to my Father and your Father, to my God and your God.'"

Reflect:

Peter and John went home, Mary Magdalene stayed at the tomb and cried. It is no wonder that Mary was heartbroken; remember, Luke wrote that Jesus had set her free from demons. She was a woman who had experienced liberty and now she had to be confused. She knew the demons submitted to Jesus, but now he was dead. If Jesus were dead, then who would stop the demons from returning to her? Whether Jesus rose from the dead or not had implications for more than just the life to come. For Mary, it was the difference between living in confident freedom or in fear of being taken back into demonic bondage. If Jesus was dead, who stood between her and the demons? No one. Perhaps this is why she stood at the tomb and wept. Was she hoping against hope that Jesus would appear? Was she terrified to leave even his burial site because she remembered what it was like to be controlled by demonic forces? Of course she stood outside the tomb crying, who wouldn't? She had lived in freedom and now it seemed there was no one who could keep her from being dragged back into dark bondage. Paul wrote that if Christ has not been raised from the dead, then you are still in your sins. Whether he rose from the dead or not has direct bearing on your liberty or bondage every bit as much as it did for Mary. If you have experienced the liberty of the gospel, your sins have been forgiven. Since Christ has risen, this liberty is a life-altering reality. It is not merely religious "mumbo jumbo" that makes guilty people feel better about themselves. Mary did not just feel badly; her life was bad. She was controlled by evil and then she was set free. The guilt of sin is not merely feeling bad, it is a terrible weight that drags us down and away from God and others.

Since Jesus has risen from the dead, then he stands between us and condemnation always. He intercedes for you even now. Close the gap on gratitude today. There is now no condemnation for those who are in Christ Jesus. Since Christ has risen, he stands, alive, between you and condemnation. Thank him now for liberty.

Day 4
Read:
John 20:13 They asked her, "Woman, why are you crying?" "They have taken my Lord away," she said, "and I don't know where they have put him." At this, she turned around and saw Jesus standing there, but she did not realize that it was Jesus. "Woman," he said, "why are you crying? Who is it you are looking for?" Thinking he was the gardener, she said, "Sir, if you have carried him away, tell me where you have put him, and I will get him." Jesus said to her, "Mary." She turned toward him and cried out in Aramaic, "Rabboni!" (which means Teacher). Jesus said, "Do not hold on to me, for I have not yet returned to the Father. Go instead to my brothers and tell them, 'I am returning to my Father and your Father, to my God and your God.'"

Reflect:
It seems that Mary did not immediately recognize Jesus when he appeared. Bowed down with grief, or maybe fear, she did not look at him right away. Perhaps her face was in her hands and her eyes blurred with tears as she wept. Jesus asked her an odd question, "Who is it you are looking for?" Wasn't it obvious? Jesus frequently asked questions that appeared obvious, but were designed to get at human hearts. In the Garden after the fall, God asked the first couple, "Where are you?" Jesus asked some of his first followers, "What do you want?" He asked Peter, "Who do you think I am?" Now he asked this grieving woman, "Who is it you are looking for?" He was not playing games with her; he never played games with people's hearts. Perhaps he was challenging her thinking..."Mary, remember what you have seen and heard. You saw me be Lord of life as I set you free and raised the dead. Now, who are you looking for and why would you be looking for the living among the dead?" Maybe the wheels started turning in her head, her senses starting to clear up, when he said her name, "Mary." That was it, the fog was gone in an instant. She knew that voice and, finally, she turned her face towards him and saw Jesus alive. "Teacher!" she cried in joy. Then she grabbed him and hung on for dear life. He finally had to tell her, "Don't hold on to me. I am going to return to my Father." Before his crucifixion and resurrection, Jesus limited himself to single places and times, just like us. He could be here with me or there with you. Now he lives in a resurrection reality where he is not limited by time and space, he is available to you and to me, all the time. This is no science fiction story; this is the gospel truth story.

Years after his experience at the empty tomb, Peter wrote, "Though you have not seen him, you love him; and even though you do not see him now, you believe in him and are filled with an inexpressible and glorious joy, for you are receiving the goal of your faith, the salvation of your souls." (1 Peter 1:8-9) Jesus could choose now to make himself available to your physical senses, but you do not have to see him in order to know him, to love him, and to experience his joy and salvation. Think for a few minutes of the reality of Jesus' presence with you right now. Take your mind to the fact of his presence with you throughout this day. His presence is an unseen reality in your life; embrace that reality by faith.

Day 5
Read:

John 20:17 Jesus said, "Do not hold on to me, for I have not yet returned to the Father. Go instead to my brothers and tell them, 'I am returning to my Father and your Father, to my God and your God.'"

Reflect:

What is the bad news of the day? What natural disaster has devastated lives somewhere near you or far from where you sit and read? What manmade horrors are unfolding today? Wars, refugee crises, murder...the list is long and it is ever-present. Perhaps the bad news is very close to you. Maybe disaster has struck in your own life or in the life of someone you love. Does the fact that a man lived in the Middle East in the first century and was executed at around age thirty-three, and then supposedly rose from the dead have any bearing at all on the bad news of this day? It depends on whether he actually rose from the dead or not. If he did not, then no, there is nothing there to mediate today's bad news. There is no echo of future hope in Christ's death. But if he did, then yes, the resurrection is the good news that impacts all bad news. At the very least, it is the good news that tells bad news that its days are numbered. When difficult things happen, one of the first places people go in their minds is to the question, "Is there meaning in this suffering?" Their question is "Why?" When they find no meaning, their suffering is multiplied; when they find purpose in it, their suffering takes on a very different tone. It remains suffering, but when there is perceived purpose in it, it's just not the same. Another question that comes with suffering is, "How long?" When will I be free from this? Will I ever be free? That question is "When?" When the answer is unknown or "No, you will not be free," then suffering can become unbearable for many people. When the answer is, "Yes, you can be free of this, but it will take some time", life remains hard, but it becomes hopeful. How does the gospel good news potentially impact all current bad news? If you are in Christ, then to the "why" question, "Is there meaning in this?" The answer is "Yes!" To the "when" question, "When will this end?" The answer is "Soon!"

Though the soon may be years away, it will someday be experienced as having been "soon." Are you in feeling despair? Don't lose heart! "Though outwardly we are wasting away, yet inwardly we are being renewed day by day. 17 For our light and momentary troubles are achieving for us an eternal glory that far outweighs them all. 18 So we fix our eyes not on what is seen, but on what is unseen. For what is seen is temporary, but what is unseen is eternal." (2 Corinthians 4:16-18)

Week 14/Day 1
Read:
Gal. 6:1-5 Brothers, if someone is caught in a sin, you who are spiritual should restore him gently. But watch yourself, or you also may be tempted. Carry each other's burdens, and in this way you will fulfill the law of Christ. If anyone thinks he is something when he is nothing, he deceives himself. Each one should test his own actions. Then he can take pride in himself, without comparing himself to somebody else, for each one should carry his own load.

Reflect:
You can't live this way alone and no one can do it for you. This is the tension of the Christian life. There is a tendency to lean one way or another; if you lean too far and too long in either direction, you will eventually fall. One approach leans too much on self and believes that you do not need others to remain faithful and fruitful. This is not how God has designed us to live. The other approach looks too much to others and fails to take full responsibility for self. This causes us to look to external solutions for internal problems and opportunities. This tension explains why Paul writes that you should "carry each other's burdens", but then he follows with "each one should carry his own load." The burden we are to share is something too heavy for one person to carry. The load is more like a backpack; it is something we must bear ourselves. Paul is giving us the balanced approach of both sharing the heavy burdens *and* carrying your own load. Which way does the wind blow in your life? Are you prone to be a spiritual loner? Perhaps you have friends and talk with people, but you do not let them into your struggles. Do you believe that you should be able, with God's help, to make life happen without the assistance of others? Will you repent of this pride? You need to let others help you carry your burdens, both for your sake and for theirs. Perhaps you lean the opposite way. Are you prone to look to others too much to do for you what you should do for yourself? This approach can often turn into a demanding spirit. Sometimes people who struggle with this can come across externally as independent, while on the inside they are very dependent on others. The "pull" these people have on others can be conflicting. On the one hand, they can act indifferently to needing help; while on the other hand, they can become angry or sulk when the "right" kind of help is not offered.

Don't play these games! Will you repent of this demanding spirit? Carry the burdens of others and also let them help you carry yours. Carry your own load and do not look to others to do what God has called you to do. Close the gap on loving others. Look today to let others more deeply into your life and look for ways to invest more deeply in the lives of others.

Day 2
Read:
Gal. 6:1-5 Brothers, if someone is caught in a sin, you who are spiritual should restore him gently. But watch yourself, or you also may be tempted. Carry each other's burdens, and in this way you will fulfill the law of Christ. If anyone thinks he is something when he is nothing, he deceives himself. Each one should test his own actions. Then he can take pride in himself, without comparing himself to somebody else, for each one should carry his own load.

Reflect:
Pride separates people; love brings them together. Pride makes us foolish. It does not allow us to see ourselves as we truly are and it prevents us from seeing others as they are. Pride loves to play the comparison game and it is that comparison that keeps us from deep, transformational engagement in the lives of others. Love is not blind to our own strengths or to others' weaknesses. Love is not afraid of our own weaknesses or others' strengths. Love does not play games with people. Love is interested in what is real and good. When we think too highly of ourselves, we have lost touch with reality. We are nothing apart from Jesus. What do you have that you have not been given? Even if you have "earned" something or worked hard to get to a certain level of achievement or knowledge, you were given that opportunity and that capacity. To look down on anyone in any way is foolish. To do so is to be self-deceived. Often, when people are aware that they are near the end of their lives, they finally lose interest in the comparison game. Not always, but often, things become much clearer. What others think of them becomes much less important. How they compare to others in regards to looks, possessions, or popularity tends to become a non-issue. The problem with end-of-life clarity, as valuable as it is, is that it comes at the end of your life. Solomon urged his readers to "remember your Creator in the days of your youth" (Eccl. 12:1). Has pride kept you from loving well those people God has put in your life? Are you tired of playing the empty comparison game? Will you close the gap on how you see life now and how you will see life when it is over? You do not have to wait until the end to have end-of-life clarity. This clarity will grow as you learn to look first at Jesus, then in the mirror. Look first at Jesus, then at others.

Day 3
Read:
Gal. 6:1-5 Brothers, if someone is caught in a sin, you who are spiritual should restore him gently. But watch yourself, or you also may be tempted. Carry each other's burdens, and in this way you will fulfill the law of Christ. If anyone thinks he is something when he is nothing, he deceives himself. Each one should test his own actions. Then he can take pride in himself, without comparing himself to somebody else, for each one should carry his own load.

Reflect:
Life ebbs and flows for everyone. There are times when you are not struggling, but your brother or sister is. You must help them with gentleness and humility because you are never above struggle or failure yourself. Maybe right now you are the struggler and you desperately need gentle and humble assistance from one who is spiritual. What does it mean to be "spiritual"? In the Scriptures, it is simply a contrast between what is 'of Christ' and what is 'of the sinful flesh.' To be spiritual means to be currently living in obedience to Jesus. No one is perfect in thought and deed and everyone struggles against the desires of the flesh. But, this is not about perfection; it is about a heart that is surrendered to Jesus. This heart is revealed in the way you treat others. The one who is spiritual does not accept the sin, but neither does he reject the sinner. The spiritual believer does not think himself beyond sinning or above the sinner. If he does, he must be careful because that kind of pride will set him up for a potential fall. If you are in a situation to help someone who has been caught in sin, then approach with caution. First, understand they are "caught." Of course, they chose this path, but at the same time they are not living in freedom. Sin is indeed a trap. See the other person as being in need. Second, speak as one speaking the words of God and act with the strength that God provides. How did Jesus speak to those caught in sin? How has he spoken to you when you were caught? He speaks with gentleness and with compassion and you must do the same. Finally, see yourself as a brother or sister, not as a judge. See yourself as one who has received, but has not earned God's grace. Now, go to the one caught in sin and "pay the debt of love" that you owe then. Go with the attitude and the words of one who has been forgiven much.

Day 4
Read:
Gal. 6:1-5 Brothers, if someone is caught in a sin, you who are spiritual should restore him gently. But watch yourself, or you also may be tempted. Carry each other's burdens, and in this way you will fulfill the law of Christ. If anyone thinks he is something when he is nothing, he deceives himself. Each one should test his own actions. Then he can take pride in himself, without comparing himself to somebody else, for each one should carry his own load.

Reflect:

Trust is earned over time through authentic love expressed and experienced in real life situations. When trust is present, good things can happen very quickly. Words do not have to be perfect because the heart behind the words is seen as good. When trust is present, misunderstandings can happen yet grace is given. Trust gives the benefit of the doubt. When trust is absent, everything good slows down. When trust is absent, every word and facial expression is scrutinized and held in suspicion. When trust is absent, misunderstanding is the norm, even good intentions are misjudged and rejected. Do you trust the people God has put in your life to the point that, if they must restore you when you are caught in a sin, you will listen to them? What if their words are not perfect? What if their perception of the circumstances is not completely accurate? What if their timing is way off? Will you demand perfection from them? Or will you accept the liberty that God is offering you through them? Has someone tried to help you recently and you rejected them because they didn't get everything just right? Were they partially right? Was there a single pearl in the basket of shells? If so, will you cast off that pearl because of the shells? Perhaps God has given you help in shouldering your burdens, but you have treated God's provision as less than the gift of grace that it is. The wise love correction, and they will take it from less than perfect sources. Maybe you have a burden to help someone caught in sin. Have you done the work to earn their trust? If not, then do not assume that you have the privilege of speaking truth to them. They may allow you to have a voice in their life, but remember that trust is earned; it is never forced on someone. Start closing the gap today between the level of trust you have with others and where it could be. Be gentle with people. Act humbly towards them. Carry their burdens.

Day 5
Read:

Gal. 6:1-5 Brothers, if someone is caught in a sin, you who are spiritual should restore him gently. But watch yourself, or you also may be tempted. Carry each other's burdens, and in this way you will fulfill the law of Christ. If anyone thinks he is something when he is nothing, he deceives himself. Each one should test his own actions. Then he can take pride in himself, without comparing himself to somebody else, for each one should carry his own load.

Reflect:

Carrying others' burdens will often be inconvenient. People don't normally plan their problems (even if they caused them). You can't necessarily put "carry someone's burden" on your calendar in advance. However, there is something you *can* do ahead of the time. You can decide that, if able and if given the opportunity, you will love the ones God has put in your life to love. You can decide, then live decided, rather than still deciding.

If you approach carrying the burdens of others in a "deciding" fashion, then you may help when needed, but you may also grumble and begrudge the fact that it is not convenient for you. When you have this attitude, then the one you are helping will likely "feel like the burden" rather than being a person "with a burden." Decide who you want to be, then go and live decided. You will still find helping people difficult and often inconvenient, but you will also find, if you continually take on this mindset of Christ, that you grumble less and enjoy helping others more. Christ, for the joy set before him, endured the cross (Heb. 12:2). You need never feel like your life is a burden to Christ. Carrying your sin was part of his joy, even though it was an unthinkable burden. Will you help others in ways that make their burdens lighter, rather than making them feeling like they themselves are your burden? Decide, then go live decided. Make your question, "*How* do I love?" rather than, "*Will* I love?" Prepare your minds for action. Ask God to help you have his heart for people. Reflect now on the fact that all that God wants from you can be summed up by this statement, "Carry one another's burdens." Don't miss the largeness of God's opportunity for you today because it looks small and it feels inconvenient.

Week 15/Day 1
Read:
1Thess. 5:9-11 For God did not appoint us to suffer wrath but to receive salvation through our Lord Jesus Christ. He died for us so that, whether we are awake or asleep, we may live together with him. Therefore encourage one another and build each other up, just as in fact you are doing.

Reflect:
"Will everything be alright?" This is the question people ask when they are afraid. Sometimes friends and family will say, "Yes, everything is going to be fine." Is that a promise that anyone can really make? It is understandable and laudable that people will try to instill courage into failing hearts with those comforting words. But it can be false courage, a promise that will fail them in the end. We may try to make things turn out "alright," but no human has the ultimate power or authority to ensure this will happen. James reminds us that we don't even know what will happen tomorrow, because our lives are like "a mist" (James 4:14). We cannot control all the outcomes. We can't know if "everything will be alright." Or can we? It depends on what you mean by "everything" and "alright." God did not appoint us to suffer wrath, but to receive salvation through Jesus Christ. This is the fact of the gospel that is to be the ultimate source of our courage. Will you keep your job? Maybe. Will your loved ones be healthy? Perhaps, but all will die in the end. Will I suffer God's wrath if I have believed the gospel? No. When I die will all be lost? No. If I trust Christ and live for his glory, will all I give my life for be a waste in the end?

No. So, will everything "be alright?" Have you believed the gospel? Then, yes! Now go and encourage one another with these truths. You can act courageously and still feel fear. Feeling fear is a normal human response. The question is, "Will you be courageous?" The question is not, will you be "free of fear"? Courage that is fact-based is courage that is gospel-based. Pour courage into your friends, your family, and yourself, all while thinking often and deeply about the gospel. As fear rises up in your own heart over things that are out of your control, do not try to stop "feeling afraid." Instead, remember what the foundation for your courage is. He died for you so that you will live together with him.

Day 2
Read:
Heb. 3:12-13 See to it, brothers, that none of you has a sinful, unbelieving heart that turns away from the living God. But encourage one another daily, as long as it is called Today, so that none of you may be hardened by sin's deceitfulness.

Reflect:
It is obvious that to be "encouraged" is the opposite of to be "discouraged." But, what is not obvious, is that hardness is often a consequence of long-term discouragement. When your heart is discouraged, it has become low on, or empty of, courage. Not courage as a "lack of fear," but courage as "the presence of hope." Discouragement opens the door to the lies of sin. "Why keep trying this? It's not working." Or, "Look at you. What difference is there in your life than someone who doesn't claim to know Christ? Except maybe they are doing better than you are." Or even, "You deserve a break, indulge that habit; give into that temptation." When we listen to and obey the lies of sin, then our hearts become hard. Hardened to encouragement. Hardened to the help of others. Hardened to the Holy Spirit. Hardened to hope. See to it that it doesn't happen to you or to your friends. This must not happen and it is your responsibility to see to it that it does not. You must pour courage into your friends and they must pour courage into you for as long as it is called Today. When would today not be called today? When "The Day" has come, the day of the Lord's final salvation when all is made new. When "today" has become "the Day," courage will flow without end like a river into our hearts. But today, see to it, brothers and sisters, that you stay encouraged.

Day 3
Read:
Heb. 10:23-25 Let us hold unswervingly to the hope we profess, for he who promised is faithful. And let us consider how we may spur one another on toward love and good deeds.

Let us not give up meeting together, as some are in the habit of doing, but let us encourage one another—and all the more as you see the Day approaching.

Reflect:
Encouragement is person relative. What might encourage you, might not encourage someone else. Effective encouragement requires the work of careful consideration. To consider is to make the effort to understand what is real, true, and best. "The purposes of a man's heart are deep waters, but a man of understanding draws them out" (Pr. 20:5). A man or woman of understanding is not simply a smart person, but rather a person who lives with a level of consideration. A person of understanding does the work to think about others and not just think about self. This kind of understanding is very different than judgment. Judgment (at least the wrong kind) is to come to conclusions about a person's motives and intentions in order to criticize or condemn them. Consideration is to think deeply about another person's life in order to know how to best encourage and serve them. Paul wrote to the Philippians and challenged them to not act out of selfishness or vanity, "but in humility consider others better than yourselves" (Phil. 2:3). This doesn't mean to think less of yourself; it means to become a person who thinks first of others. Consideration here means that you are to become a person whose first thought is, "What is best for them?" Think about who has encouraged you in your life. How did they do it? Why was it encouraging? It is very likely that they had given careful consideration to who you are and what encourages your heart. It is also likely you had a level of trust for them because you believed they wanted the best for you. Give consideration to how you can learn to encourage others. You can do better and you want to do better. Close the gap. Move towards being a person who is known as an encourager. Proverbs 25:11 says, "A word aptly spoken is like apples of gold in settings of silver." A word that pours courage into a person's heart because it is "aptly" or appropriately spoken is a thing of real beauty to everyone.

Day 4
Read:
Heb. 10:23-25 Let us hold unswervingly to the hope we profess, for he who promised is faithful. And let us consider how we may spur one another on toward love and good deeds. Let us not give up meeting together, as some are in the habit of doing, but let us encourage one another—and all the more as you see the Day approaching.

Reflect:
If you show up, good things can happen; if you do not, they will not. Meeting together and encouragement are directly connected. If this is true, then why would some give up on meeting together? Doesn't everyone like to be encouraged?

Some give up on meeting together because the impact is not always immediately evident. The encouragement that comes from being active in community can be subtle. Your heart may be encouraged in such a small way that it is barely perceptible when it happens. But the cumulative impact of even 'small' encouragement is enough to keep you in the fight. When you fail to meet together with other believers, you may not feel any immediate difference. But if you continue to neglect meeting together, you certainly will experience a difference. Or something worse may happen, you may not feel any difference at all because the cumulative impact of not meeting with others has hardened your heart and discouragement has become the accepted norm in your life. Do not give up. Show up and keep showing up! Meeting together in community in all its various forms is a good thing. Do not become weary in doing this good thing, because you will reap a harvest if you do not give up. The harvest takes planting, watering, and waiting, but if you continue to do what is good to do, then the harvest will come in due time. When you meet together with other believers, remember why you are there – to encourage one another. Pour the courage of the gospel into one another when you meet. Let others complain, let them blame, let them talk about things that don't matter. But let *us* continue to meet together and, when we do, let us encourage one another.

Day 5
Read:
1Thess. 5:9-11 For God did not appoint us to suffer wrath but to receive salvation through our Lord Jesus Christ. He died for us so that, whether we are awake or asleep, we may live together with him. Therefore encourage one another and build each other up, just as in fact you are doing.

Heb. 3:12-13 See to it, brothers, that none of you has a sinful, unbelieving heart that turns away from the living God. But encourage one another daily, as long as it is called Today, so that none of you may be hardened by sin's deceitfulness.

Heb. 10:23-25 Let us hold unswervingly to the hope we profess, for he who promised is faithful. And let us consider how we may spur one another on toward love and good deeds. Let us not give up meeting together, as some are in the habit of doing, but let us encourage one another—and all the more as you see the Day approaching.

Reflect:
Encourage is a verb; it is what you do. Your goal in encouragement is not to evoke a feeling, but to help others continue to move towards Christ in faith and towards others in love. They may feel encouraged or not, but the goal of encouraging others is to spur movement in the direction of courage.

If they are encouraged, they will continue on whether or not they feel a certain way. Encouragement towards faith and love is based on the settled facts of the gospel. Those facts are to be the foundation of your encouragement for others and their encouragement for you. Whether the discouragement has come because of poor health, broken relationships, or disappointment over unfulfilled expectations, the courage to continue is based on the fact that God's purposes will prevail. His glory and your ultimate good are not dependent on temporary circumstances. This fact will not always help you or others *feel* encouraged, but this fact can help you *be* encouraged. It can help you continue to move forward in courage and in faith. The gospel truth can encourage your heart all by itself, if comprehended by our minds and applied to our hearts by the Holy Spirit. However, the way God has designed us is such that maximal encouragement happens when the gospel truth comes in the form of a friend who walks side-by-side with us. Communicated truth is powerful; demonstrated truth is transformational. Encourage someone today, not merely by throwing words their way, but by walking side-by-side with them. Let someone encourage you today. If you need to humble yourself and ask for encouragement, do so. You will encourage them if you let them encourage you. People will be challenged by your strengths, but they will encouraged by your weakness.

Week 16/Day 1
Read:
Rom. 12:9-16 Love must be sincere. Hate what is evil; cling to what is good. Be devoted to one another in brotherly love. Honor one another above yourselves. Never be lacking in zeal, but keep your spiritual fervor, serving the Lord. Be joyful in hope, patient in affliction, faithful in prayer. Share with God's people who are in need. Practice hospitality. Bless those who persecute you; bless and do not curse. Rejoice with those who rejoice; mourn with those who mourn. Live in harmony with one another. Do not be proud, but be willing to associate with people of low position. Do not be conceited.

Reflect:
Love that it is real, with substance, cannot hang in midair with no foundation. Many try to begin their definition and expression of love with love itself. Love must have a foundation and that foundation is God. He describes what love is and he prescribes how it should be expressed. How do we know what love is? We look to God, because he is love. How do we know how love is expressed? We look to Jesus, because he shows us how. "This is how we know what love is, Jesus Christ laid down his life for us and we ought to lay down our lives for each other" (1 John 3:16). Because love begins with God, he is love's moral foundation. Love hates what is evil and clings to what is good. Love does not keep a record of wrongs, but love is not blind to what is wrong.

Love judges actions and attitudes that are a threat to its health. It is clear-eyed in its assessment of evil and it clings desperately to what is good. Love always protects, not self, but the relationship. Begin your judgment with yourself. Those attitudes of self-pity, or defensiveness, or pettiness that keep you at a distance from loved ones, judge them. Those words that are not in line with love, judge them. Those acts of selfishness that put you first over those you are called to love, judge them. Judge all of these – your attitudes, words, and selfish acts – as the enemies of that which is most valuable, love. Then, judge the threats to love that you see in your friends and family. Do not judge the people; judge the threats. How you do this will vary from person to person and from situation to situation. It will be complicated at times to know how to judge the threat without condemning the person. But, if you begin with the right heart, you will be positioned to come to the right conclusion. Begin here: Jesus Christ laid down his life for others. And we must do the same.

Day 2
Read:
Rom. 12:9-16 Love must be sincere. Hate what is evil; cling to what is good. Be devoted to one another in brotherly love. Honor one another above yourselves. Never be lacking in zeal, but keep your spiritual fervor, serving the Lord. Be joyful in hope, patient in affliction, faithful in prayer. Share with God's people who are in need. Practice hospitality. Bless those who persecute you; bless and do not curse. Rejoice with those who rejoice; mourn with those who mourn. Live in harmony with one another. Do not be proud, but be willing to associate with people of low position. Do not be conceited.

Reflect:
Notice the repetition of "one another" in the passage you just read. One another simply means each other. It is how Philippians 2:4 happens in practice, "Each of you should look not only to your own interests, but also to the interests of others." If each one is looking to the interests of the other, there is going to be harmony with one another. If each one is looking first to what is best for themselves, there can be no harmony. What happens when one is looking to the interests of the other, but the other is not reciprocating? What if you are in a family or friend relationship where you cannot find harmony because it seems that much or all of what you try to do is misunderstood or rejected? You must control what you can control and leave the rest with God. It takes two people to live in harmony, but it only takes one to live in faithfulness. Will you trust God in this difficult relationship? This is the kind of situation where faith is tested by the fires of real life. Few things can be as difficult as having a broken or strained relationship and knowing you cannot do anything to change the other's perception. What can you do then? You can be faithful. You can do *your* half of the "one another."

You can make whatever appropriate choices you have in order to live in harmony with the other, even if they do not make those same choices. This is enormously challenging and it does not guarantee that everything will work out between you in the end. The other person may not respond well, no matter what good choices you make. But if faithfulness is your goal, in the end you will be whole. Broken relationships can be heartbreaking, but faithfulness to what God has called you to will, in the end, lead to a "whole heart."

Day 3
Read:
Rom. 12:9-16 Love must be sincere. Hate what is evil; cling to what is good. Be devoted to one another in brotherly love. Honor one another above yourselves. Never be lacking in zeal, but keep your spiritual fervor, serving the Lord. Be joyful in hope, patient in affliction, faithful in prayer. Share with God's people who are in need. Practice hospitality. Bless those who persecute you; bless and do not curse. Rejoice with those who rejoice; mourn with those who mourn. Live in harmony with one another. Do not be proud, but be willing to associate with people of low position. Do not be conceited.

Reflect:
A musical harmony occurs when multiple notes or pitches are played at the same time. Relational harmony occurs when multiple people act together for common purposes and with common values. In harmony, neither the musical notes nor the people are identical, but they come together with the same aim – whether to create a song or something much grander. The common cause for those who follow Christ is the glory of God. God is both the goal of the Church's harmony and its cause. He empowers very different people to come together as one people. The church is unique in the world in many ways, but one of the more evident ways is how a group of such diverse people can operate in harmony. It is not surprising that there are problems in the church; it is surprising that there is such harmony among people who are so different from one another. It has been said that Sunday morning is the most segregated time of the week. This belief fails to take into account the many ways in which people are different from one another. You may be of a different race than someone else and yet have much in common with them, such as personality, preferences, economics, and the like. You may be of the same race as someone and yet totally different from them in most other ways. The fact is, each individual represents a unique "inner culture." For any two people to live in harmony requires that they consider more than their own needs, interests, and perspectives. They must find a common cause and a common point of interest. If you are a Christ follower, your fundamental life purpose is to glorify God. A very practical way this happens is when you live in harmony with others.

72

Jesus said that people know we follow him when we love one another (John 13:35). Make God's glory your goal, because it is your greatest good. Practically, this means you must look for ways to live in harmony with others. Don't be distracted by the "small stuff," but focus on the "largeness" of God's glory in your relationships with others.

Day 4
Read:
Rom. 12:9-16 Love must be sincere. Hate what is evil; cling to what is good. Be devoted to one another in brotherly love. Honor one another above yourselves. Never be lacking in zeal, but keep your spiritual fervor, serving the Lord. Be joyful in hope, patient in affliction, faithful in prayer. Share with God's people who are in need. Practice hospitality. Bless those who persecute you; bless and do not curse. Rejoice with those who rejoice; mourn with those who mourn. Live in harmony with one another. Do not be proud, but be willing to associate with people of low position. Do not be conceited.

Reflect:
A person who is moody tends to interact with others largely based on what he is currently feeling on the inside. The opposite is a person whose interior feelings do not dictate his exterior demeanor. Everyone has moods, but not everyone is held captive to them. What is your mood right now? Are you feeling happy or sad? Are you feeling hopeful or discouraged? Are you ambivalent, caught between competing emotions? To live in harmony with others requires that you enter into their lives and that you do not live entirely out of your own circumstances and moods. How can you rejoice with those who rejoice and mourn with those who mourn in an authentic way? Remember – and believe – that there are people who care about you who are reading this passage as well. They must be aware of your joy and your sadness, if they are to practice this kind of love towards you. Be authentic and be open about the reality of your internal and external circumstances. This does not mean that if others are sad, you must disguise your joy, or if they are happy, you must hide your sadness. God desires for his children to live in harmonious relationships. When people living in very different life situations move towards each other in love, for God's glory and for their own good, it creates a beautiful harmony. Furthermore, when each person enters into another's joy and sadness in *appropriate* ways, there is an ongoing opportunity for balanced living. Their joy gives perspective to your sadness and their sadness gives perspective to your joy. Joy and sadness are both valid expressions of a gospel life. When joy lacks the perspective of sadness, it can become "earthbound" and lose its eternal foundation. When sadness lacks the perspective of joy, it can take over a person's soul and remove gospel hope. Live in harmony by choosing to enter into the lives of others and by letting them enter deeply into yours.

73

Day 5
Read:
Rom. 12:18 If it is possible, as far as it depends on you, live at peace with everyone.

Reflect:
The Bible *describes* reality and *prescribes* reality-based thinking and living. It is no surprise, then, that Paul was a realist. He understood that God is ultimate reality. He knew that the gospel was the real power of God to change lives and to bring men and women into relationship with God. So, as important and beautiful as harmony with others is, it is not always possible. It takes two to build a relationship, but it only takes one to break it. Peace with everyone cannot be the goal because it is not something we have control over. The goal in all relationships must be the glory of God revealed in faithfulness to God. You *can* control whether or not you are faithful in thought and deed. You *cannot* control all the outcomes of your faithfulness. Never mind that you will not always be faithful, the point is that you are oriented that way. Faithfulness, not fruitfulness, is your calling. God determines the fruit that will result from your faithfulness. "Now it is required that those who have been given a trust must prove faithful" (1 Cor. 4:2). You have been entrusted with the gospel and with the opportunity to live out the gospel in your life. What God requires of you related to that trust (and everything else he has given) is that you be found faithful. You may desperately want peace with someone in your life. You may believe that if you could just do more, pray more, give more, then surely harmony would result. By all means, do all you can do to have peace with others, as long as it is done within the boundaries of faithfulness to God. As far as possible, as much as it depends on you, live at peace with others. Of course, the implication is that peace is not always possible because it doesn't just depend on you. Set your heart and set your habits on faithfulness. This is what God requires from you. While faithfulness on your part will not guarantee your favored outcomes, it will guarantee God's favor in your life. Live in harmony when you can; live faithfully always.

Week 17/Day 1
Read:
Gal. 5:13-16 You, my brothers, were called to be free. But do not use your freedom to indulge the sinful nature; rather, serve one another in love. The entire law is summed up in a single command: "Love your neighbor as yourself." If you keep on biting and devouring each other, watch out or you will be destroyed by each other. So I say, live by the Spirit, and you will not gratify the desires of the sinful nature.

Reflect:

Jesus took "the very nature of a servant, being made in human likeness" (Phil. 2:7). What this says about you is that your very nature, as a human, is that of a servant. This is offensive to some who might believe that it is beneath them to be called or treated as a servant. The great push in society is to maneuver into a position where others will serve you. Those who are highly esteemed in most cultures are those who have servants, not those who are servants. However, when you consider that Jesus did not come to be served, but to serve, it should give an entirely different perspective on what it means to be a servant. Contemplate the sun for a moment. It is a vast nuclear reactor, with a core temperature of 27 million degrees. A single solar flare could be 35 times the size of our planet. Now, think about the fact that the sun is one of billions in our galaxy and our galaxy is one of billions in the universe. Push your mind out of the room you are in, off the planet you are on, and into the vastness of the universe. Now, with that larger perspective, think about the men and women who live for a very short time on a very small planet, but who often believe they are above being a servant and detest being treated like one. Think of yourself and your own attitude in this regard. Now, consider the following facts: "Through [Jesus] all things were made" (John 1:3). Jesus "did not come to be served, but to serve, and to give his life" for others (Mark 10:45). The one who spoke the universe into existence came as a human to redeem humanity and, in the process, also demonstrated what true greatness is; it is to serve others. In your life today, you will have opportunity to serve. You may be treated like a servant. How will you respond in your thoughts and your actions? Will you embrace the greatness of service to others?

Day 2
Read:

Gal. 5:13-16 You, my brothers, were called to be free. But do not use your freedom to indulge the sinful nature; rather, serve one another in love. The entire law is summed up in a single command: "Love your neighbor as yourself." If you keep on biting and devouring each other, watch out or you will be destroyed by each other. So I say, live by the Spirit, and you will not gratify the desires of the sinful nature.

Reflect:

The entire law is summed up in a single command: "Love your neighbor as yourself" (Matt. 22:39). To understand what God wants in regard to others is not complex; he wants you to love them. However, to consistently do this in practice is not easy; in fact, it is very difficult. Of course, there are those people who are easier to love than others.

There are also times when people are easier to love than other times, but to move towards consistency in loving others requires the work of the Holy Spirit in our lives and ongoing attention on our part. In competition for our constancy in loving others is the ongoing compulsion to indulge ourselves. To love others well, we must put their interests ahead of our own, yet our sinful nature does not take kindly to being in "second place." "Indulge and satisfy" versus "love and serve" are the battle lines in your life. You must continually decide to move your attitudes and actions fully into the realm of "love and serve." Live by the Spirit and you will not live your life on the wrong side of the battle. You will live to serve others, not to serve yourself. To live by the Spirit simply means to operate within the realm of the Spirit's desire for your life. The realm of his desire is the realm of his power. To move out of that realm of his will and into the desires of the flesh is to live without his power operating in you. He will not empower you for rebellion and selfishness. Why would he? Are you struggling to love and serve others? Do you feel trapped in the gravitational pull of your own selfish desires? The first step is to repent. Ask God to forgive you and ask the Holy Spirit to fill you. Move back into the realm of his will for your life and you will find that is the realm of his power for your life as well. Power to live as he would have you live, loving and serving one another.

Day 3
Read:
Gal. 5:13-16 You, my brothers, were called to be free. But do not use your freedom to indulge the sinful nature; rather, serve one another in love. The entire law is summed up in a single command: "Love your neighbor as yourself." If you keep on biting and devouring each other, watch out or you will be destroyed by each other. So I say, live by the Spirit, and you will not gratify the desires of the sinful nature.

Reflect:
Altruism is the selfless concern for the well-being of others. There is a correlation between this approach to life and personal happiness. There are many theories as to why this is, but the bottom line reason is that this is how God has made you. His design specifications for humanity are such that, when we live selfishly, our unhappiness increases. When we pursue selfless lifestyles, our personal satisfaction and sense of purpose increases. But isn't it self-serving to serve others in order to be more personally satisfied? Perhaps, but the problem is not wanting to be satisfied and happy, the problem is when we pursue those things outside of the will and ways of God. The pursuit of life apart from God is always a lose-lose scenario. We do not find anything good in that lifestyle. Those around us, likewise, fail to experience good from our lives as well. However, serving one another in love is a win-win scenario; others find increased joy from our lives, as do we.

76

The commands of God are always win-win. They may appear to be burdensome, but they are the way of liberty. "I run in the path of your commands, for you have set my heart free" (Ps. 119:32). "Love your neighbor as yourself" is God's invitation to join him in his joyful and free life. It doesn't always have to *feel* good to *be* good. Putting the interests of others ahead of your own today may not bring any immediate feel-good feedback. Nevertheless, it *is* good. Run that good path often enough and your joy will increase as will your experience of liberty. You will have increasing freedom from the heavy burden of selfish living. Has selfishness "worked" in your life yet? No? That's because it never will. Pursue a better path today.

Day 4
Read:
Gal. 5:13-16 You, my brothers, were called to be free. But do not use your freedom to indulge the sinful nature; rather, serve one another in love. The entire law is summed up in a single command: "Love your neighbor as yourself." If you keep on biting and devouring each other, watch out or you will be destroyed by each other. So I say, live by the Spirit, and you will not gratify the desires of the sinful nature.

Reflect:
You were called to be free. Freedom is the ability to do what you ought to do and to be who you were made to be. Freedom is not doing anything you want to do; it is wanting to do what is best to do. The sinful nature pursues freedom apart from God, but that pursuit leads to decreasing liberty. The Spirit of God leads you in the pursuit of God and that path leads to real liberty. The liberty of God is expressed in love for others. Love for others will often include willfully limiting your personal freedoms for the good of others. It is a bit of a paradox. You are free to limit your freedoms in order to love others well. When you live a life of those "love limits," your freedom increases. What might these limits look like? Perhaps you choose to forgive, even though the other person does not see how they wronged you. Maybe you stop trying to convince someone of your position and simply accept them where they are. Whatever the case, when you take the strong position and love people where they are, then you grow on the inside. It is there, on the inside, that your liberty increases. These willing "love limits" free your heart from bitterness, from jealousy, and from a desire to exact revenge. These chosen limits can, over time, decrease anxiety, discouragement, and other emotions that hamper your personal liberty to enjoy God, life, and other people. Use your freedom to serve one another, not yourself. When you do, your freedom will increase, as will your joy. This is where faith and love intersect. Believe God when he tells you, "Walk here, this is the path of liberty." That path is the path Jesus walked, the path of laying down your life for others.

Day 5
Read:

Gal. 5:13-16 You, my brothers, were called to be free. But do not use your freedom to indulge the sinful nature; rather, serve one another in love. The entire law is summed up in a single command: "Love your neighbor as yourself." If you keep on biting and devouring each other, watch out or you will be destroyed by each other. So I say, live by the Spirit, and you will not gratify the desires of the sinful nature.

Reflect:

You cannot control the attitudes and actions of others. Yet, those attitudes and actions have a tremendous impact on your life. What are you to do then? The most common approaches are to wallow in worry, to escalate attempts to control others, to become bitter, or to disengage from people altogether. These approaches lead to Paul's vivid description of "biting and devouring each other" with the final outcome of being "destroyed by each other." There is a striking contrast in this passage between "serving one another" and "biting and devouring each other." To serve is to give what you have that someone else needs. To "bite and devour" is to try and forcefully take what you are demanding from them. You are a child of God under the control of the Spirit. You are not meant to live like an animal under the control of impulses and instincts. Do you have a demanding heart or a trusting heart? Do you demand that God, others, and life give you what you believe you must have to be fulfilled? Are you quick to judge, to pout, or to become angry when others do not behave in a way that you want them to? Are you easily offended and ready to blame others for your unhappiness? You do not have to think or to live this way. You can, if you choose to do so, but you do not have to. Will you move away from this bitter and hard country of "demanding" and, instead, travel to the pleasant and beautiful country of "trusting?" You cannot control the choices of others; you can only control your own choices. God has given you both that privilege and that responsibility. Choose to trust God for what you need and relinquish the impulse to control others. The practical application of trusting God is to serve others. Faith in God is revealed in the way we respond to others. Do you believe God is 'enough'? Do you want to experience that reality more and more in your life? Then trust God by serving others and see him both meet your needs and reveal his love to others more fully through your life.

Week 18/Day 1
Read:

Eph. 4:25 Therefore each of you must put off falsehood and speak truthfully to his neighbor, for we are all members of one body...29

Do not let any unwholesome talk come out of your mouths, but only what is helpful for building others up according to their needs, that it may benefit those who listen.

Reflect:

Paul exhorts us to not allow any unwholesome talk out of our mouths. James, on the other hand, warns that only a perfect man will never be at fault in what he says (James 3:2). What are we to do? We cannot be perfect, yet we must always speak in helpful ways. James' point was primarily that words originate in the heart, not in the vocal cords. Paul would agree with James. That's why Paul writes: "put off falsehood, speak truthfully, and do not let unwholesome words out of your mouth." The implication is that we choose our words. They do not just "come out"; we have to *let* them out. You have operational control over your words because you have a choice in what is happening to your heart. If your words are not truthful and helpful and designed to bless others, then you must begin with an examination of the heart, not the tongue. Perhaps you have habitualized unwholesome talk. Have half-truths, exaggerations, complaining, and criticizing become reflexive for you? First, you must decide who it is that you want to be. Do you want to be the person who leaves others better off after having been with you? Do you want to leave others hopeful and encouraged because they have been touched by your words? If you want to be (or become) this type of person, then you must begin to build habits into your heart that will find their way to your tongue. You *can* do this! Many people have leveraged new heart habits into wholesome talk. Wholesome words are words that leave people "whole." Their souls are refreshed by their interaction with you. The world needs more people like this. You can be one of them. Peter cast this compelling vision, "If anyone speaks, he should do it as one speaking the very words of God" (1 Peter 4:11). Take that vision to heart and, then, let that vision out of your mouth for the glory of God and the good of others.

Day 2
Read:

Eph. 4:21 Surely you heard of him and were taught in him in accordance with the truth that is in Jesus...25 Therefore each of you must put off falsehood and speak truthfully to his neighbor, for we are all members of one body...29 Do not let any unwholesome talk come out of your mouths, but only what is helpful for building others up according to their needs, that it may benefit those who listen.

Reflect:

To speak truthfully to one another is to honor Jesus with authentic speech. Falsehood can take direct forms like an outright lie.

But more subtly, untruth can come in the form of flattery, which is telling people what they want to hear for your own personal benefit. It can come as exaggeration, where you willingly inflate the facts to make your position more compelling. It can be intended deception, where you allow people to believe something you know is not true without correcting them because you are proud, or ashamed, or insecure. Or maybe you just hold back relevant and important things because of fear or pettiness. We must avoid all these forms of falsehood in our speech. Speaking truthfully to each other goes way beyond falsehood to being appropriately honest with who we are. It doesn't mean we always tell all that we could tell, but it does mean that what we do tell others is in accordance with the truth that "is in Jesus". It is authentic speech, true to the facts as best we know them, out of respect for the Lord Jesus, who is the "truth." We must be "truth tellers," not in the sense that we are quick to correct others, but in the sense that we are always on guard against words that are less than accurate and authentic. It does not mean our words are going to always be perfect. Oftentimes, we don't know which words to choose and even when we don't mean to, we can say things that are wrong. This is more about a heart direction than words of perfection. The direction of our heart must be oriented towards God-honoring love for others. When our heart's desire is that our words benefit those who hear them, then over time, our words will become increasingly in-line with the truth that is in Jesus. Our words will encourage others to move in his direction.

Day 3
Read:
Eph. 4:25 Therefore each of you must put off falsehood and speak truthfully to his neighbor, for we are all members of one body...29 Do not let any unwholesome talk come out of your mouths, but only what is helpful for building others up according to their needs, that it may benefit those who listen.

Reflect:
Satan is the father of lies; Jesus is the truth. Lying destroys relationships; truth builds them up. Our physical bodies require ongoing communication to function in full health. For instance, some diseases or injuries impair the brain's ability to communicate accurately with other parts of the body. When your physical body's ability to communicate "truthfully" breaks down because of some neurological problem, then your body begins to fall into a state of disease and disintegration. Truthful and accurate information is essential to both physical and relational health. Why do people not speak truthfully to one another since it is so important? Largely because they believe that deception, or less than the full truth, will somehow lead to better outcomes.

They believe it will be better for them in some self-protective way. In some cases, people believe lying will benefit others as they "protect" them from the truth. Speaking truthfully is not always telling people what you *could* tell them, but it is always telling people what you *should* tell them. How do you know what to tell them? The starting point is to understand the purposes of telling people anything. We are to speak to others for their benefit, not for our own. It doesn't mean we don't benefit from these conversations. It means that in our speech, as in our actions, we are to put the interests of others ahead of our own. How would it change your conversations if your primary objective were to build others up according to "their" needs? Move away from lies and move resolutely towards the truth. If you have practiced self-protective and deceitful speech for a long time, it may take some time to change, but you can. You will need to pray about, plan for, and practice truth-telling. God will help you, but you must decide and move into that decision daily. Pray now, plan now, and then move out today and practice.

Day 4
Read:
Eph. 4:25 Therefore each of you must put off falsehood and speak truthfully to his neighbor, for we are all members of one body...29 Do not let any unwholesome talk come out of your mouths, but only what is helpful for building others up according to their needs, that it may benefit those who listen.

Reflect:
Every word you speak, along with every action you take, is supposed to be "in the name of the Lord Jesus" (Col. 3:17). This means that your words should represent him well. It is as if Jesus has given you "power of attorney" to speak for him. At the end of your conversation you should be able to sign his name to what you just said. Does that give you pause? It should. Jesus said that we will give account for "every careless word" we speak (Matt. 12:36). This does not mean we should only talk about "spiritual stuff" and we must never engage in small talk. That would be tiresome and unhelpful in relationships. It does mean that words are vitally powerful and important things. The accountability that Jesus refers to is tied to the fact that our words betray our hearts. They "speak" to who we are on the inside. The opportunity to speak to one another is so common that we can lose sight of how powerful and important words are. They originate from our hearts and they can penetrate into the hearts of others. Can you remember specific words spoken to you years ago? Of course, you can. What was the content of those words? Either they cut you down or they built you up. In either case, the power of the words seared them into your memory. But they are not just in your memory; they have ongoing shaping power in your life.

The vibrations of the vocal chords pushing sound waves to vibrate your eardrums have long ceased. However, the power of those simple words has not ended; they continue to be a force in your life for good or for ill. Don't take yourself too seriously. Be good at small talk, but remember that even small talk has the power to build others up or tear them down. In all of your talk, big and small, have a big goal...the building up of others for the glory of God. Speak words that Jesus would be happy to sign his name to.

Day 5
Read:
Eph. 4:25 Therefore each of you must put off falsehood and speak truthfully to his neighbor, for we are all members of one body...29 Do not let any unwholesome talk come out of your mouths, but only what is helpful for building others up according to their needs, that it may benefit those who listen.

Reflect:
C.S. Lewis said, "Sarcasm is the language of the devil." This doesn't mean there is never a place for sarcasm as a type of speech, but it does mean that it is very often destructive in people's lives. "Like a madman shooting firebrands or deadly arrows is a man who deceives his neighbor and says, 'I was only joking!' " (Pr. 26:18-19). Sarcasm is often like shooting someone with a painful arrow and then claiming, "I was just kidding." Using words as a weapon is never a joke. Words are tools and raw materials that should be used to "build" others up. There is a place for joking and laughing; in fact, humor is a key component of human resiliency and healthy relationships. However, the humor that is a *tool* leaves people refreshed, joyful, and lighter in their spirits. The humor that is a *weapon* leaves people tarnished, guilty, and further from God. What is "unwholesome" talk? It is speech that tears down instead of building up. It could even be a "spiritual conversation," but if it is transacted in such a way that others are judged, condemned, and unloved, then it was unwholesome. You are not fully responsible for how others "feel" about your words, although you should care about this. You are, though, fully responsible for the motive of your words. Why are you saying this? Where is it coming from? Are you speaking words merely because you want to speak them or mainly because others need to hear them? People don't need to hear your words because they are so impressive, but because God wants to speak encouragement to them through you. This is an awesome privilege and responsibility. Speak in a way that moves people towards God. The "pull" of your words should not be that others are impressed with you, but that they are drawn to God. Is speaking in this way beyond you? Is it too much to ask? Not at all! God will help you, but you must decide to put his help into regular practice.

Week 19/Day 1
Read:

Eph. 4:29-32 Do not let any unwholesome talk come out of your mouths, but only what is helpful for building others up according to their needs, that it may benefit those who listen. And do not grieve the Holy Spirit of God, with whom you were sealed for the day of redemption. Get rid of all bitterness, rage and anger, brawling and slander, along with every form of malice. Be kind and compassionate to one another, forgiving each other, just as in Christ God forgave you.

Reflect:

If we can grieve the Holy Spirit, then it stands to reason we can bring him joy as well. When we express kindness, compassion and forgiveness to each other, it brings him joy. These choices reflect the Holy Spirit's presence in our lives. Did you notice the word "choices"? It is important that you do, because there is a tendency to think of kindness, compassion and forgiveness as feelings. The fruit of the Spirit is not primarily feelings; it is actions. "The fruit of the Spirit is love, joy, peace, patience, kindness, goodness, faithfulness, gentleness and self-control" (Gal. 5:22-23). You might wonder about "joy and peace." Aren't those feelings? Joy and peace certainly can involve feelings, but peace is a reality that exists between the Christian and God, regardless of feelings. Peace is also a state of affairs that exists between two people who are not at odds. To have peace means you have done the things, or taken the actions, that lead to peace. Joy is often a choice, a decision to experience what God is offering to us in the midst of circumstances that are not in themselves joyful. Do not wait to *feel* kind or compassionate or forgiving or gentle, but, instead, *do* these things to one another. As you choose to move into these actions, then they will move more deeply into you. In other words, as you do what you are called to do, you will become who you are called to be. As a follower of Christ, you have the Holy Spirit resident within you. This is mysterious and beyond our ability to fully comprehend, but is it not beyond our ability to experience. His presence and power in your life are available for you to live in a way that brings him joy. You can rest assured that if it brings him joy, it will do the same for you. You must see acting with kindness, compassion and forgiveness as decisions empowered by the Spirit, not mere human feelings. If you wait for or pursue feelings of love, joy, and peace (and the other fruits of the Spirit) before choosing them, you are moving in the wrong direction. Say "yes" to God in the choices you have, then act on that "yes" in the way you treat others. As you live out this "yes" in your actions, you will live in the realm of the Holy Spirit's fruit. He is *in* you. Say "yes" to him and his fruit will come *out* from you.

Day 2
Read:

Eph. 4:29-32 Do not let any unwholesome talk come out of your mouths, but only what is helpful for building others up according to their needs, that it may benefit those who listen. And do not grieve the Holy Spirit of God, with whom you were sealed for the day of redemption. Get rid of all bitterness, rage and anger, brawling and slander, along with every form of malice. Be kind and compassionate to one another, forgiving each other, just as in Christ God forgave you.

Reflect:

Who has hurt you the most? It was probably someone close to you. The deepest wounds come from those who have made their way deepest into our hearts. Maybe you don't feel deep wounds, just a thousand little "cuts" that accumulate over time. Whatever the case, the standard for how we are to deal with others is high. We are to forgive as, in Christ, God forgave us. What does this mean exactly? Well, it doesn't mean we can bear the sins of others, only Christ can do that. It doesn't mean we can forget what others do to us. It doesn't mean that we cannot protect ourselves from others who might want to continue to wound us. Then what does it mean? It means we do not continually hold the sins of others against them. So, in our words and actions we do not attempt to bring them harm in any way. In our hearts we release their sin and our hurt to God, so that if we had the power to "pay them back," we would not do so. You can forgive a person and still not trust them in every way. Forgiveness is related to past actions, trust is related to future reliability. This does not mean we are to say to others, "I forgive you, but I will never trust you again." In that case, you would be playing the role of God, but the future is not yours to predict or to declare. When asked and when appropriate, you must be prepared to simply say, "I forgive you." In your heart, they are forgiven. You must let grace "marinate your mind" in your view of them, but in your actions you are responsible. You must let wisdom guide your choices. If someone has stabbed you in the back, you would be wise to not turn your back towards them, but, at the same time, you must not harden your heart towards them.

Day 3
Read:

Eph. 4:29-32 Do not let any unwholesome talk come out of your mouths, but only what is helpful for building others up according to their needs, that it may benefit those who listen. And do not grieve the Holy Spirit of God, with whom you were sealed for the day of redemption. Get rid of all bitterness, rage and anger, brawling and slander, along with every form of malice. Be kind and compassionate to one another, forgiving each other, just as in Christ God forgave you.

Reflect:

There are likely people in your life who you cannot help but step on their toes. It seems you cannot always know what will offend them, only that you will eventually offend them. What are you to do about this? Certainly, you cannot always try to live your life to avoid offending people. This would be impossible, if for no other reason than the choices necessary to avoid offending one person might, at the same time, be offensive to someone else. You must live your life doing all you can to be at peace with all people, while also realizing that you cannot always actually be at peace with others. There is something else you can do with this reality of people in your life who seem to have perpetually "large toes." You can learn from their negative lesson and be careful to not be like that yourself. It can be hard to see in ourselves what we do not like in others, but it is important that we do. Be honest. Are you easy to offend? Do you find that people are often "stepping on your toes?" Then perhaps you should pray that God would decrease the "size of your toes" and increase the "size of your heart." Don't be a petty person. You do not have to let things bother you like they do. I am not speaking of large, truly hurtful wrongs done to you. This is about the ongoing things that others, who mean you no harm, do that offend you. You must become more generous in your heart towards others. To be continually offended by multiple, smaller offenses is an indication that you have made life about you. It is not. Pray that God will give you a "larger heart" and "smaller toes." You might find that you have fewer things to forgive others for than you thought you did.

Day 4
Read:

Eph. 4:29-32 Do not let any unwholesome talk come out of your mouths, but only what is helpful for building others up according to their needs, that it may benefit those who listen. And do not grieve the Holy Spirit of God, with whom you were sealed for the day of redemption. Get rid of all bitterness, rage and anger, brawling and slander, along with every form of malice. Be kind and compassionate to one another, forgiving each other, just as in Christ God forgave you.

Reflect:

What if others don't deserve to be forgiven? What if they are not sorry for what they have done? What if they continue to do hurtful and wrong things? No one really "deserves" forgiveness, but everyone needs it. However, some people do not seem to realize they need it, or they just don't care. But, not only does everyone need forgiveness, everyone needs to forgive as well. Even when others do not care about your offers of forgiveness, it is right that you give it to them. Even if they refuse to benefit from grace offered to them, you can benefit by giving grace to others. It takes two to have a relationship.

When relationships have been broken, it requires that forgiveness be both offered and received, if the friendship is to be restored. However, it only takes one to forgive. Forgiveness does not mean forgetfulness or foolishness, but it is essential that you give it to those who need it. It is not your concern whether they want it or deserve it. You give forgiveness because it has been given to you. You give forgiveness because you want to live in the liberty of Christ. What if you offer forgiveness and the offer is rejected? What if they reject you, misunderstand you, and misrepresent you? Then you have the chance to live what you say you believe. Jesus is Lord of your life and he is the one you live to please. Now you have a real chance to demonstrate this fact. He has seen your offer of forgiveness and he is pleased. Let his pleasure be enough.

Day 5
Read:
Eph. 4:29-32 Do not let any unwholesome talk come out of your mouths, but only what is helpful for building others up according to their needs, that it may benefit those who listen. And do not grieve the Holy Spirit of God, with whom you were sealed for the day of redemption. Get rid of all bitterness, rage and anger, brawling and slander, along with every form of malice. Be kind and compassionate to one another, forgiving each other, just as in Christ God forgave you.

Reflect:
You must get rid of all the manifestations of the old life from your life. You must be rid of bitterness, which is the opposite of kindness, not of sweetness. Rage and anger must go, as well as their verbal expressions of brawling and slander. In fact, every form of malice must be continually "shown the door." Malice is depravity; it is the manifestation of the old "us" without Christ. Is the Christian life nothing more than an exercise in futility? Do not let any unwholesome talk out of your mouth. Do not grieve the Holy Spirit. Get rid of all this bad stuff. Be kind and forgive as Christ forgave you. All of these direct commands to consistently be and do and to not be and not do may just seem impossible. Reorient yourself to the reality of God right now. Your life in Christ is not a pass/fail endeavor. It is a relationship, a growing relationship. God is not growing, but you are. If you are a Christian, you are accepted in Christ Jesus. You are okay; you cannot earn what has been freely given to you. Now look again at all of these "impossible" things you are asked to do and be. It is not an exercise in futility; it is an invitation to liberty. Believe that it is possible for you to be this kind of person, more and more as time and choices go by. Expect that your choices matter. God has given you the privilege of being a part of what happens to you. Decide to move into the choices that will shape you into this kind of person. This really is about a life of direction, not a life of perfection.

Week 20/Day 1
Read:
Rom. 15:1-7 We who are strong ought to bear with the failings of the weak and not to please ourselves. Each of us should please his neighbor for his good, to build him up. For even Christ did not please himself but, as it is written: "The insults of those who insult you have fallen on me." For everything that was written in the past was written to teach us, so that through endurance and the encouragement of the Scriptures we might have hope. May the God who gives endurance and encouragement give you a spirit of unity among yourselves as you follow Christ Jesus, so that with one heart and mouth you may glorify the God and Father of our Lord Jesus Christ. Accept one another, then, just as Christ accepted you, in order to bring praise to God.

Reflect:
In the secular worldview, the law of the strong defines reality. Survival of the fittest is both a description of how humans have become what they are and a prescription of how humans are to deal with life and others. You demonstrate your fitness by winning. The highest good is survival, so only the best survive. In the end, it doesn't matter how you survive just that you did. Consequently, in some societies laws are in place to keep people's survival tactics inside some acceptable boundaries. In lawless or despot-ruled societies, however, the "strong" consume the weak without limits. In the end, what eventually becomes of the strong in all these scenarios? They ultimately become the weak. The tables are turned on them and they are no longer the fittest. Therefore, they do not survive in the end. It is all a demonic lie. No one is "fit" and, in the end, there are no survivors. The mad rush for survival that describes the lives of many is a chasing after illusion. Stop for a moment and take a deep breath of sanity. "We who are strong ought to bear with the failings of the weak and not to please ourselves. Each of us should please his neighbor for his good, to build him up." Life is not about survival; it is about God's glory. When you live your life like he is truly alive, his glory is revealed in your life. Since he is alive, you do not have to live to protect yourself. Since he is alive, you do not have to live for what you believe will bring pleasure. Since he is alive, you do not have to "win." Since he is alive, he is your protection, your purpose, and your pleasure. Christ has won so that you can share in his "winnings." He won because he was the "fittest," but in his fitness he sacrificed for all those who are not "fit" and do not deserve to survive. In his strength, he died for the weak so that that the weak might survive. The survival of the unfit – which includes you, me and everyone else – is completely dependent upon the willing sacrifice of the only one who has ever been truly "fit", the Lord Jesus. Become like him in his "weakness" and experience him in his strength. Look to the good of others not just your own.

Day 2
Read:
Rom. 15:1-7 We who are strong ought to bear with the failings of the weak and not to please ourselves. Each of us should please his neighbor for his good, to build him up. For even Christ did not please himself but, as it is written: "The insults of those who insult you have fallen on me." For everything that was written in the past was written to teach us, so that through endurance and the encouragement of the Scriptures we might have hope. May the God who gives endurance and encouragement give you a spirit of unity among yourselves as you follow Christ Jesus, so that with one heart and mouth you may glorify the God and Father of our Lord Jesus Christ. Accept one another, then, just as Christ accepted you, in order to bring praise to God.

Reflect:
Accepting one another is difficult when the other person does and says things that are unacceptable. It is important to remember how or, rather, when Christ accepted you. "While you were still a sinner, Christ died for you" (Rom. 5:8). We must take people where they are and love them just as they are. That is exactly what Christ did, and continues to do for us. This, of course, does not mean that we must accept all that people do and say. Jesus does not accept all that you think, do, and say. However, if you belong to him, he does accept you. His love for you cannot allow him to accept what is unacceptable about you and, at the same time, it means you are completely acceptable just as you are. Is this a contradiction? No, it is just two different ways of looking at the same person. A loving father might tell a child, "I love you no matter what you do. You will always be my accepted son or daughter." That same father will say to the rebellious child, "What you did is completely unacceptable. You can do better and I am disappointed." The father is not confused and, likely, neither is the child. The difference is clear in principle and practice. It is sometimes described as, "Love the sinner, not the sin." When you accept someone where they are, and they understand what they really means, you have empowered them to change. When we feel like we can only fail, we probably will. When others believe in us and accept us as we are and, yet, call us forward towards much more, we are likely to become much more. Live the tension by accepting others without accepting all that they do; you will be used by God to help them become more like Christ over time. How does God want you to express acceptance to someone in your life? In your attitude, words, and actions you help them understand they are valuable and worthwhile...just as they are. From that position of acceptance, how can you then encourage them to become more than they are? Acceptance and encouragement are powerful forces in the lives of people. Use them today for the glory of God, for the good of others, and for your own joy.

Day 3
Read:

Rom. 15:1-7 We who are strong ought to bear with the failings of the weak and not to please ourselves. Each of us should please his neighbor for his good, to build him up. For even Christ did not please himself but, as it is written: "The insults of those who insult you have fallen on me." For everything that was written in the past was written to teach us, so that through endurance and the encouragement of the Scriptures we might have hope. May the God who gives endurance and encouragement give you a spirit of unity among yourselves as you follow Christ Jesus, so that with one heart and mouth you may glorify the God and Father of our Lord Jesus Christ. Accept one another, then, just as Christ accepted you, in order to bring praise to God.

Reflect:

We are not merely to accept others; we are to accept "one another." You must accept others as Christ has, but you must also allow them to do the same for you. For some, allowing others to accept them may be a greater challenge than to be the one accepting others. To allow others to accept you means you will be known by them. They must know you adequately and accurately enough to be able to have an authentic relationship with you. You will not be able to do image management and, at the same time, allow others to accept you as Christ accepted you. But you may wonder, isn't this a contradiction? If they are going to accept me as I am, wouldn't that indicate they should accept my insecurities, and even my desire to put forth a "good image," though it will be inaccurate and incomplete? No, it's not a contradiction; it is looking at accepting one another from different perspectives. When you look at others in their weaknesses and failures, you must choose to accept them right where they are. In regard to being accepted by others, you are not to demand they accept you, but you are to allow them to do so. You must do your level best to let them see who you really are, both in your strengths and weaknesses, in order that they can accept the real you, not some fabrication of a false you. Is this a double standard? No, it is a single standard, sometimes called the "Great Commandment." You are to love others in the same way that you would want others to love you. So, in regard to accepting others, you take them right where they are. In regard to being accepted by others, you offer them the real you. This is a dual application of a single standard. You cannot choose for others, but you must choose for yourself. Make the good and God-blessed choice of accepting one another. Do both. Accept them as they are and allow them to accept you, as you actually are.

Day 4
Read:
Rom. 15:1-7 We who are strong ought to bear with the failings of the weak and not to please ourselves. Each of us should please his neighbor for his good, to build him up. For even Christ did not please himself but, as it is written: "The insults of those who insult you have fallen on me." For everything that was written in the past was written to teach us, so that through endurance and the encouragement of the Scriptures we might have hope. May the God who gives endurance and encouragement give you a spirit of unity among yourselves as you follow Christ Jesus, so that with one heart and mouth you may glorify the God and Father of our Lord Jesus Christ. Accept one another, then, just as Christ accepted you, in order to bring praise to God.

Reflect:
There is an old parable of a man who put his ladder against a wall, then spent his entire life climbing that ladder. Finally, at the end of his life he realized he had put the ladder against the wrong wall. Many people are guessing as to what life is all about and hoping that what they value will actually prove to be valuable in the end. But, humans are terrible guessers and there are no do-overs. These two facts make it vitally important that we actually get it right in terms of what we trade our lives for. You don't have to be a prophet in order to make accurate predictions of the future, but you do have to be a historian. What has happened in the past is a great way of understanding what is likely to occur in the future. But, even then, is it a guarantee? Yes and no. No, it is not a guarantee in terms of absolute confidence that past outcomes will repeat themselves in the future. However, you do have a guarantee that who God was in the past, he will also be in the future. He does not change. He does not grow or get smarter or stronger or better. He is perfect in every way. You can look in the Bible and see how God has interacted with people and you can see the outcomes of their ways of life. From those interactions, you can learn both negative and positive lessons for your own life. You can escape the negative and embrace the positive without having to go through all of the pain of learning either lesson from personal experience. Personal experience is an important teacher, but learning from the experience of others can be even better. So, in looking into the Scriptures what do you find that tells you what you should give your life for? Of course, there are many things, but the one thing that stands out is that Christ did not live merely to please himself. He lived for the glory of his father and for the good of others. His life was and is one of abiding joy. If you chase happiness, it will surely flee from you. If you pursue the glory of God by accepting and loving others, then happiness will chase you and, over and over again, it will find you.

Day 5
Read:

Rom. 15:1-7 We who are strong ought to bear with the failings of the weak and not to please ourselves. Each of us should please his neighbor for his good, to build him up. For even Christ did not please himself but, as it is written: "The insults of those who insult you have fallen on me." For everything that was written in the past was written to teach us, so that through endurance and the encouragement of the Scriptures we might have hope. May the God who gives endurance and encouragement give you a spirit of unity among yourselves as you follow Christ Jesus, so that with one heart and mouth you may glorify the God and Father of our Lord Jesus Christ. Accept one another, then, just as Christ accepted you, in order to bring praise to God.

Reflect:

C.S. Lewis spoke of a quest that drives people to be included in "The Inner Ring." It could be at work, at school, at a social club, or even at church. These "rings" are not inherently bad; in fact, any group of people with a common story and struggle will form one. They are made into something bad, however, by our propensity to want to be included and to exclude others. Lewis said that the Inner Ring exists for the purpose of exclusion. It would not be meaningful to be an insider if there were no outsiders. The invisible line that forms the ring would have no meaning unless most people were on the wrong side of it. Exclusion is the essence of the Inner Ring and the quest to be "in" will ruin your heart unless you act decisively against this urge. The gospel both forms an Inner Ring and, at the same time, breaks down the barriers that divide people. In the church, all who are in Christ are in his "Ring" and they are to accept one another even as he has accepted them. So, in Christ, there is "neither Jew nor Greek, slave nor free, male nor female, for you are all one in Christ Jesus" (Gal. 3:28). It is not that these cultural and gender distinctions don't exist, but, rather, it is that they don't divide people anymore because Christ has made them one. So, you are in Christ, included by him through faith into his Inner Ring and, therefore, you must not exclude anyone intentionally from your life. It doesn't mean you can't have close friends or that there won't be people you like more than others; it simply means that you will "accept one another… just as Christ accepted you." In your heart and in your home, you must make room for people you would not likely be friends with, apart from Christ in you. To accept one another in the way Paul intends is not merely to tolerate others, but it is to embrace them into your friendship. How has Christ accepted you? What conditions has he put on his acceptance? Did you clean up your act first? Did you become free of things that displease him? No, he accepted you as you are and then proceeded to help you become better than you are. This is how you are to accept one another.

Take each other as you are, in order that each person will become far more than they are or even thought they could be. Others in Christ's Inner Ring will likewise accept you as you are. You will find, and perhaps you already have, that some of your most treasured relationships are with people you would never have let into your "ring," if Christ had not already let both of you into his.

Week 21/Day 1
Pray:
Ask God to reorient you to Himself. Confess any known sin. Thank Him for His forgiveness. Be still and reflect on Jesus and His sacrifice for you. Ask the Holy Spirit to open your heart and mind to God's Word. Pray for others in your life that they, too, would know and love God today.

Read:
James 5:16-18 Therefore confess your sins to each other and pray for each other so that you may be healed. The prayer of a righteous man is powerful and effective. Elijah was a man just like us. He prayed earnestly that it would not rain, and it did not rain on the land for three and a half years. Again he prayed, and the heavens gave rain, and the earth produced its crops.

Matt. 5:23-24 Therefore, if you are offering your gift at the altar and there remember that your brother has something against you, leave your gift there in front of the altar. First go and be reconciled to your brother; then come and offer your gift.

Reflect:
It is not surprising that Christians can get at odds with one another, but what is surprising is how often they work through their differences and are able to have restored relationship. Sinning against each other is not necessary. But it is likely; therefore making peace with confessing your sins to others is always going to be an important part of your spiritual journey. If you are going to live in close relationships with others, and you should, you will need to confess your failures when they happen. Confession of failure can be challenging for several reasons. It may be that you do not feel you are completely at fault. Perhaps you believe the blame for the problems between you and someone else is shared equally between you. It could be that you believe they are more at fault than you are. An important guiding principle is to learn to take total responsibility for your own sin. Even if you believe you are only 10 percent of the problem, then take 100 percent responsibility for your 10 percent. Leave their 90 percent to them and to God. Another issue that can make confession difficult is insecurity. You may feel it will make you more vulnerable or make you look weak if you admit to having failed.

Think of a time when someone confessed their failure or sin to you or, perhaps, you saw a person admit they were wrong to someone else. How did you feel about that person? Did your respect for them decrease or increase? Confession of sin, on the whole, increases respect because it shows maturity to be able to be wrong. Confessing your sins to each other is like healing medicine applied to a wound. Because of our sinful nature we are going to wound one other, but since Christ is in us we can apply the healing power of confession to those wounds. Confess your sins to one another. It may feel like it is going to be such a difficult and painful experience until you actually do it. Then, afterwards, you will realize that avoiding or dreading confession is worse than actually doing the confessing.

Day 2
Read:
James 5:16-18 Therefore confess your sins to each other and pray for each other so that you may be healed. The prayer of a righteous man is powerful and effective. Elijah was a man just like us. He prayed earnestly that it would not rain, and it did not rain on the land for three and a half years. Again he prayed, and the heavens gave rain, and the earth produced its crops.

Matt. 5:23-24 Therefore, if you are offering your gift at the altar and there remember that your brother has something against you, leave your gift there in front of the altar. First go and be reconciled to your brother; then come and offer your gift.

Reflect:
The prayer of a righteous man or woman is powerful and effective. But who is righteous? It is likely you do not feel like you are, but being righteous is not being perfect, it is being forgiven. When you have confessed your sins to God and to others, you are forgiven and therefore you are righteous. Elijah was a man of powerful and effective prayers, but he was certainly not a perfect man. He was, in fact, just like you. This fact is both encouraging and challenging. It is encouraging in that there is no good reason why you cannot experience powerful and effective prayers. It is challenging because to experience that kind of praying requires keeping short accounts with God and with others. Look again at the order of events James gives here: confess your sins to one another, be healed, and pray powerfully and effectively. This is no magic formula, but it is a description of how important it is to confess our sins to one another. Paul wrote that the "only thing that counts is faith expressing itself in love" (Gal. 5:6). Obviously, if we sin against one another, then love would require that we confess that sin and do all we can to make things right. As a result, our faith is seen in our love to one another. Our love to one another is seen in continually keeping short accounts with each other.

93

Unconfessed sin between you and someone else is a hindrance to effective prayer. Jesus said that if you are offering your gift to God but remember you have sinned against another person, then you are to stop what you are doing, go make things right with the person, and only then can you offer your gift to God. If you are not right with others, it will not be possible for you to be right with God. Prayer is conversation with God, talking with him about things that are important to you both. If you are at odds with another person, God is interested in that situation, not in the other things you might want to talk to him about. You will find he has a one-track mind when it comes to these things. Go. Confess your sins to each other. Then come back to God and you will find your conversations with him are powerful and effective.

Day 3
Read:
James 5:16-18 Therefore confess your sins to each other and pray for each other so that you may be healed. The prayer of a righteous man is powerful and effective. Elijah was a man just like us. He prayed earnestly that it would not rain, and it did not rain on the land for three and a half years. Again he prayed, and the heavens gave rain, and the earth produced its crops.

Matt. 5:23-24 Therefore, if you are offering your gift at the altar and there remember that your brother has something against you, leave your gift there in front of the altar. First go and be reconciled to your brother; then come and offer your gift.

Reflect:
There is no promise in Scripture that all disease or injury will be healed if only you just believe or pray or do the right things. After all, death is a final failure of the physical body, so in the end all will die of something. However, there are times when God does desire to heal people of physical ailments in order to reveal his glory in those circumstances. You are free at any time to ask him to heal, but you should at all times trust him with his purposes in your life. There may be times when the root of your physical problem is sin. Unforgiveness and bitterness are known causes of disease. To harbor a grudge - to refuse to give and to receive forgiveness - can literally make us sick. To forgive and to be forgiven is good for you in many ways. In addition to the practical physical and mental benefits, the willingness to make things right with others opens up our hearts to God in ways that can make our praying more effective. If we ask God to bring healing (or anything else for that matter) and, yet, we harbor unconfessed or unforgiven sin, then we should not wonder why our prayers are ineffective. Confess your sins to one another. Ask for forgiveness when necessary and give forgiveness when you have the opportunity. This is fairly simple to understand and apply, but enormously important for your physical, mental, and spiritual well-being.

Not to mention your relational well-being, both with others and with God. Confess your sins and pray for each other so that you may be healed. Do this so you may be healed of physical "sin-sickness" as well as relational "sin-sickness." To live in the fullest possible health it is necessary that, as far as it is within your own ability, you live in right relationship with others. This is both right to do and good for you to do.

Day 4
Read:
James 5:16-18 Therefore confess your sins to each other and pray for each other so that you may be healed. The prayer of a righteous man is powerful and effective. Elijah was a man just like us. He prayed earnestly that it would not rain, and it did not rain on the land for three and a half years. Again he prayed, and the heavens gave rain, and the earth produced its crops.

Matt. 5:23-24 Therefore, if you are offering your gift at the altar and there remember that your brother has something against you, leave your gift there in front of the altar. First go and be reconciled to your brother; then come and offer your gift.

Reflect:
King Saul liked to do things his own way while, at the same time, pretending he was obeying God. The final straw that cost him his kingdom was when he decided God needed an "offering" from him more than obedience. Samuel confronted Saul regarding his rebellion and Saul essentially said, "Yeah, I knew what God wanted, but I had a better idea. Rather than destroying all this good stuff, I kept it as a sacrifice for God." Samuel replied, "Does the LORD delight in burnt offerings and sacrifices as much as in obeying the voice of the LORD? To obey is better than sacrifice, and to heed is better than the fat of rams" (1 Sam. 15:22). Jesus would echo the same principle when he taught that if you were making an offering (a sacrifice) in worship and remembered that you had sinned against someone, then stop what you are doing! Go and do your best to be reconciled to your brother or sister, then come back and make your offering. God does not want your worship or your sacrifice unless he has your obedience. Why? Because if he is not seen as sovereign Lord, then it's really not worship. If he is not obeyed, then he is not seen as sovereign Lord. Saul saw himself as a 'sort of' junior partner to God. This would be humorous if it were not so blatantly wrong. God does not need our help, or our advice, or our sacrifice. He *needs* nothing from us, but he *wants* obedience from us. Living in healthy relationships with one another is bottom-line obedience to God. As far as it is within your power, maintain clear relationships with one another. Only then will your "offerings" be acceptable to God. Because only when he is fully obeyed are we actually perceiving him as he really is.

He is the Lord of heaven and earth and he needs nothing from us, but there are things he wants from us. Forgiving one another is one of those things.

Day 5
Read:
James 5:16-18 Therefore confess your sins to each other and pray for each other so that you may be healed. The prayer of a righteous man is powerful and effective. Elijah was a man just like us. He prayed earnestly that it would not rain, and it did not rain on the land for three and a half years. Again he prayed, and the heavens gave rain, and the earth produced its crops.

Matt. 5:23-24 Therefore, if you are offering your gift at the altar and there remember that your brother has something against you, leave your gift there in front of the altar. First go and be reconciled to your brother; then come and offer your gift.

Reflect:
Consistently confessing your sins can help you see the futility of those sins. Sinning against one another is empty and unfulfilling. Everyone, if they are paying attention, will experience this emptiness. The problem is that the experience of the emptiness of sin is most acute after the fact. How can we learn to see the emptiness of sin before the act of sinning? Getting perspective after failure is important; it leads to repentance, confession, and restoration. Getting perspective before failure is ideal; it leads to wisdom and the avoidance of sin altogether. Perspective by itself will not always be enough to keep you from making bad choices. Often people will "see" what is right to do, but still plow ahead into sin anyway. However, perspective over time can and does shape our choices. If we see at the beginning the futility that will come in the end because of some choice we are considering, it can help us avoid that choice. Confession can help with that perspective. Often people will sin against someone and then just wait for time to take away its "edge." An unkind word, a bad attitude, or a sinful action against someone needs to be dealt with directly, not passively. Do not just "wait it out." Instead, take action. Go to the person you have sinned against and ask for forgiveness. Use these words: "I was wrong. Would you forgive me?" Be direct. Do this every time you sin. In the first place, it is the right thing to do. In the second place, it will help you make better choices in the future. When you have asked for forgiveness for the same bad attitude or the same foolish choice over and over again, it can help you learn to just skip the sin altogether. If you get "sick" of confessing the same sin over and over, don't stop confessing. Instead, move that perspective backwards on the timeline. As you are about to make the bad choice, remember where you will end up if you do so. Do the math. Has this bad choice ever really been worth it? What are the chances it will be worth it this time?

There are other factors that are important in dealing with and avoiding sin, but consistent and full confession of sin to one another is clearly an important one. Confess your sins to one another and you will be healed.

Week 22/Day 1.
Read:
Mark 1:35 Very early in the morning, while it was still dark, Jesus got up, left the house and went off to a solitary place, where he prayed.

Deut. 29:29 The secret things belong to the LORD our God, but the things revealed belong to us and to our children forever, that we may follow all the words of this law.

Reflect:
If God knows everything, why pray? If God is in control and is going to do whatever he knows is best, why pray? Since I am limited and can't see the big picture, why pray? What do I know, how can I presume to know what should happen? You should pray because the scriptures say you should. In fact, they say you should pray a lot...you should pray continually (1 Thess. 5:17). We should seek to understand God's will and ways as much as possible, but we must understand that there is a limit to the capacity of our understanding. This is offensive to adults, but not to children who tend to be aware that they have limits. We are not adults in our relationship to God. We are children. We should try to learn how to better pray and we should also try to pray more often. But in terms of understanding *why* we should pray even though God is in control, we only need to know that we are told to do so. The fact that God is in control should be an encouragement to pray, not a discouragement from praying. If someone or something else was in control, we should be addressing our prayer and attention to them or it. But since God is in control and he has told us to pray, we are wise to direct our attention and our petitions to him. He can answer prayers because nothing can stand in his way. So ponder the deep things of God all you want, but in the end do the simple things he has told you to do. Pray at all times about all things. This is what he has told us to do and the mysteries of how it all works together is not our concern. Will you wait until you have figured God out before you experience God in your life? If you do, you will wait indefinitely. You don't have to figure him out to experience him, but you do have to obey him. Pray today. Pray about everything that concerns you and learn to pray about everything that concerns him as well.

Day 2
Read:
Mark 1:35 Very early in the morning, while it was still dark, Jesus got up, left the house and went off to a solitary place, where he prayed.

Deut. 29:29 The secret things belong to the LORD our God, but the things revealed belong to us and to our children forever, that we may follow all the words of this law.

Reflect:
Jesus prayed. From eternity past God the Father, Son, and Spirit have lived in loving relationship. God is three persons in one being. This is not hard to understand; it is impossible to fully understand. But this inability to fully understand is fully understandable. We understand by analogy, "This is like that." There is no analogy to God. He is completely unique. But the fact that we cannot fully understand does not mean we cannot have adequate and accurate understanding of God. We know that because God exists as the Trinity he does not need us in order to express and experience love and relationship. Within the uniqueness of who he is there has always been friendship, relationship, and love. This fact helps us understand why Jesus prayed. His existence had always been one of intimate friendship. Now as he dwelt among us as the "Word made flesh" (John 1:14), he continued to live in that friendship. He got up early in the morning, at the beginning of his day, and left his new friends to spend time with his old friends. Why pray? It's because you were made for relationship with God. Relationships require regular communication in order to flourish and grow. Your relationship with God is no different in this regard than the ones you have with other people in your life. There are many forms that prayer can take, just as there are many forms that communication between any two people can take. In all relationships there is asking, and listening, and confessing, and thanking, and on and on. You should pray because Jesus did. But you should also pray because you understand why Jesus did. He was in a friendship and so he prayed because he wanted to. He liked to pray. It may have been hard for him to get up early in the morning just like it can be for us, but he did it because he wanted to pray and not because he had to pray. Do you "want" to "want" to pray? You can learn to "want to" pray if you begin by seeing prayer as a conversation in a very important relationship.

Day 3
Read:
Mark 1:35 Very early in the morning, while it was still dark, Jesus got up, left the house and went off to a solitary place, where he prayed.

Deut. 29:29 The secret things belong to the LORD our God, but the things revealed belong to us and to our children forever, that we may follow all the words of this law.

Reflect:

A "secret thing" is how human prayer and God's sovereignty work together. A "revealed thing" is that they *do* work together. You can wait until you have it all worked out in your mind before you enter deeply and consistently into a conversational relationship with God. However, if you do, you will wait indefinitely. God is sovereign; all things are under his control and, at the same time, you are still told by God to pray. The sovereign God has set things up in such a way that your act of praying matters in terms of outcomes. Don't spend much time trying to figure it out. It's not a math problem; it's a relational reality. You really only need to be convinced of the fact that God has told you to pray and that your prayer matters. If you are convinced of this one thing, then whether or not you figure out any number of other things will not make a significant difference. The best place to look for how to live the Christian life well is to look to Christ himself. He prayed and you should too. He asked God for what he wanted and he trusted God for what he gave. You can try to "get off the hook" by telling yourself that, since he was the Christ, it's really not helpful to look to his life as a model for yours. However, scripture points us directly to his life as a model for how to live ours. Of course he was not just a role model, he was the atonement for our sins. But though he was more than a role model, he was certainly not less than one. Look to him, do what he did, and try to live like he lived. Jesus prayed. You should as well.

Day 4
Read:

Mark 1:35 Very early in the morning, while it was still dark, Jesus got up, left the house and went off to a solitary place, where he prayed.

Deut. 29:29 The secret things belong to the LORD our God, but the things revealed belong to us and to our children forever, that we may follow all the words of this law.

Reflect:

A mystery is not a contradiction. A contradiction implies that an error is involved, while a mystery means there is more to be known than what we currently know. God is completely in control *and* our prayers make a difference in outcomes. This is a mystery, but it is not a contradiction. Part of seeing how this works together is to view prayer as more than getting God to agree with us on what we want to happen. Prayer can become mostly bargaining, or even attempts at manipulation, if we don't see our relationship with God as a sort of partnership. Not partnership in that we are his equal or that we can somehow "out vote" him on some issue. But a partnership in that you and God are both working towards the same goals. You both desire to see your life maximize his glory and the good of others.

Prayer is not trying to get God to see things your way. It is first and foremost about fostering the health of the relationship. In human relationships, it is common for two people to sometimes see each other as opponents. Each one is vying for their own position and each one is somehow trying to "win." The truth is, in any healthy relationship what matters most is the relationship itself. When there is disagreement on key issues, then the ultimate goal is not to "win" but to protect the relationship so that it can continue to thrive. People will sometimes plead with God regarding some issue of great importance to them. As they plead it is hard to imagine how something so important to them could not be as important to God. When God does not "come through" as asked (or demanded), disillusionment can set in. Perhaps what happens is that they disagreed with God on a certain outcome and for them getting the desired outcome became the most important thing, not the relationship itself. Will you make prayer primarily about the relationship itself? Communication among friends and family should not be just about getting the other person to see things your way. It should be, ideally, about building the relationship itself. You can ask him for anything, and your asking does matter in the outcomes. But how will you respond when he doesn't agree with you on some matter of great importance? Move towards him, not away from him and in so doing you will be positioned to better understand what is of great importance to him.

Day 5
Read:
Mark 1:35 Very early in the morning, while it was still dark, Jesus got up, left the house and went off to a solitary place, where he prayed.

Deut. 29:29 The secret things belong to the LORD our God, but the things revealed belong to us and to our children forever, that we may follow all the words of this law.

Reflect:
Why pray? Because you can. If God did not exist, you could speak words to the ceiling or to the sky, but it would still not be prayer. It would be self-talk. If God existed but did not care, you could speak words to him but he would not listen. If he did not listen, it would not be prayer. It would be "wish-talk." You should pray because you can pray. You can pray because God exists and he cares for you. The fact is, most people do pray. Even about 1 in 5 atheists or agnostics prays daily. Which makes you wonder if they actually are what they think they are – atheist or agnostic. But although most pray, it is unlikely that most see prayer as the privilege that it is. Many people dream of being able to speak to some wise, famous or powerful person. They would love to be able to get that person's help, or their perspective, or just to have relationship with them.

Prayer is a conversational relationship with the all-wise, eternally famous, all-powerful God. We may know this as "brute fact," but we may not see this as the beautiful truth it is. If we would take the time to remember, reflect, and rehearse out loud these truths, it would likely make our praying seem more like the privilege that it is. It's good to pray "as you go" about all kinds of things and, of course, you can't always recite the greatness of God before every prayer. However, sometimes when you pray, it would be good and helpful if rather than beginning by "asking in prayer," you would "tell in prayer." Tell God (and yourself) of the greatness and goodness of God. Speak to him (and yourself) of his power and love and "smartness." His ways are best for you because he is both really smart and really good...try to remember this as you pray. Position yourself to pray by turning your thoughts to who it is you are praying to. Learn to see prayer as the privilege it is. You don't have to pray, you get to pray.

Week 23/Day 1
Read:
1 Thess. 5:16-18 Be joyful always; pray continually; give thanks in all circumstances, for this is God's will for you in Christ Jesus.

Reflect:
It is God's will that you "be joyful always," "pray continually," and "give thanks in all circumstances." Surely this means we will often live our lives outside the will of God because after all who can accomplish these lofty goals? We are sometimes joyful, sometimes prayerful, and sometimes thankful. So, is this a goal we aim for which is clearly unattainable? Is this a rebuke for how often we fall short of the will of God? Not at all. It *is* possible, even for a "regular" Christian to live a life of "always, continually, and in all circumstances." First, it is important to understand what these words imply. To be joyful always does not mean you will always "feel" a certain way. Jesus for the "joy set before him endured the cross" (Heb. 12:2). There is no question that he did not feel what we would normally call joy in the moments of his suffering. But it was the reality of joy that took him to the cross. His joy was a settled inner disposition that flowed from his relationship with God the Father. He had lived so well and for so long in relationship with God the Father that his heart was "trained for joy." But his joy was also a choice. He chose to move continually into the joy that is available to all who live in continual fellowship with God. So, "joyful always" and "pray continually" are two sides of single coin. When we live in a conversational relationship with God, we live in his joy. When we live in his joy, we will live in a conversational relationship with God. To experience his joy and to be able to live in his presence continually are both his gifts to us and our choices in regard to him. We are told to accomplish these things..."be joyful" and "pray continually."

We are not told to merely wait for them to be done to us or for us. Close the gap on where you are right now and where you (and God) want you to be. Do not merely regret how far you might be from continual joy and prayer. Move a step closer today to this lifestyle. God is offering it to you. Will you take him up on his offer and practice his presence starting today?

Day 2
Read:
1 Thess. 5:16-18 Be joyful always; pray continually; give thanks in all circumstances, for this is God's will for you in Christ Jesus.

Reflect:
Continual joy, prayer, and thankfulness are linked together like the molecules that combine to make water. These three choices come together to shape a clear picture of God's will for you. People will often search frantically to discern God's unknown will on the particulars of their lives. Who to marry, what to do vocationally, whether to make major purchases, where to go to school, where to live, or what church to join. It is odd that sometimes these same people are not as diligent to pursue the known will of God for their lives... which is to keep on being joyful, praying, and giving thanks. This is clearly the will of God for your life. Continual joy is a by-product of living in his presence in prayer. Giving thanks in all the circumstances of your life flows naturally from living in his presence and experiencing his joy. This kind of life is available to you. You don't have to wonder about it or say, "If it be your will, I would like to pray more, live in your joy and be thankful." It *is* his will, now move more faithfully and diligently into his will for your life. You can be sure that if God is all for something, then all that remains is for us to be all for it as well. He could keep us from this kind of life, but he won't. We can keep ourselves from this kind of life, though, and we often do. Close the gap. Move further into the will of God for your life - an ever joyful, prayerful, and thankful life.

Day 3
Read:
Rom. 12:12 Be joyful in hope, patient in affliction, faithful in prayer.

Reflect:
Practice makes permanent. What you do repeatedly over time shapes who you are. What we repeat (intentionally or unintentionally) becomes reflexive for us. What you do reflexively is who you have become. If anger has been practiced, then anger now comes quickly and easily for you. You have become an angry person. If kindness has been practiced, then kindness comes "naturally" for you and you have become a kind person. You think it's not that simple? Yes, in fact, it is that simple.

102

But it's not by any means easy to change your reflexes. This is especially true once you have practiced "wrong" for a long time. Now you have to both undo bad reflexes and train good ones. To be faithful in prayer simply means to practice prayer. It means to do it, over and over again. At first, you will need to remind yourself to pray as you go through your day. In response to these reminders to pray and also through the practice of praying, you are being faithful in prayer. How does your praying life compare to someone else's? That is not your concern other than maybe how you can be challenged by their example. But in terms of "measuring" how much you pray or how well you pray as compared to someone else, this is not to be your focus. Focus on faithfulness. Faithfulness is practice. Faithfulness is a lifetime of closing the gap between where you are and where you could be. What will you do today to remind yourself to pray? What will you do today in practice that will make prayer a bit more reflexive for you?

Day 4
Read:
Col. 4:2 Devote yourselves to prayer, being watchful and thankful.

Reflect:
The Scriptures frequently present prayer as a kind of wrestling or labor. This makes sense because most of us have experienced the reality of prayer as being difficult at times. The difficulties can take many forms. Some find it difficult to pray at all; their prayer life is inconsistent at best. Others struggle to focus in prayer or to know how they should pray. Many find it hard to pray in faith, they constantly wonder if praying is really worthwhile at all. The fact is, virtually all good and helpful things in life are difficult to maintain. To have good physical health over a long period of time takes constant attention. The same is true for relational health. Even if you desire something as relatively simple as a healthy lawn, you understand it takes a sort of devoted attention in order to accomplish this "yard health." Spiritual health is no different. It requires devoted attention. You must give ongoing attention to your relationship with God. This requires ongoing conversation with God. Don't be surprised if and when this conversational relationship proves to be difficult. Difficult is normal, there is nothing unusual about struggling in your prayer life. Some people do not struggle to pray and they are blessed, but they are not the norm. The reality of having difficulty is not an excuse to not pray. Rather, it is an encouragement to continue to wrestle in prayer. Devoting yourself to prayer means to continue to pray even when (especially when) it is a struggle. Don't be surprised that it can be hard to pray, just remember that hard is not bad or wrong...it's just hard. Devote yourself to prayer, being watchful and thankful.

Day 5
Read:
1 Thess. 5:16-18 Be joyful always; pray continually; give thanks in all circumstances, for this is God's will for you in Christ Jesus.

Col. 4:2 Devote yourselves to prayer, being watchful and thankful.

Reflect:
Prayer is communication. The number one problem with communication is the illusion that it has occurred. In human-to-human communication the message that is intended to be sent is often not the message that is received. It could be practical reasons like one person is a poor communicator or the other is distracted. It could also be personal reasons like one has an "anger filter" in place while the other has a "distrust filter." But in prayer God has no filters. All communication breakdowns are on our side of the conversation. There are some implications here for our hearing from God, but let's focus now on our speaking to God. Since God "hears" everything with perfect clarity, including our hearts and not just our words, it seems our hearts and not our words should get most of our attention. This is why you can pray another person's prayer, like the Psalms, and they can still be "your" prayer. When their words match what is in your heart, it becomes your prayer. It's also why Jesus warned against using "many words" to try and get God's attention. He is paying attention to our hearts, not just our lips. Of course, often the words are the authentic cries of our hearts, but not always. Sometimes the prayers of the lips don't match the condition of the heart. In this case, God is not "hearing" the words, he is only hearing the "heart." What does this mean practically for prayer? It means it is worth the time to be still and reflect on what is really in your own heart. God always knows, but we often don't. Reflect and then pour out your true heart to God. Confusion, disappointment, anger, doubt, joy, anticipation, passivity - all of these heart issues are known by God, but as we pray with "heart-honest" words we are in a heart-conversation with God. This kind of praying positions us to be changed by God. God can increase your joy if you are honest with him about your current lack of joy. Speak to him honestly from your heart, then listen to him speak honestly from his. To hear his heart will change your heart.

Week 24/Day 1
Read:
Matt. 6:9-13 This, then, is how you should pray: "Our Father in heaven, hallowed be your name, your kingdom come, your will be done on earth as it is in heaven. Give us today our daily bread. Forgive us our debts, as we also have forgiven our debtors. And lead us not into temptation, but deliver us from the evil one."

Reflect:

Jesus did not say this is "what" you should pray. He said this is "how" you should pray. This is not a formula to merely be repeated by using these words. It is an approach to God that involves both the head and the heart. It is possible to pray the "intent" of this prayer without using the actual "content" of the prayer. What is the intent? It is to approach God in a way that is in line with who he is. Who is he? He is our Father and he is in heaven. In Jesus' time, people did not often address God as Father, but Jesus did it frequently. Because we are familiar with addressing God as Father, we are prone to miss how profound this really is. The God who is too holy and awesome for a mere mortal to even glance at and whose power and might are beyond comprehension is our Father. This term implies relationship, love, care, and closeness. God's closeness to his children is also known as his immanence. God is not far off and he is not too great and powerful to be concerned with insignificant humans. He is close and he is engaged because he is our Father. But he is "our Father in heaven." Heaven is not some distant geographical space. It is the realm of his holy and transcendent existence. As "immanence" describes his closeness, "transcendence" describes his distance in terms of how much greater he is than we are. He is our Father and we can have relationship with him. He desires for us to draw near to him so he can draw near to us, but he is still our Father in heaven. We must not take him lightly or for granted. He is God. His "rank," so to speak, is God. His relationship to us is Father. That we can call him "Father" is our great privilege. That he remains our God is his great right.

Day 2
Read:

Matt. 6:9-13 This, then, is how you should pray: "Our Father in heaven, hallowed be your name, your kingdom come, your will be done on earth as it is in heaven. Give us today our daily bread. Forgive us our debts, as we also have forgiven our debtors. And lead us not into temptation, but deliver us from the evil one."

Reflect:

It is no small thing that Jesus said we are to pray "our Father" rather than "my Father." Of course we are to pray in private, but this passage that has been called the "model" prayer is given to us as a public or community prayer. It has been recommended that we "pray long in private and short in public." This prayer is short and it is public. Praying with others need not be formal, or long, or uncomfortable. It does not need to be tied to meals or special occasions. When you are with a friend or a family member enjoying time or enduring a difficult time, pray together. When you are having trouble connecting with a friend or family member, or having trouble working through a difficult problem, pray together.

Peace with God through the gospel brings peace with others in relationships. Our salvation is personal and our relationship with God is personal, but our salvation and relationship with God is revealed interpersonally. Surely, he is "*my* Father" and "*your* Father," but the Lord Jesus said to pray like this, "*Our* Father." He didn't use very many words to tell us how to pray. Therefore, we should pay careful attention to those words he did use. Private prayer is assumed, most do it. Praying regularly with others is not as frequent for most people. It is very likely that as you pray "Our Father" with others you will grow in your depth of understanding and appreciation for the fact that he is "My Father."

Day 3
Read:
Matt. 6:9-13 This, then, is how you should pray: "Our Father in heaven, hallowed be your name, your kingdom come, your will be done on earth as it is in heaven. Give us today our daily bread. Forgive us our debts, as we also have forgiven our debtors. And lead us not into temptation, but deliver us from the evil one."

Reflect:
You are moving right now. The earth is spinning 1,000 miles per hour on its axis. It is traveling 67,000 miles per hour around the sun. In spite of this incredible speed of movement, you have no perception of any of it. What is true doesn't always feel true. God is the one true King. He is the eternal, all-powerful, and all-wise creator. This remains true whether you feel it is true or not. Whether it's when you read or hear the news or as you drive to work or school. Or even as you live "inside your head" and contemplate your own struggles and fears, you may or may not perceive of God as King, but he still is. The fact that he is the one true King should have bearing on how you perceive the world around you and the world inside of your mind. But you must "practice" perceiving what is real. Close your eyes for a moment and think of yourself as sitting on a planet that is spinning and speeding around the sun. Use your imagination to "feel" this movement. Can you do it? You can, if you practice. When you use your imagination like this, you are not trying to make yourself believe something that is not real. Instead, you are connecting your mind with something that is real. It takes what we often call imagination to make this connection because the reality of the earth's movement is not immediately available to our senses. In a similar way, when you stop and contemplate the reality of God, you are using your imagination to consider a reality that is not normally immediately available to your physical senses. Close your eyes and contemplate God, the mighty King, living before he created time and space. Alive and powerful now, the transcendent God is greater than all of the time and space he has made.

Practice this so that your mind will more consistently "see" what is real but not immediately available to your eyes. *Practice* his presence so you will more consistently *experience* his presence in your life. This is not about "pretending" that something is true. It is about more consistently "remembering" what is true.

Day 4
Read:
Matt. 6:9-13 This, then, is how you should pray: "Our Father in heaven, hallowed be your name, your kingdom come, your will be done on earth as it is in heaven. Give us today our daily bread. Forgive us our debts, as we also have forgiven our debtors. And lead us not into temptation, but deliver us from the evil one."

Reflect:
"Hallowed" be your name, means "holy be your name." Jesus is not, of course, praying that God would become holy, but rather that he would treated with the respect and reverence that is due him. This is more than not using God's name as profanity; it is to live in such a way that demonstrates a belief in his utter holiness. His "name" is who and what he is. It is God as he has revealed himself to men and women. Holiness is less an attribute of God than it is a description of him. It means "separateness." He is set apart from all other beings in a way that is utterly unique. Christians have been declared to be holy by God, but this is a description of how God relates to us in light of the gospel. Christians can also choose to *act* in ways that are holy. But God *IS* holy; he is utterly set apart from all of created reality. To "hallow his name" means that we approach him as he truly is. He is the uncreated creator. We are not to approach him casually or flippantly, but with reverence and awe. Yet, it is "our Father" whose name is to be hallowed. How do we deal with this apparent contradiction? Can we approach him confidently, joyfully, even playfully? Of course, we can. After all, what do fathers enjoy more than the knowledge that their children enjoy them? But what about his holiness, how do we deal with this fact as well? There are many answers to that question, but one answer is that we rejoice in the fact that our Father is the holy God. For the child who has a heart to obey, having a "Holy Father" is a source of supreme comfort. For the child whose heart has turned away, having a "Holy Father" is a source of supreme discomfort. There is no conflict between "Holy" and "Father" when our hearts are set in his direction. It is the fact that he is holy that makes him such a good Father.

107

Day 5
Read:
Matt. 6:9-13 This, then, is how you should pray: "Our Father in heaven, hallowed be your name, your kingdom come, your will be done on earth as it is in heaven. Give us today our daily bread. Forgive us our debts, as we also have forgiven our debtors. And lead us not into temptation, but deliver us from the evil one."

Reflect:
Solomon wrote that "God has set eternity in our hearts" (Eccl. 3:11). In general, people think more often about God than any other thing. Even those who do not really love him, think about him. But these thoughts can be quite different, depending on the kind of relationship they have to him. For some, God is a sort of elderly figure, looking down on them in a sort of detached way. He is sometimes amused, sometimes annoyed, but he is largely impotent. He is their "grandfather in heaven." Others think of God as their "policeman in heaven." He lurks on the side of life's highways, ready to bring judgment if any laws are broken. Fortunately for them, they do not believe he is always attentive to them, sometimes he is too busy pulling someone else over to notice what they are doing. Still others believe God is "my buddy" in heaven. He is understanding, reasonable, and able to be negotiated with. In fact, he exists entirely for their perceived good. He is a sort of wealthy benefactor who doesn't judge and has no real standards other than "a good time is had by all." There are, of course, many other perceptions of God that people hold in their minds and often those perceptions shift from one view to another. This is a terrible thing. It is commonly believed that, in regard to matters of faith, it doesn't really matter *what* you believe only that you *do* believe. We certainly don't think this about how airplanes operate, or what foods humans should consume, or virtually any other aspect of reality. Because we know that in the "real world" it is of vital importance that we believe and act in line with is actually true. The same is true in regard to who God is, but with even more importance. It is even more important because getting it right regarding who God is impacts both time and eternity. Jesus said he is our "Holy Father." We must hold his revealed nature consistently in our minds. Who he actually is must overthrow any false ideas of him in our minds. We must believe, value, and live in line with the reality that he is "Our Father" and his name is to be "hallowed."

Week 25/Day 1
Read:
Matt. 6:9-13 This, then, is how you should pray: "Our Father in heaven, hallowed be your name, your kingdom come, your will be done on earth as it is in heaven. Give us today our daily bread. Forgive us our debts, as we also have forgiven our debtors.

And lead us not into temptation, but deliver us from the evil one."

Reflect:

Jesus inaugurated the Kingdom in his first advent. He will consummate the Kingdom in his second advent. Right now, we live "between" the times of the first and second advents. The Kingdom is "already, but not yet." It is "already" in that Christ reigns in the hearts of his people, and he is transforming them from the inside out. It is "not yet" in that his reign is not yet fully visible and experienced in its power. Therefore, in this in-between time, we pray for his kingdom to come and his will to be done on earth as it is in heaven. The Kingdom of God is the place where what God wants done, is done. Because God has given human beings choice, we can choose to not do his will (and very often this is what we choose). This prayer for his kingdom to come has many implications, but one that is very important is that as his people, we must come to fully and joyfully yield to his will in our lives. If you are a follower of Christ, his kingdom has come in your life. But you still live in a personal "already, not yet." You are his and you want what he wants and, yet, you often find yourself wanting what is in opposition to what he wants. This prayer for his will to be done is not a generic prayer of global impact, but it is a personal prayer of immediate impact. Today, make it your prayer and your intention that his kingdom and his reign be fully manifested in your life. Today, move through your day as a joyful, loyal subject of a kingdom, a kingdom with a good and wise king. Believe this to be true so that you will value his will for your life. As you value his will, as his will actually seems like the highest good you could do, you will be positioned to do his will. Believe that you are a subject in a kingdom. *Value* the king's will for your life. *Do* what the king wants done. *Experience* the beauty of life in the kingdom of God today. You can close the gap in your life today. Choose your trajectory by pointing your heart and mind in his direction.

Day 2
Read:

Matt. 6:9-13 This, then, is how you should pray: "Our Father in heaven, hallowed be your name, your kingdom come, your will be done on earth as it is in heaven. Give us today our daily bread. Forgive us our debts, as we also have forgiven our debtors. And lead us not into temptation, but deliver us from the evil one."

Reflect:

The kingdom of God is not political, but it changes the hearts of politicians. It is not a military, but it changes the minds of generals. It is not a public policy organization, but it changes the morals of all who enter it. We enter the kingdom by faith in the gospel of Jesus. When we enter the kingdom, we find that, in fact, the kingdom has entered into us.

It grows inside us like a tiny bit of yeast in a lump of dough, taking over more and more "inner" ground in our hearts until it permeates us thoroughly and, in ever-increasing ways, directs the course of our lives. In the gospel of Mark, a religious teacher asked Jesus to tell him which was the most important commandment. "The most important one," answered Jesus, "is this: 'Hear, O Israel, the Lord our God, the Lord is one. Love the Lord your God with all your heart and with all your soul and with all your mind and with all your strength.' The second is this: 'Love your neighbor as yourself.' There is no commandment greater than these." (Mark 12:29-31) The teacher then replied to Jesus, "Well said... these things are more important than all the burnt offerings and sacrifices." Jesus, THE teacher, then replied "You are not far from the kingdom of God" (Mark 12:34). We do not know if that religious teacher ever did enter the kingdom, but he was standing on the border looking in when he acknowledged that the kingdom of God is not merely external and ceremonial. This kingdom is love that begins internally and reveals itself externally in our relationships. When we pray for his Kingdom to come, we are praying that our lives would be more and more dominated by love for God and love for others. Do not despair if you believe you are not growing in these areas. Pray, from your heart, right now: "Your kingdom come!" Then go into your day, taking what he brings into your life as his answer to that prayer. You can move through your day trusting God to manage things for your good. You can live with gratitude and not grumbling because the king is in charge.

Day 3
Read:
Matt. 6:9-13 This, then, is how you should pray: "Our Father in heaven, hallowed be your name, your kingdom come, your will be done on earth as it is in heaven. Give us today our daily bread. Forgive us our debts, as we also have forgiven our debtors. And lead us not into temptation, but deliver us from the evil one."

Reflect:
In his agonizing prayer in the garden, Jesus poured out his heart to God the Father. He confessed that all things are possible for his Father (Mark 14:36) and he also asked that if possible this "cup" be taken from him (Matt. 26:39). The cup is the wrath of God that was to be poured out on Jesus for us. There is no contradiction in these passages. As Jesus prayed on that dark night and his disciples heard and remembered his prayers, they heard him say both things. In a sense, all things are possible for God because he can do anything that can be done. He can create the universe from nothing. He can raise Jesus from the dead. But he cannot lie. He cannot die. He cannot choose to not be God. God cannot make a square circle because that is not a real thing that can be done it is a contradiction.

Jesus asked, "Father, you can do all things, is there another way this can be done?" Then Jesus immediately confessed, "But let me be clear, if there is no other way to do what must be done, then what I most want is what you want." The fact is that God could not redeem humanity apart from the death of Christ and his bearing our wrath in his body. His love could not allow us to remain in our sins without a means of salvation. His justice could not allow us to escape his wrath without a means of justice. All things that can be done are possible for God, but God could not save us apart from the death of the Savior. Jesus did not want to bear the cup of God's wrath *and* Jesus wanted to bear the cup of God's wrath. He wanted another way, but what he most wanted was his Father's way. What about you? Are there things in your life now in which you do not want to submit to God? Do you fear the future and find yourself hesitant to fully give your life and hopes to Jesus? It is okay to pray, "God your will be done, but if there is another way than this one, I'll take it." Jesus prayed in that way and we can as well. But in the end, when the answer is, "No, there is no other way except this one," what will you do? Will you pray: "Your will be done, your kingdom come"?

Day 4
Read:
Matt. 6:9-13 This, then, is how you should pray: "Our Father in heaven, hallowed be your name, your kingdom come, your will be done on earth as it is in heaven. Give us today our daily bread. Forgive us our debts, as we also have forgiven our debtors. And lead us not into temptation, but deliver us from the evil one."

Reflect:
Paul wrote, "The god of this age has blinded the minds of unbelievers, so that they cannot see the light of the gospel of the glory of Christ, who is the image of God" (2 Cor. 4:4). The "god" of this age is Satan. "This age" refers to this period of time prior to the return of Christ. This age has made Satan its god, so all across the globe in nations, cities, homes, and hearts, "his" kingdom has come. It doesn't often come in terms of overt Satan worship, but mostly in the more subtle worship of self. Satan comes in disguise; he doesn't normally show his true evil form. What he offers is satisfaction, fulfillment, and the opportunity to live life on our own terms and get what we want. When we live to please self as opposed to God, we fall right into Satan's hands. We are operating in his kingdom. Life in the enemy's kingdom feels initially like liberty. We may believe we are free from the bonds of that seemingly eternal tyrant, God. We are the masters of our own lives and we set our own course. We get to decide what is right, real, and good. Then, when the god of this age has set his trap, he demands his due. We have not been living freely; we have been living as his puppets. God brings liberty, while the enemy only brings misery.

111

God offers freedom through submission to his will and ways. Satan offers freedom from submission to God. God's offer brings increasing joy, peace, and love - all the blessings of his great kingdom. Satan's offer brings ever-decreasing life satisfaction and a final loss of real liberty. In the enemy's kingdom, we increasingly experience the loss of the desire and the ability to do what we ought to do, because we are trapped in the gravitational pull of doing only what we want. Now, do you see? Cry out to God right now, "YOUR kingdom come, YOUR will be done!" Never mine, never mine...always yours!

Day 5
Read:
Matt. 6:9-13 This, then, is how you should pray: "Our Father in heaven, hallowed be your name, your kingdom come, your will be done on earth as it is in heaven. Give us today our daily bread. Forgive us our debts, as we also have forgiven our debtors. And lead us not into temptation, but deliver us from the evil one."

Reflect:
"Then Jesus came to them and said, 'All authority in heaven and on earth has been given to me. Therefore go and make disciples of all nations, baptizing them in the name of the Father and of the Son and of the Holy Spirit, and teaching them to obey everything I have commanded you. And surely I am with you always, to the very end of the age' " (Matt. 28:18-20). Authority is power, dominion, and jurisdiction. It is a word used to describe a king and his kingdom. Kings have some power; they have limited jurisdiction over specific geographical regions. But Jesus has all power and unlimited jurisdiction over all of heaven and earth. His kingdom comes now as he reigns in the hearts of men and women. "Therefore," Jesus said, "Go and make citizens of my kingdom." He tells us, "Immerse them in the name of the Triune God and teach them the opportunity and necessity of obedience to me as their king." Then he finished this royal commission of sending us, his people, as emissaries of his kingdom with a powerful and encouraging reminder: "I am always with you, even until I return again." Pray for his kingdom to come, his will to be done on earth as it is in heaven. His kingdom comes as people submit to Jesus as king. His will is done as his people go into the world and make him known. He has not given some edict from a throne and then sent us off to succeed or fail. He is a king who has sent us and has also promised to go with us. He has sent us as his ambassadors, not as someone who will go and "sell" what we have to others who do not have. He has sent us to go and "tell" what a great king he is. We are to tell of the opportunity of the good news. "Selling" is often about pressure. "Telling" is about confidence; it is simply letting people know what you know to be true.

Pray for his kingdom to come. As you go into the world today see to it that his will is done in your life. As you have opportunity, tell of the king and his kingdom.

Week 26/Day 1
Read:
Matt. 6:9-13 This, then, is how you should pray: "Our Father in heaven, hallowed be your name, your kingdom come, your will be done on earth as it is in heaven. Give us today our daily bread. Forgive us our debts, as we also have forgiven our debtors. And lead us not into temptation, but deliver us from the evil one."

Reflect:
In the New Testament, the word translated "bread" is often used to indicate a meal or food. A prayer for "daily" food is a prayer for what we need today; it is a practical request, but it is also a request that provides perspective. It is a constant reminder of our need and his provision. This is especially true for those who live in countries where the daily eating of food is commonplace rather than a rare occurrence. The food chain in a modern society is quite complex. It begins with those who sow and harvest the food at the "ground" level to those who transport it, process and package it, then sell it at local groceries or restaurants. Where is God in all of this? How is he "providing" daily food? In the wilderness God provided "bread from heaven." The Israelites called it "manna" (a word that literally means "what is it?"). For the wandering Israelites, it was quite obvious that God was the entire food chain. It was clear that God was providing the daily bread. In fact, except for the day before the Sabbath, they were forbidden from collecting any more manna than they needed for today. If they tried to collect more than their daily bread, the manna would be rotten and inedible the next day. God wanted them to trust him each day for today. But apart from that specific group of people during a specific time in history now called the "Exodus," God's role in the food chain is not nearly as obvious. In fact, many (and probably most) people would not dream of giving thanks for a meal because God was not responsible for their food, they were. They earned the money to purchase it. Some farmer grew it and a trucker transported it. God is not providing daily food, they are. Jesus said pray like this, "Give us today, our daily bread." Why? Because it is true that he is providing our daily food. More importantly, it is true that we are prone to miss this fact. Even those who believe God is not providing anything for them are, in fact, enjoying his provision. However, they are not enjoying God, the provider. As you go to your grocery store, restaurant, or kitchen to obtain a meal today, ask God to provide your daily needs. Do this because the assumption that the human food chain cannot fail is a false assumption; it can fail.

Do this because even if the human agents active in providing your meal do not fail, it is God who is providing all that is needed along the way. Sun, rain, crops, human wisdom and strength are all gifts from God. Ask for his daily provision today and give thanks for it today. Position yourself not merely to enjoy God's provision but also to enjoy God the provider.

Day 2
Read:
Matt. 6:9-13 This, then, is how you should pray: "Our Father in heaven, hallowed be your name, your kingdom come, your will be done on earth as it is in heaven. Give us today our daily bread. Forgive us our debts, as we also have forgiven our debtors. And lead us not into temptation, but deliver us from the evil one."

Reflect:
How do you ask God to provide food when it is in your kitchen right now? All you need to do is get up and go eat it. Does this prayer not apply to you? Has it already been answered and you can pray for something else instead? No, if this prayer has been answered for you, then pray not for <u>something</u> else, but rather pray right now for <u>someone</u> else. Remember this is an "us" prayer, not merely a "me" prayer. "Oh God, give <u>us</u> our daily bread!" Do your brothers and sisters around the world have food today? Are there not many who are hungry and crying out to God for food? Not just for food, but for peace, safety, and relief from war. Some have it and some do not. This is not just a prayer for self, this is a prayer for others as well. Why do some people lack daily bread? Often it is because of the sins of those in positions of power in their countries. Of course, there are droughts and famines, but lasting misery among large groups of people are not traced to "natural" disasters, but to sinful and corrupt leadership whose wickedness and ineptitude prolong and multiply the suffering. So, pray not just for bread, but also for leaders in places where people are suffering. "I urge, then, first of all, that requests, prayers, intercession and thanksgiving be made for everyone — for kings and all those in authority, that we may live peaceful and quiet lives in all godliness and holiness. This is good, and pleases God our Savior, who wants all men to be saved and to come to a knowledge of the truth" (1 Tim. 2:1-4). As you pray for others who are desperate for daily bread, do not feel guilty that you have access to food. Guilt is something to be confessed and left behind. Do not live in guilt. It robs you of productive, forward movement towards God and others. Let the needs of others produce gratitude in you. Be grateful for daily bread and do not take it for granted. Let the needs of others produce a sense of stewardship in you. If you have been given more than others, then along with that increased privilege comes increased responsibility. Pray, be grateful, and then ask yourself, "What else does God want from me today?" Not to earn his grace, but to express it to others.

114

"From everyone who has been given much, much will be demanded; and from the one who has been entrusted with much, much more will be asked" (Luke 12:48).

Day 3
Read:

Matt. 6:9-13 This, then, is how you should pray: "Our Father in heaven, hallowed be your name, your kingdom come, your will be done on earth as it is in heaven. Give us today our daily bread. Forgive us our debts, as we also have forgiven our debtors. And lead us not into temptation, but deliver us from the evil one."

Reflect:

Many 1st century workers were paid one day at a time. This meant that a few days of illness or an injury could have tragic consequences. This prayer for daily bread reflects this kind of short-term lifestyle. Long-term planning is wise, but we do not have ultimate control over our future. It's not wrong to save money or put away food for a time of disaster or need. It is wrong to rely on our own planning and saving. Listen to what Jesus said in this regard: "Watch out! Be on your guard against all kinds of greed; a man's life does not consist in the abundance of his possessions." And he told them this parable: "The ground of a certain rich man produced a good crop. He thought to himself, 'What shall I do? I have no place to store my crops.' "Then he said, 'This is what I'll do. I will tear down my barns and build bigger ones, and there I will store all my grain and my goods. And I'll say to myself, "You have plenty of good things laid up for many years. Take life easy; eat, drink and be merry."' "But God said to him, 'You fool! This very night your life will be demanded from you. Then who will get what you have prepared for yourself?' "This is how it will be with anyone who stores up things for himself but is not rich toward God." (Luke 12:15-21) Can you see how a daily prayer for daily bread can be a protective barrier against the folly of pursuing personal security over the pursuit of a rich faith in God? How many have lived exactly as that parable describes? They have lived with no sense of need, no prayers for daily bread, no need for God in their present or their future. Then, suddenly, all their planning has come to nothing. Oh God, give us today our daily bread and give us today the wisdom to understand our daily need for you. Today, tomorrow, and forever make us rich in faith towards you.

Day 4
Read:

Matt. 6:9-13 This, then, is how you should pray: "Our Father in heaven, hallowed be your name, your kingdom come, your will be done on earth as it is in heaven. Give us today our daily bread. Forgive us our debts, as we also have forgiven our debtors.

And lead us not into temptation, but deliver us from the evil one."

Reflect:
Praying for daily bread does not substitute for work. Of course, there are those who are unable to work in order to provide for their own needs and to help with the needs of others. But for most people, faithfulness to God means they will take responsibility for themselves. "Make it your ambition to lead a quiet life, to mind your own business and to work with your hands, just as we told you, so that your daily life may win the respect of outsiders and so that you will not be dependent on anybody" (1 Thess. 4:11-12). The phrase "work with your hands" does not apply only to those who engage in physical labor. It applies to everyone, no matter what is actually done for a "living." The phrase "for a living" is interesting. What most people do vocationally takes up a good bit of their lives. These jobs take most of our waking hours for most of our adult lives. It is also true that these jobs "pay" for our living, including housing, food, transportation, entertainment, etc., all of the things of our lives. So, we do work "for a living." It is not tragic that people spend much of their lives working a job. Work is a gift. We are designed to be productive and creative. It is a gift to enjoy your work, but it is also a gift just to have good work to do whether you enjoy it or not. What is tragic is when people trade their lives "away" for a job without recognizing what the purpose of their lives actually is. Our lives are to be spent for his glory and one way we bring him glory is by working. Some, maybe most, labor in vain because they do not do what they do for the glory of God and the good of others. "And whatever you do, whether in word or deed, do it all in the name of the Lord Jesus, giving thanks to God the Father through him" (Col. 3:17). Consequently, prayer for daily bread does not substitute for daily work, it compliments it. As you do what you do "for a living," remember why it is that you live. You live for his glory and for the good of others. Praying for your daily bread should include praying for your work, your health, your boss, and your co-workers, all those things that are a part of "earning" your daily bread. There is a sense in which you do "earn" a living, there is a higher sense in which nothing you have is earned; it is all received. "What do you have that you did not receive?" (1 Cor. 4:7).

Day 5

Read:
Matt. 6:9-13 This, then, is how you should pray: "Our Father in heaven, hallowed be your name, your kingdom come, your will be done on earth as it is in heaven. Give us today our daily bread. Forgive us our debts, as we also have forgiven our debtors. And lead us not into temptation, but deliver us from the evil one."

Reflect:

There are two mistakes we can make in regard to how we think and pray about our daily, or more mundane, needs. First, we can determine that God is much too busy to be concerned with trivial things. I must only ask for things that are of great importance. The second mistake is to pay so much attention to our daily needs that we forget there are bigger things going on in the world. How do we hold these things in balance? That word "balance" is the key. God is not "busy" in the normal sense of the word. His omnipotence (all-powerful) and his omniscience (all-knowing) mean that nothing he does is taxing or distracting for him. He doesn't grow tired or overwhelmed. All that he does, he does without effort. All there is to know, he knows immediately and completely. This means there is no detail that is big or small in terms of scope for God. All details are equally small or big, depending on how you want to think about it. You have an all-powerful, all-knowing Father in heaven. Your daily bread is a concern to him, as are the multitude of other things that happen in your life day-to-day. It is no compliment to God your Father to think, "I'll not bother him with insignificant things." Don't good fathers value what is important to their children? A very small child might be concerned with something that is trivial, but the good father will not make light of what is important to the child. On the other hand, we must grow up in our faith. We must not approach life like a perpetual child where the earth revolves our own needs. We must see there are many people with many needs all around us. We must see that God has multi-generational purposes of which I am one part. We must work to have perspective as we pray for our daily needs, but not our daily "greeds." So, balance is the path forward. Pray as a child to a good father. Whatever is on your heart you can take to God, no matter how small. But seek to grow up in your faith as well. As you pray for your needs and wants, move to the place where you consider the needs of others more consistently. Pray for "*our*" daily bread. Have a heart for what God is doing in your life as well as the lives of people all around you and all around the world.

Week 27/Day 1
Read:

Matt. 6:9-13 This, then, is how you should pray: "Our Father in heaven, hallowed be your name, your kingdom come, your will be done on earth as it is in heaven. Give us today our daily bread. Forgive us our debts, as we also have forgiven our debtors. And lead us not into temptation, but deliver us from the evil one."

Reflect:

"Forgive us our debts, as we also have forgiven our debtors." In the passage which immediately follows the Lord's model prayer, we see this idea repeated.

117

"For if you forgive men when they sin against you, your heavenly Father will also forgive you. But if you do not forgive men their sins, your Father will not forgive your sins" (Matt. 6:14-15). Does this mean that we must earn our own forgiveness by forgiving others? No, it doesn't. Clearly the Gospel indicates that we cannot earn forgiveness, we can only receive it. In that case, then what are we to do with these passages? You see in Jesus' prayer both an assumption and a confidence. The assumption is that we will forgive those who sin against us. The confidence is that God will likewise forgive us. This is not about earning forgiveness; it is about the fruit of having been forgiven. Jesus ministered to a woman who was said to have "lived a sinful life." Of course everyone sins, so the implication is that she "sinned for a living." This broken woman came to Jesus in repentance, weeping so profusely that her tears splashed on his feet as she washed and anointed them with perfume. The people around Jesus failed to understand what they were seeing. They believed Jesus didn't know "what kind of woman this was." They assumed if Jesus knew how much of a sinner she was, then he would send her away. Jesus knew who she was and he also knew what was in the hearts of those who condemned her. He told the story of two men who both had debts that were forgiven. One debt was much larger than the other. He asked, "Which one would love more?" The answer was obvious, the one who had been forgiven more. Jesus then said to those with hard hearts, "Therefore, I tell you, her many sins have been forgiven — for she loved much. But he who has been forgiven little loves little" (Luke 7:47). How does this story speak to this verse in the Lord's Prayer? It shows us the heart behind the simple phrase, "Forgive our debts as we also have forgiven our debtors." There is the assumption that those who have been forgiven much will have hearts to forgive. There is the confidence that those who have hearts to forgive have been and will continue to be forgiven. Close the gap on gratitude for having been forgiven much. Close the gap on readiness to continually forgive those who sin against you.

Day 2
Read:
Matt. 6:9-13 This, then, is how you should pray: "Our Father in heaven, hallowed be your name, your kingdom come, your will be done on earth as it is in heaven. Give us today our daily bread. Forgive us our debts, as we also have forgiven our debtors. And lead us not into temptation, but deliver us from the evil one."

Reflect:
Often we pray for things not knowing for sure if they are God's will and our will or only our will. If they are only our will, then we must learn to pray, "Not my will, but yours be done" (Luke 22:42). Because, in the end, we "want to want" what God wants.

But here in the model prayer, we have clear guidance on what God wills for us. We can ask God to "forgive our debts, as we also have forgiven our debtors" and we know that it is done. His answer to this request will always be, "Yes." "This is the confidence we have in approaching God: that if we ask anything according to his will, he hears us. And if we know that he hears us — whatever we ask — we know that we have what we asked of him" (1 John 5:14-15). Can we be sure that it is his will to forgive our sins if we ask? Look at what John wrote earlier in his letter: "If we confess our sins, he is faithful and just and will forgive us our sins and purify us from all unrighteousness" (1 John 1:9). So yes, we can pray with confidence to be forgiven, knowing that when we do we are praying in line with God's will. That being said, it is important to remember the whole context of this prayer. The prayer is, "forgive us as we have forgiven others." Again, this is not about earning forgiveness it is about living as one who has been forgiven. The one condition for forgiveness is repentance. Repentance literally means a "change of mind," but a real change of mind leads to a change of heart and life direction. The reason repentance is a condition of forgiveness is because without it we do not really want what forgiveness brings to us. Forgiveness from God brings restored relationship with God. Sin is doing things our own way; it is living in opposition to the will and ways of God. Think about it, how could we be forgiven (have restored relationship with God) if we do not repent (desire relationship with God)? You can ask God to forgive your sins and you can be sure he will do so. But this is not merely a "get out of jail free" card where we desire to be disconnected from our actions and attitudes so that we will not be held to account for them. This is a prayer for relationship. Our sins break fellowship with God, while our confession leads to restoration with God. Ultimately we must be learning to confess because we love God, not merely because we fear punishment. If we are secure in our faith, we know that we have escaped condemnation. Since we have received this great gift of salvation, our hearts long for intimacy with God. Our sins are a wedge between God and us. We know that God wants that wedge removed because he wants relationship with us, and all that remains is for us to want what he wants and to ask, "Forgive us our debts." When you ask, he will answer you: "Done!"

Day 3
Read:
Matt. 6:9-13 This, then, is how you should pray: "Our Father in heaven, hallowed be your name, your kingdom come, your will be done on earth as it is in heaven. Give us today our daily bread. Forgive us our debts, as we also have forgiven our debtors. And lead us not into temptation, but deliver us from the evil one."

119

Reflect:

Forgiveness is a prerequisite for worship. Jesus said, "Therefore, if you are offering your gift at the altar and there remember that your brother has something against you, leave your gift there in front of the altar. First go and be reconciled to your brother; then come and offer your gift" (Matt. 5:23-24). In this passage, Jesus is instructing us on the place which having right relationships with one another has in our relationship with God. When we come to God in worship and, right there at the altar, we remember we have sinned against someone else, then we leave the offering and go seek reconciliation. Once we have done so, we are then ready to return and continue our worship. Pay careful attention to the order here: "First go and be reconciled… then come and offer your gift." Many operate under the delusion that they can treat the people around them poorly, and yet still be in a healthy relationship with God. They believe that it is possible to be "wrong" with people and "right" with God. Jesus was instructing; he was not praying for himself. Jesus had no debts with either his Father or other people. He lived in perfect, sinless liberty. So, pay careful attention to the instruction which Jesus gives for your life: "Pray and live like this...forgive us our debts, as we have forgiven our debtors." It is assumed that those who move toward God looking for grace would also move toward others with grace as well. As you offer God your time, your prayers, and your attention right now, stop and ask. Ask God to bring to your mind if there is someone from whom you need to seek forgiveness. If there is not, then continue with your "devotional offering." If there is someone, however, then finish your time with God right now with a prayer of commitment and a request for strength. Commit to go, as soon as you are able, to make things right with the person(s) with whom there is a relationship breach. Then, ask God for the strength to follow through with grace. If the breach in relationship is on "their end", that is if they have sinned against you, then will you forgive them right now? You do not always have to seek restoration of relationship; it is sometimes not possible or wise. You do need to forgive them from your heart it is always possible and it is always wise. Forgiving and seeking forgiveness from one another is essential for true worship.

Day 4

Read:

Matt. 6:9-13 This, then, is how you should pray: "Our Father in heaven, hallowed be your name, your kingdom come, your will be done on earth as it is in heaven. Give us today our daily bread. Forgive us our debts, as we also have forgiven our debtors. And lead us not into temptation, but deliver us from the evil one."

Reflect:

There may be someone in your life that has done great harm to you. Perhaps this person remains a danger and should be avoided. These situations are not uncommon and often require very specific guidance and responses in order to handle them in healthy ways. However, the vast majority of the "debtors" we are to forgive are of the "garden variety." They are people who are rude, or unkind, or uncaring, or at least we perceive them to be so. They are people who seem to put their own interests first and who hurt with words, actions, and attitudes in ways that make us feel diminished, or stupid, or without real value. These people are the sorts of debtors we are most often called to forgive. But how? Especially when they continue to stack up debts against us. How can we continually forgive them? What did Jesus say? "Forgive us, as we forgive them." How often do you want Jesus to forgive you of your debts against him? How fully do you want him to forgive you? If we could see the enormity of our offense against God, then we would see how often we exaggerate the offenses of others against us. Do not begin with their sin, begin with your own. Do not begin with how much you will need to forgive them of, instead begin with how much you have been forgiven for. When we learn to move towards others with grace like this, we will begin to see things we did not see before. Maybe we will see how much our own selfishness has colored our perspective of others. Perhaps they did not intend to hurt you. Perhaps we were more at fault than we first believed. When we move toward others in grace with the desire for restored fellowship, we will learn to emphasize what is good between us and others rather than simply focusing on what is not. How do you really want to live? Are you feeling justified in your judgment? Do you believe you are not to blame for the breach in relationship so you will not make the first move? Again, how do you want to live? Do you want joy, peace, and relationship or do you mostly want to feel justified for your judgment on others? Choose his life, choose his truth, and choose his way. Choose to approach others as you would have them approach you and as Jesus does approach you.

Day 5
Read:

Matt. 6:9-13 This, then, is how you should pray: "Our Father in heaven, hallowed be your name, your kingdom come, your will be done on earth as it is in heaven. Give us today our daily bread. Forgive us our debts, as we also have forgiven our debtors. And lead us not into temptation, but deliver us from the evil one."

Reflect:

The good news of the gospel is that God forgives us more quickly and more completely than we forgive others.

Of course we are to forgive as we have been forgiven, but the fact remains that we are just not as good at forgiving as God is. As much as we might intend to not hold people in their past, we cannot help "seeing" past choices in the present as we deal with others. We cannot help but to "remember" the sins of others. God on the other hand, though his memory is perfect and immediate, is able to "not remember" our sins. "I, even I, am he who blots out your transgressions, for my own sake, and remembers your sins no more" (Isa. 43:25). Of course this doesn't mean God forgets, it is a figure of speech that indicates God is able to see the "present us" untainted by the "past us" because he sees us through the window of Jesus' death for us. "He does not treat us as our sins deserve or repay us according to our iniquities. For as high as the heavens are above the earth, so great is his love for those who fear him; as far as the east is from the west, so far has he removed our transgressions from us" (Ps. 103:10-12). Do you believe God truly sees you right now, if you have received his Son, as forgiven? Think carefully about this question. Your sins are forgiven and your sins are forgotten. As you look at the "real you", you see failure. As he looks at the real you, he sees forgiven. This is not an easy thing to grasp, so it is important that you take the time to grapple with it. Finish your time right now by reflecting carefully on this verse: "If we confess our sins, he is faithful and just and will forgive us our sins and purify us from all unrighteousness" (1 John 1:9). Glance at your sins...then confess them. Gaze at your savior...and consider him. This kind of spiritual and mental exercise of the truth will be a powerful factor in changing you into a person who more and more remembers less and less the sins of others towards you.

Week 28/Day 1
Read:
Matt. 6:9-13 This, then, is how you should pray: "Our Father in heaven, hallowed be your name, your kingdom come, your will be done on earth as it is in heaven. Give us today our daily bread. Forgive us our debts, as we also have forgiven our debtors. And lead us not into temptation, but deliver us from the evil one."

Reflect:
"When tempted, no one should say, 'God is tempting me.' For God cannot be tempted by evil, nor does he tempt anyone; but each one is tempted when, by his own evil desire, he is dragged away and enticed" (James 1:13-14). How does what James wrote jibe with what Jesus said? Is there a contradiction? No, because God does not tempt people to disobey him. When Jesus said we should pray to not be led into temptation, the word can have the connotation of "testing." But then there is another problem because James also wrote, "Consider it pure joy, my brothers, whenever you face trials of many kinds" (James 1:2).

In that case, why would we pray to escape trials if we are to consider them pure joy? The solution, once again, is in finding a biblical balance. Jesus, when in severe soul agony in the garden, prayed that God would deliver him from the trial of the cross, but then immediately afterwards he prayed that God's will would be done. Therefore, in order to "pray the biblical balance," we are to ask God to keep trial and testing from us and we are also to pray for his will to be done in our lives. Pray for deliverance from trial, but if he still takes you there, trust his good purposes and pray for endurance and JOY in the face of testing. Rejoice and be grateful when God takes you "around" trials and also trust God and find his joy when he chooses to take you "through" them. The Bible does not contradict itself and neither, of course, does God. However, the Bible is not a "simple" book. How could it be? It is the book of God and though he is not intentionally vague or hard to understand, it would be an understatement to say he is complex. As you wrestle with what sometimes appear to be competing truths, be sure you understand that they are, in fact, complementary truths. To pray for escape from temptation and to also pray for safe passage through temptation are not prayers that contradict each other; they are prayers that together comprise a single principle. The principle is this, "Father in heaven, hallowed be your name, your kingdom come, your will be done in my life as it is in heaven...whether you take trials from me, or take me through them. Amen."

Day 2
Read:
Matt. 6:9-13 This, then, is how you should pray: "Our Father in heaven, hallowed be your name, your kingdom come, your will be done on earth as it is in heaven. Give us today our daily bread. Forgive us our debts, as we also have forgiven our debtors. And lead us not into temptation, but deliver us from the evil one."

Reflect:
"No temptation has seized you except what is common to man. And God is faithful; he will not let you be tempted beyond what you can bear. But when you are tempted, he will also provide a way out so that you can stand up under it" (1 Cor. 10:13). Not everyone has the exact same temptations, but everyone is tempted in the same ways. Everyone is tempted to put self first, to trust self over God, to live for pleasure and not for God, and to make idols and cherish them. Our temptations are common and they cross all cultural boundaries. In sin, there truly is racial solidarity. This is an unhappy truth about human nature, but it does help to understand this fact for several reasons. First, it might help you to not feel sorry for yourself. Being sorry for sin is a healthy habit/choice, but feeling sorry for yourself is an unhealthy one.

To believe that your struggles are harder than anyone else's does not prepare you to withstand temptation; in reality, it prepares you to give in to them. A second reason it helps to understand the commonality of our temptations is that we can be "encouraged" by the struggles of others. Not that it is good to gloat over the troubles of others, but we can be helped in our own battles by realizing that other people are just like us. We are not alone and, in fact, others are successfully doing battle in the very same kinds of struggles we experience, so we can do the same. There is some value in understanding that others are tempted like we are, but there is power in understanding the second part of that verse: "God is faithful"! He will not allow us to be tempted beyond our ability to withstand it and he will provide a way out for us. You may very well feel like this verse has not proven true in experience; however, our experience of "what is" is not the same as "what could be." If you moved through the battlefield of temptations armed with the confidence that God is going to provide a way out – which he will and you can - how would that change how you live? Think about it. If you believe there are temptations out there that are simply too strong to resist, how likely are you to give your full energy to not giving in? But if you believe God is faithful and there is a way out and what is required of you is that you actually take it, what then? If you believe you are able to resist, you are much more likely to actually do so. But think clearly about this "way out." It may not be an escalator; it may be a difficult climb up a rock wall, but it is a way out, nonetheless. God is faithful and what remains is for us to be faithful as well.

Day 3
Read:
Matt. 6:9-13 This, then, is how you should pray: "Our Father in heaven, hallowed be your name, your kingdom come, your will be done on earth as it is in heaven. Give us today our daily bread. Forgive us our debts, as we also have forgiven our debtors. And lead us not into temptation, but deliver us from the evil one."

Reflect:
"For we do not have a high priest who is unable to sympathize with our weaknesses, but we have one who has been tempted in every way, just as we are — yet was without sin" (Heb. 4:15). When Jesus, our high priest, was tempted by Satan in the wilderness, he countered the temptations with truth. Temptations are lies. How do they lie? They offer what they cannot deliver. They offer freedom to do as you please and then to have liberty from unhappiness or discontentment. Instead, they deliver bondage and loss of liberty. They offer fulfillment and opportunity to truly be satisfied. Then they deliver disappointment and lasting dissatisfaction. Jesus countered the enemy's lies with truth. Truth exposes the false advertisement of the temptation to sin. In culture at large, resisting temptation is seen as a form of

suppression of what is natural. In a way, this is true since sin has become "natural." But many things that are natural must be suppressed, if we are to live as free people. It is "natural" to strike back when people hurt you. It is "natural" to put yourself first at all costs. It is "natural" to let physical pleasure drive the course of our lives. All these natural things, if allowed to run their course, will lead us into pure bondage and far from true liberty. The truth of God is a spotlight on the dark deceit of temptations. Jesus knew this and deployed God's truth expertly. Contrast Jesus' approach to that of our first parents, Adam and Eve. When Satan cast doubt in Eve's mind by asking, "Did God really say?" her response was confused. She added to what God had said rather than simply repeating what he had said and confidently exposing Satan's lie. Satan then took the gap left open by her confusion and directly contradicted God's word. "'You will not surely die,' the serpent said to the woman" (Gen. 3:4). She believed the serpent rather than God and the rest is "history." But it is not just history, it is contemporary reality. All over the world today people will believe the lie and trade liberty for bondage. Will you see the lie, believe the truth, and live in the liberty of God? You should pray, "Lead us not into temptation, but deliver us from the evil one" with a heart and a mind ready to believe truth and to see temptation as the lie that it is. Temptations on the surface look appealing, but they never deliver on what they promise. Pray now for the day ahead: "Lead us in to truth and deliver us to the Holy One."

Day 4
Read:

Matt. 6:9-13 This, then, is how you should pray: "Our Father in heaven, hallowed be your name, your kingdom come, your will be done on earth as it is in heaven. Give us today our daily bread. Forgive us our debts, as we also have forgiven our debtors. And lead us not into temptation, but deliver us from the evil one."

Reflect:

"My prayer is not that you take them out of the world but that you protect them from the evil one" (John 17:15). Jesus prayed for us that we would be protected from the "evil one," who is Satan. Satan is a word that means "adversary." He opposes us because he opposes God. Why hasn't God just "ended him?" For that matter, why hasn't he just "ended sin" as well? God is in the process of ending both Satan and sin. That is why the time we live in is called the "last days." We are living in the middle of the end. It might help if you consider that all time is "now" for God and that his "lifespan" is eternal. He is working his purposes out on his eternal time scale while we live out our lives in a cosmic microsecond. The life, death, and resurrection of Jesus marked the beginning of the end. Satan's back has been broken and he is an adversary with an expiration date.

125

Yet even so, Satan remains fierce and dangerous. Sin, likewise, has lost the war but continues to win many battles in our lives. So, we attempt to live for God's glory, but remember that we do so in a world that remains in opposition to him. We must endeavor to demonstrate that the final victory is sure by living lives of daily victory. Our deliverance, in the end, is final and complete. Our deliverance in the meantime is trust-by-trust and choice-by-choice. You must not become complacent. Many have died from battle wounds even after the war has been declared over. Your enemy is defeated and yet he can still do you great harm. Pray today and pray every day, "deliver us from evil." Then go into your day with confidence and with caution. Close the gap on your faith and on your humility. You do not have what it takes to stand up to Satan, but Jesus does. Lean into God today and pray throughout the day, "Deliver me from the evil one and deliver me to your liberty."

Day 5
Read:
Matt. 6:9-13 This, then, is how you should pray: "Our Father in heaven, hallowed be your name, your kingdom come, your will be done on earth as it is in heaven. Give us today our daily bread. Forgive us our debts, as we also have forgiven our debtors. And lead us not into temptation, but deliver us from the evil one."

Reflect:
Jesus taught us how to pray, not what to pray. You can repeat this very prayer, word for word, over and over and that would be a very helpful thing...if. If you are praying and not merely repeating words. There is no magic in these or any words. There is no "power in prayer" either. God is powerful and he is able to accomplish his purposes. To say prayer is powerful is like saying an extension cord is powerful. An extension cord is a means of tapping into and directing power towards a purpose. But an extension cord that is unplugged has no power. Prayer is an important way of aligning our will with God's and making requests accordingly. Prayer without a yielded relationship with God is like expecting an unplugged extension cord to power a machine; it will not. The realm of God's power for your life is the realm of God's will for your life. To live in his power for your life, you must continually return to the realm of his will for your life. "Not my will, but yours be done" is always a very good prayer. He will not empower you towards a life that is away from him, so surrender is a prerequisite in effective prayer. His power in your life is always to more fully and accurately reveal himself in your life. Many religions around the world pray mindless prayers, repeating words over and over. Sometimes prayers are put in a sort of "wheel" that is able to be spun without thinking and then you are able to pray constantly without giving any attention to those prayers. This is tragic

because it turns prayer into magic. Prayer is communication with God and from God. Prayer is built on relationship. Prayer requires engagement and commitment. It is never "mindless" activity; it always requires all of who we are. There are times when we don't know what to pray, perhaps we are overcome with grief or confusion. During these times our prayers may be a sort of "groan," but even then our minds and hearts are turned fully to God. We are not distracted; we are focused because our pain or confusion has turned our full attention to God. This daily prayer for daily bread, and for his will in our lives, and for forgiveness and protection is an ongoing reminder to pay attention. Do not move through life with a distracted relationship with God. Be still, remember, pay attention, and pray with attention: "Our Father in heaven, hallowed be your name, your kingdom come, your will be done on earth as it is in heaven. Give us today our daily bread. Forgive us our debts, as we also have forgiven our debtors. And lead us not into temptation, but deliver us from the evil one."

Week 29/Day 1
Read: Matt. 6:5-8 "And when you pray, do not be like the hypocrites, for they love to pray standing in the synagogues and on the street corners to be seen by men. I tell you the truth, they have received their reward in full. But when you pray, go into your room, close the door and pray to your Father, who is unseen. Then your Father, who sees what is done in secret, will reward you. And when you pray, do not keep on babbling like pagans, for they think they will be heard because of their many words. Do not be like them, for your Father knows what you need before you ask him."

Reflect:
To get clarity on important ideas and practices, it is helpful to both know what to think and do as well as what not to think and do. Jesus taught us how to pray in the model prayer, but in the verses prior to that he also taught us how not to pray. He first warns against praying like the "hypocrites." Religious hypocrisy is a frequently misunderstood concept. When a Christian fails to live up to the faith they profess, they might be considered to be a hypocrite by some around them. Sin or failure is not hypocrisy. Hypocrisy is when a person is "playing at faith." To say, "I never sin" and then to judge those who do is hypocrisy. It is hypocrisy because all people sin and it is playing games to believe or try to imply that you are sinless. The word "hypocrite" originally meant a stage player, an actor. This is not about "perfect praying"; it is about authentic versus "pretend praying." What makes this person an "actor" is not their location, whether synagogues or street corners. It is not their posture, "standing." There are many authentic prayers in the Scriptures that were prayed in a variety of locations from various physical postures. The problem here, that turns this prayer into hypocrisy, is the posture of the heart.

You see, the real issue is apparent in the phrase, "they love...to be seen by men." Stage actors love to be seen by others, and there is nothing wrong with that. They use their gifts and talents to entertain. Prayer is not entertainment; it is a conversational relationship with God. Prayer is directed at God, not to those who might be listening or praying with you. Again, this is not about perfection in prayer. Anytime you are praying in a public setting, whether with one another person or with many, it is impossible to forget others are there. It is not even wrong to pray to God in a way that speaks to those around you. Jesus did it. "Then Jesus looked up and said, 'Father, I thank you that you have heard me. I knew that you always hear me, but I said this for the benefit of the people standing here, that they may believe that you sent me' " (John 11:41-42). Jesus spoke to his Father, but also to those around him. The difference is that Jesus did not pray in order to please people. You can pray a "pretend prayer" even if others are not around. If your heart is far from God, then it's possible you are praying because you just want to hear yourself pray. Don't "pretend pray," but also don't get "locked up" in looking for perfection in prayer. Just pray because you want to have relationship with God. He's not looking to see if you get "it" right in prayer. He is looking to your heart; he wants you to want him. He certainly wants you.

Day 2
Read: Matt. 6:5-7 "And when you pray, do not be like the hypocrites, for they love to pray standing in the synagogues and on the street corners to be seen by men. I tell you the truth, they have received their reward in full. But when you pray, go into your room, close the door and pray to your Father, who is unseen."

Reflect:
Jesus said that when we pray we should go into our rooms and pray in secret so that only God will hear. This must be taken in context. Clearly public prayers are important and not under the Lord's condemnation. The Psalms contain notable examples of public prayer. Jesus said that when two or three gather in his name, he is there with them. Surely this gathering would, at times, include praying together. There are many other examples of public prayer. In Acts chapter one, Luke wrote that the early church was constantly praying together. One implication of this warning from Jesus about how not to pray is that public prayer has a direct link to private prayer. If there is no unseen prayer, then the seen prayer is likely to be playing at prayer. On the other hand, if you pray with a person in public and you find yourself feeling like you are "listening in" to a conversation with a good friend or a beloved father, it is likely because that person has a meaningful private prayer life. Jesus is not teaching that we should never pray in public, but rather that our public prayer life will not outrun our private prayer life. The reason why we pray in public is the same as why we pray in private.

We pray so we can take our requests, our hearts, and our desires to God as our Father. To pray in order to sound spiritual or to look impressive is ridiculous. Imagine trying to "show off" in prayer. Can you think of many things more absurd than that? Yet that is what Jesus is addressing here. He is telling us to beware of "pride prayers," because when you pray for the applause of people, you better enjoy it because that is all you will get from it. Your reward for pride-filled praying is the illusion that others are impressed. The people who would possibly be impressed with this kind of thing are, at the same time, too busy trying to be impressive to actually be impressed with you. Can you see how this is all like actors on a stage? There is nothing of reality in it. The gospel of Luke gives the clearest example of both playing at prayer and really praying...both done in a public setting. To some who were confident of their own righteousness and looked down on everybody else, Jesus told this parable: "Two men went up to the temple to pray, one a Pharisee and the other a tax collector. The Pharisee stood up and prayed about himself: 'God, I thank you that I am not like other men — robbers, evildoers, adulterers — or even like this tax collector. I fast twice a week and give a tenth of all I get.' But the tax collector stood at a distance. He would not even look up to heaven, but beat his breast and said, 'God, have mercy on me, a sinner.' I tell you that this man, rather than the other, went home justified before God. For everyone who exalts himself will be humbled, and he who humbles himself will be exalted." (Luke 18:9-14) Do not play at prayer. God is not impressed by you, but he does want to talk with you.

Day 3
Read:

Matt. 6:5-8 "And when you pray, do not be like the hypocrites, for they love to pray standing in the synagogues and on the street corners to be seen by men. I tell you the truth, they have received their reward in full. But when you pray, go into your room, close the door and pray to your Father, who is unseen. Then your Father, who sees what is done in secret, will reward you. And when you pray, do not keep on babbling like pagans, for they think they will be heard because of their many words. Do not be like them, for your Father knows what you need before you ask him."

Reflect:

Praying the same prayer over and over is not a problem. In fact, one of the most heartfelt and meaningful prayers that can be prayed is, "Help me Jesus. Help me Jesus." Repetition is not the problem in this passage, it is the "babbling." Babbling is meaningless and mindless speech. We are not to babble like the pagans, literally "Gentiles." This critique was directed at the non-Jews who believed that their gods were moved to action by the words of their followers. However, Jesus was not limiting his critique to non-Jews, he was warning the Jewish people to not fall into that same trap.

In the world of man-made religions with man-made gods, prayers can be a kind of incantation. You must get the words just right, like combining different elements in a chemical compound. Then you must repeat them over and over until they "work." Do you see how this whole enterprise is void of anything that resembles a relationship? Can you imagine talking to anyone else you know in this manner and expecting anything good to come from it? It is very helpful to consider actual relationships you have with people in order to make sense out of certain Scriptures that have bearing on our relationship with God. What do you want from people you enjoy and desire relationship with? You want honesty. You want to hear their hearts and minds. You certainly don't want to feel like they are trying to manipulate you or treating you as if you are not a real person, but rather some kind of barrier they have to get through to get what they really want. The difference between "babbling" and "help me Jesus" is not in the words, but in the source of the words. Jesus said, "The good man brings good things out of the good stored up in his heart, and the evil man brings evil things out of the evil stored up in his heart. For out of the overflow of his heart his mouth speaks" (Luke 6:45). Prayers that are repetitive but not "babbling," flow from a heart that wants relationship with God. As you consider closing the gap on a conversational relationship with God, ask him to help you to "want to want him" more deeply and authentically in your heart of hearts.

Day 4
Read:
Matt. 6:5-8 "And when you pray, do not be like the hypocrites, for they love to pray standing in the synagogues and on the street corners to be seen by men. I tell you the truth, they have received their reward in full. But when you pray, go into your room, close the door and pray to your Father, who is unseen. Then your Father, who sees what is done in secret, will reward you. And when you pray, do not keep on babbling like pagans, for they think they will be heard because of their many words. Do not be like them, for your Father knows what you need before you ask him."

Reflect:
Jesus said we are not to think that God responds to the quantity of our words, but rather to the quality of our words or, actually, to the quality of our hearts. His reasoning is, "Your Father knows what you need before you ask him." On the surface, this doesn't seem like an encouragement to pray at all. If he knows what I need before I ask him, then why ask him? Again, think in terms of actual relationships. If you are a parent and you know what your child needs, does this mean you will give it to her regardless of whether she asks or not? What if what you really want for your child is something deeper than merely for them to "get what they need" from you? What if you want deep relationship with them?

What if you want them to see what they actually need and not just what they want? What if you want them to grow into maturity and part of that growth requires them learning to humble themselves and ask? There are many reasons why a good parent would want a child to ask for what they need, even though the parent knows. Think about it another way, how could God NOT know what you need? Is he not God? Is he not all-knowing? Of course he knows, but that does not change the fact that he wants you to pray. What this indicates is that he is not just about "getting stuff done." We often turn life into a series of tasks and days to be completed in order to get to the next one and then, when we run out of days and tasks, we die. God, I think, views our lives as journeys with him. We must learn to think that way as well. On a journey we are going somewhere, but on this journey "where" we are going is the same as "who" we are going there with. We are journeying to God, with God. This being the case, our praying is part of the journey. So, it may seem silly or inefficient to ask God for what God could easily provide since he knows already, but then again, this is seeing life as other than it actually is. It is not silly in a relationship to do things that may seem inefficient, but also very effective. Your loved one may know you love them, so why continue to tell them so? Because it is part of the relationship to do so. Your friends may know your story, but want to hear it again anyway. Why is this? Because they are your friends and they enjoy hearing about and living "in" your life with you. No, God doesn't respond to "babbling" because he already knows what you need, so he doesn't need to be convinced or coerced (as if this were even possible). But yes, God does respond to simple, honest prayer because it is an important part of relationship with him.

Day 5
Read:
Matt. 6:5-8 "And when you pray, do not be like the hypocrites, for they love to pray standing in the synagogues and on the street corners to be seen by men. I tell you the truth, they have received their reward in full. But when you pray, go into your room, close the door and pray to your Father, who is unseen. Then your Father, who sees what is done in secret, will reward you. And when you pray, do not keep on babbling like pagans, for they think they will be heard because of their many words. Do not be like them, for your Father knows what you need before you ask him."

Reflect:
There are no rules for praying, either in this warning against how not to pray or in the model prayer that comes after this passage. There are, however, important principles for prayer here. The largest principle is that of trust. Prayer is about developing a trust relationship with God. When trust is low between two individuals, it is important to get every word just right.

Any word that is misspoken can be taken the wrong way, even if the intention was good. When trust is low, conversation is slow because every word must be carefully measured to ensure the other person will not take it out of context or misunderstand a single meaning. The principles Jesus gives here and in the following passage are much more about heart direction than word perfection. A relationship with God is based on trust. We are only able to come to him at all because of Jesus and the way which he has opened up for us. Now, because of this trust relationship with God, we do not have to get every word right. In fact, we can come to him when we are confused, or angry, or doubting. We can speak directly and honestly from our hearts because that is what he desires from us. Some people use only pre-written prayers to be sure they say the "right" things to God. There is nothing wrong with pre-written prayers, but there is something wrong with a perspective that drives praying such prayers mostly because of the fear of getting it "wrong." The one thing that we must be concerned with not getting wrong is our hearts. A single word prayer such as "help" or "thanks" or "why" that comes from a heart set in God's direction is more profound than a long and eloquent prayer that comes from a disinterested heart. As you consider how to close the gap on a conservational relationship with God, do not be concerned with methods and patterns of prayer. Give great attention to a surrendered and honest heart. "A bruised reed he will not break, and a smoldering wick he will not snuff out, till he leads justice to victory" (Matt. 12:20). When we see our great need for God and talk to him out of that need, we don't have to get all the words just right because our hearts will be right. When we come to him as the "bruised reeds" that we are, we experience his compassion. Jesus said, "Your Father knows what you need before you ask." What exactly does he know that we need? First and foremost, we need him. He knows that and it remains for us to more fully know that as well.

Week 30/Day 1
Read:
1 Kings 19:2-5 So Jezebel sent a messenger to Elijah to say, "May the gods deal with me, be it ever so severely, if by this time tomorrow I do not make your life like that of one of them." Elijah was afraid and ran for his life. When he came to Beersheba in Judah, he left his servant there, while he himself went a day's journey into the desert. He came to a broom tree, sat down under it and prayed that he might die. "I have had enough, LORD," he said. "Take my life; I am no better than my ancestors." Then he lay down under the tree and fell asleep.

Reflect:
Elijah was a man called by God to speak truth about the spiritual corruption in his culture. This corruption started at the highest levels of government and trickled down to the false prophets and the people who listened to them.

Elijah had been trained by God in faith and prayer through a program that included a great deal of time alone as well as increasingly challenging opportunities to trust God. His faith journey culminated in a dramatic encounter with a large group of false prophets where the true God showed himself powerful and the false gods of the culture were defeated. Immediately following this dramatic experience, Elijah found himself on the run from the wrath of the queen whose prophets had been destroyed by God. Now the prophet of God, fresh from an amazing display of the power of God, is hiding from a murderous queen. His prayer at this point is "take my life." This prayer is surprising and, yet, it is not. It is surprising in that this man had seen so much of the power of God. He had seen God provide food for him and others in miraculous ways. He had seen a dead boy raised to life. He had seen God destroy wicked and deceitful prophets. Now, his prayer is "kill me." It ought to surprise us that Elijah had seen so much of God and, yet, still fell short in trusting God. It ought to surprise us when we are like Elijah. It seems the human race's common prayer is, "Yes, but what have you done for me today?" We need to grow up in our faith. When the things of today are discouraging, we must remember to remember what God has already done. Now, on the other hand, this prayer is not surprising. We are human and we also live in physical bodies. Not enough food, not enough sleep, or too much stress or pain can "undo" us. James wrote, "Elijah was a man just like us" (James 5:17). Take comfort in the fact that even this great man of faith was prone to the same kinds of discouragement that we are. We will always be closing the gap on where we are and where we could be in our faith. But don't take too much comfort in his weakness; instead, be challenged by it as well. Just because it is often true that our faith in God's faithfulness falls short, it doesn't mean it has to. You have reason to trust God today, even if today is full of discouragement and challenge. Will you?

Day 2
Read:
1 Kings 19:5-8 All at once an angel touched him and said, "Get up and eat." He looked around, and there by his head was a cake of bread baked over hot coals, and a jar of water. He ate and drank and then lay down again. The angel of the LORD came back a second time and touched him and said, "Get up and eat, for the journey is too much for you." So he got up and ate and drank. Strengthened by that food, he traveled forty days and forty nights until he reached Horeb, the mountain of God.

Reflect:
Elijah prayed an honest prayer, but it was a foolish prayer, "Take my life." The Bible records what did happen, but not always what should have happened. In his model, Jesus "prescribed" how to pray. Elijah's prayer here is "described," but it is not a model for how we should pray.

Of course, gut-level honesty is essential to praying. But that honesty is best coupled with biblical-intelligence. This was an honest, but not intelligent, prayer in regard to how Elijah should have seen his situation. At any rate, God did not despise him in his desperation. He was kind to him, providing for his needs. Notice that the answer to his prayer "take my life" was not, "Elijah, you know better than that!" It was not a theological treatise on suicide, or even a word of encouragement that all will be well. Instead, God let Elijah sleep. Then when he awoke, the angel of the Lord (angel comes from a word that means "messenger") delivered this message, "get up and eat." Then after eating Elijah fell asleep again. The messenger of God then delivered the second message, "Get up and eat, for the journey is too much for you." It was only after resting, eating, and drinking that Elijah finished his journey and went to the place where God was going to speak directly to his questions. What do we learn about prayer from this narrative? We should always speak from our hearts, but we must realize that what is in our hearts is not always what is real or true. We are spiritual/physical hybrids. When the physical "us" is worn down, no amount of "willing spirit" will be able to make up for that fact. God made Elijah and you and me. He knows what we need. Elijah did not need truth at that desperate point in his journey. He needed rest and food and drink first, and only then would he be positioned to actually hear and absorb the truth when it was given. Sometimes we must have the wisdom to know when we do not have wisdom in our perspective. Sometimes the struggles in our minds and hearts are best answered by sleep and food. Do not fail to see the physical in your spiritual struggles. Do not fail to see the spiritual in your physical struggles. Pray as a "whole" person. Be honest with what is in your heart, but realize that what is in your heart may at times be out of sync with what is actually real and true. Sometimes the answer to your heartfelt prayers may be, "sleep, eat...then we will talk more later."

Day 3
Read:
1 Kings 19:9 There he went into a cave and spent the night. And the word of the LORD came to him: "What are you doing here, Elijah?"

Reflect:
It has been said that when we speak to God it is called prayer, but when God speaks to us it is called insane. It is true that many claim that God has spoken to them when certainly he has not. Some who claim God has spoken to them are mentally ill. However, God does speak to people. He speaks most often and most clearly through the Scriptures. But he speaks to people in other ways as well. Prayer is often speaking to God, but prayer is also listening to him. Learning to discern his voice versus our own inner thoughts is a process that takes time and attention.

It is important to have others around you that you trust so you can ask them about what you believe God may be saying to you. You would be foolish to not take the counsel of wise people around you in discerning whether God is actually speaking to you or not. How does God speak to people? Certainly, as already mentioned, he speaks through the Bible. He also speaks through others, through circumstances, and in our "hearts." If you desire to better hear from God, it is very important that you understand the primary goal of hearing from him. The primary goal of hearing from God is to have a mature love for God and for others. If you miss this point, you will consistently miss the voice of God. Beyond that key principle, you must approach God with humility. If and when God does direct you, it does not indicate you are special. It simply means that God, in his mercy, wants you to understand something about him and his will for your life. It doesn't make you authoritative, because God is the authority. You can be wrong, but he cannot. Do you want to hear from God? Why? Because you are bored? Because you want him to tell you some good news? Because you don't really believe and want validation? If God speaks to you, it will have as its goal HIS glory revealed in your increasing love for him and obedience to him. Your love for him and obedience to him will show up in love for those around you. It is truly a great thing for God to speak to a person, but his speaking is not primarily about us. It is about him. God spoke to Baruch through the prophet Jeremiah, "Should you seek great things for yourself? Seek them not" (Jeremiah 45:5). God did speak to Baruch and he told him that difficult times were ahead for him and his people. But the trouble that was coming for them was ultimately about the glory of God. Sometimes what God says to us might not be what we want to hear. But we must learn to want to hear what he wants to say, because what God wants is ultimately good because it is about his glory. If you want to position yourself to hear from God, be sure that you understand life is not about you. It is about God. Your life is not to be about you. It is to be about his glory. When he speaks - and he will speak to you about things in your life - ultimately what he says to you is about his greatness revealed in and through your life. Close the gap on a conversational relationship with God. Conversation with God is called prayer and this conversation with God is always about relationship with God.

Day 4
Read: 1 Kings 19:11-12 Then a great and powerful wind tore the mountains apart and shattered the rocks before the LORD, but the LORD was not in the wind. After the wind there was an earthquake, but the LORD was not in the earthquake. After the earthquake came a fire, but the LORD was not in the fire. And after the fire came a gentle whisper.

Reflect:

Elijah's experience with God was unique. Some might envy his direct conversations with God as well as the fantastic experiences of God's power which he witnessed. However, I doubt anyone would envy the cost of his experiences. Elijah lived a very difficult and lonely life. He suffered times of dark despair and doubts. He did not doubt whether God was alive and involved, but he had doubts as to whether his own efforts and sacrifices were worth it. In the passage for this week there is a line that is easy to miss if you are not paying attention: "He traveled forty days and nights until he reached Horeb, the mountain of God." Forty days and nights would be a long journey on a train with a sleeping car, but this journey was by foot. Why did God have him make this difficult journey? Could he not have spoken to Elijah where he was? Perhaps he was still trying to escape the wrath of the murderous queen. Perhaps he needed that time to prepare to hear from God. He had no electronic devices to keep him occupied or distracted along the way. Hearing from God requires time and attention. We cannot give God a 5-minute slot on our schedule and demand he "get to the point." It takes God time to speak mostly because it takes us time to be ready to listen. I suspect that for much of the 40-day journey Elijah didn't need an electronic device to distract him. His own thoughts were probably enough. He really did believe some things that were not true and so he could not wait to tell God what was on his mind. When he finally arrived God asked him, "Why are you here?" Elijah answered the question with a complaint. He believed he was the only one living faithfully and the "reward" for his efforts was that people were trying to kill him. God's answer to Elijah's complaint was to instruct him to step out of the cave so he would experience God's presence. What happened next must have been terrifying. A hurricane force wind attacked the mountain, shattering rocks as they were swept along. Then an earthquake shook the mountain followed by a fire. Perhaps massive boulders were loosened by the wind and fell to the foot of the mountain causing the earth to shake. Maybe the storm produced lightening that struck the brush and set the mountain on fire. Whatever the effects, God was the cause. But he did not appear to Elijah in all of this awesome display. In the stillness after the storm, Elijah heard a gentle whisper. Maybe it was the same whisper he had heard as a child when he was first learning to hear from God. God was in the whisper. As God seems to do at times, he repeated his question. Elijah answered the exact same way as before but now, it seems, he was ready to hear God's mind on his situation. God spoke in the gentle whisper and gave him a correct perspective as well as a course of action to take. Are you in a hurry? Have you left no space in your mind for God to speak? How will you be ready to hear the gentle whisper of God if your own mind and life is all wind, and quake, and fire? Be still.

Day 5
Read:

1 Kings 19:13-14 When Elijah heard it, he pulled his cloak over his face and went out and stood at the mouth of the cave. Then a voice said to him, "What are you doing here, Elijah?" He replied, "I have been very zealous for the LORD God Almighty. The Israelites have rejected your covenant, broken down your altars, and put your prophets to death with the sword. I am the only one left, and now they are trying to kill me too."

Reflect:

What was the whole point of the wind, the quake, and the fire? What was God trying to show Elijah - and us - about himself? What do we learn about a conversational relationship with God from this experience? It's not a parable. It is a historical account of a real event. But the event was designed by God to teach us about him, so we must try to pay careful attention and learn. There are certainly many things that can be learned, but let's try to isolate a few. First, it is easy to see, hear, and feel a great wind, the earth quaking, and a blazing fire. It is much harder to pay attention to a gentle whisper. This explains why it may be getting harder and harder for people to hear from God because the noise around us is constant. We do not live in an age where hearing from God is going to be easy. Not because God is slow to speak, but because our lifestyles make it hard to hear. What will you do to break from the spirit of these times and hear from the timeless God? Second, when we only hear and pay attention to the noise, we will likely mistake the wind, quake, and fire for the voice of God. When we cannot hear the whisper, we will think we are hearing God in the noise. What we will hear is the voice of the current culture telling us what we want to hear. It will not challenge our thinking or our way of living; it will confirm them. It will tell us that times have changed and so has God. The noise of contemporary culture will speak a loud lie if we are not still long enough to hear quiet truth. Finally, when our physical ears have been bombarded by too many decibels, they lose their ability to hear the more quiet sounds. The noise can train our ears to only hear that which is loud. The same is true for our spiritual ears. When we live in the continual din of the loud, the proud, and the busy, we will lose our ability to hear the quiet voice of God. Thankfully, though at times it is impossible to regain lost physical hearing, there is a way to regain spiritual hearing. This way is through repentance of self-trust and a return to trusting in God. "This is what the Sovereign LORD, the Holy One of Israel, says: In repentance and rest is your salvation, in quietness and trust is your strength" (Isaiah 30:15). God, forgive us for living loud and proud and quiet our hearts so we may trust in your strength.

Week 31/Day 1
Read:

Mark 10:13-16 People were bringing little children to Jesus to have him touch them, but the disciples rebuked them. When Jesus saw this, he was indignant. He said to them, "Let the little children come to me, and do not hinder them, for the kingdom of God belongs to such as these. I tell you the truth, anyone who will not receive the kingdom of God like a little child will never enter it." And he took the children in his arms, put his hands on them and blessed them.

Reflect:

These children were very small. In fact, Luke's account calls some of them babies. They were small enough that he was able to "take them in his arms." The disciples did not dislike children, but they were probably trying to protect Jesus from interruptions. He was busy with "important" stuff and could not be bothered by small children. It shows how much they did not yet understand. Jesus was a master of turning the events of life into teaching moments. Clearly, this incident made an impression on the disciples because it was included in the gospel account. John wrote that "Jesus did many other things as well. If every one of them were written down, I suppose that even the whole world would not have room for the books that would be written" (John 21:25). Since Jesus did many more things and said many more things than are included in the gospels, it should make us very attuned to what is included. The disciples were impacted by this event and God wants us to be impacted as well. There are many things to learn about God and us in this passage. Jesus very clearly said that if we do not receive the kingdom like a child, we would not receive it all. The Kingdom of God in this context is the reign of Christ in our hearts. Entering his Kingdom brings the peace, presence, power, and purposes of God into our lives now in part and one day in full. We are to come to the King and receive his Kingdom as a child would. A child is not self-conscious when it comes to his needs. Adults may be coy, reserved, or just too proud to admit to a need or desire. But small children, when they have a need, are sure to make that need known. A proud adult would sometimes rather go without than admit weakness or need. This would be inconceivable for a small child. We are not to become childish, but childlike. Childish would make us demanding and petulant (moody, touchy). Childlike means we have some *qualities* of a child. We must be childlike in regard to our need for God. We have learned as adults to be self-sufficient. This is good and important in order that we do not become childish adults. But as childlike adults, we must know that our self-sufficiency does not apply to our relationship with God. When we enter the world as adults, we must do all we can to care for our own needs and the needs of others. But as we move through the world as "physical adults," we must remember to do so as "spiritual children."

Not children in that we are not growing in our faith, but children in that we never outgrow our desperate need for God. As you talk with God today, remember to be childlike without being childish. Do not demand from him and do not forget your utter dependence on him

Day 2
Read:

Mark 10:13-16 People were bringing little children to Jesus to have him touch them, but the disciples rebuked them. When Jesus saw this, he was indignant. He said to them, "Let the little children come to me, and do not hinder them, for the kingdom of God belongs to such as these. I tell you the truth, anyone who will not receive the kingdom of God like a little child will never enter it." And he took the children in his arms, put his hands on them and blessed them.

Reflect:

A child has both a simple and a simplistic view of the world. "Simple" means without complexity. "Simplistic" means unrealistic. Some children are forced to grow up too quickly. Because of the absence of mature adults or the presence of immature adults in their lives, they must jettison childhood simplicity much too soon. When this happens it may make them more streetwise and heart-hardened, but it does not make them healthy or more mature. There is a healthy order in human development. Children in ideal circumstances do not lie down at night and worry about whether they will eat tomorrow or whether mom and dad will stay together. They lie down to sleep in a world that is warm, safe, and sure. As they grow up, they learn mom and dad are not able to protect them from everything and that the world is not safe. But because of the foundations that were built by mature adults into their childhood, they can live in a world that is not safe without living in fear. A simplistic view is: "The world is safe, so I do not have to fear." A mature view is: "The world is not safe, but I do not have to live in fear." We are to approach the King and the Kingdom with the simplicity of a child. We do not throw away the perspective of an adult that understands the nature of the world, but rather we add to an adult perspective the perspective of childhood. We live as "grown children" by understanding the world is not safe, but knowing we do not have to fear. God, unlike a human parent, is all-knowing and all-powerful and cannot fail or die. We do not live as fools unaware of the realities of life and we do not live in fear because we aware of the reality of God our Father and his promises. Your Father will never leave you nor forsake you. Now as you approach your Father in heaven in prayer about the many things that concern you, do so as a child. Leave your fear with him and then you can go out into a dangerous world and live by faith and not in fear.

Day 3
Read:

Mark 10:13-16 People were bringing little children to Jesus to have him touch them, but the disciples rebuked them. When Jesus saw this, he was indignant. He said to them, "Let the little children come to me, and do not hinder them, for the kingdom of God belongs to such as these. I tell you the truth, anyone who will not receive the kingdom of God like a little child will never enter it." And he took the children in his arms, put his hands on them and blessed them.

Reflect:

Small children are "stream of consciousness" talkers. What is in their minds is coming out of their mouths. This is not good practice for adults, but it is endearing in a child. Adults should learn to filter their thoughts before they put them into words. If they do not, they are foolish and can cause great damage. There is an exception to this. In prayer, adults should relearn the childlike practice of "mind to mouth" communication. It's not that we shouldn't be thoughtful in prayer. We should. It's not that everything we think is good to say. It's not. It is more about remembering that God knows what is on our minds before we can speak it anyway. It can be very helpful to be honest with what is really going on in our heads. If a complaint is in our minds, then it can be good to talk to God about it. Not that our complaints are always valid, but rather it is good to talk with God about them. If doubt is in our minds, then talk to God about your doubts. Just because it is in our minds and our mouths, it does not mean we are considering it valid. But when we come to God like a child, telling him everything (even though he knows it already) the conversation can change. It can become less routine and more real. It can become more heartfelt and honest. It can open us up to what is actually true about God and our current situation, not just what we are currently thinking and feeling is true. If you have trained yourself to be careful with your words, you have done well. Now, in prayer train yourself to be honest with your words. It's never good or right to slander or accuse God of wrong. But if you are struggling to understand why he allowed or caused something, it is good to talk with him about that struggle. A child will talk with anyone they trust about virtually anything. A mature and loving adult does not despise the child for this, they love them for it. In your conversational relationship with God do you need to become more childlike? Start now. Talk to God about what is really on your mind. Perhaps you will be positioned to hear what is really on his.

Day 4
Read:

Mark 10:13-16 People were bringing little children to Jesus to have him touch them, but the disciples rebuked them. When Jesus saw this, he was indignant. He said to them, "Let the little children come to me, and do not hinder them, for the kingdom of God belongs to such as these. I tell you the truth, anyone who will not receive the kingdom of God like a little child will never enter it." And he took the children in his arms, put his hands on them and blessed them

Reflect:

"Jesus loves the little children, all the children of the world." The well-known children's song is well-grounded in Scripture. Jesus demonstrated his love for children in practical ways. But there is a sense in which all people are children before God, no matter their age. In Hosea, God spoke of the nation of Israel as his child: "When Israel was a child, I loved him, and out of Egypt I called my son" (Hosea 11:1). Of course, there is a greater degree of accountability before God as we age, but we never stop being children in relationship to God. This perspective should lead to humility. Small children are not naturally humble as in the character quality of humility. They do, however, live in "positional" humility. They have little power, skill, or ability. They mostly have needs. They live in a humble place. As adults, humility is something we must choose to grow in. Humility understands that in spite of any increase in power, knowledge, wealth, or prestige, we remain like children with utter dependence on God for life and ultimate salvation. No matter what your age, you live before God in positional humility. You are not truly strong, smart, or good. You are a child before him and always will be. Reflect on your position of humility so that you might move farther into the character of a humble person. Reflect on the fact that God is your Father and you will always be a child. Then go interact with the people in your life with a humility-empowered perspective. "The LORD is compassionate and gracious, slow to anger, abounding in love. He will not always accuse, nor will he harbor his anger forever; he does not treat us as our sins deserve or repay us according to our iniquities. For as high as the heavens are above the earth, so great is his love for those who fear him; as far as the east is from the west, so far has he removed our transgressions from us. As a father has compassion on his children, so the LORD has compassion on those who fear him; for he knows how we are formed, he remembers that we are dust." (Psalm 103:8-14)

Day 5
Read:

Mark 10:13-16 People were bringing little children to Jesus to have him touch them, but the disciples rebuked them. When Jesus saw this, he was indignant.

He said to them, "Let the little children come to me, and do not hinder them, for the kingdom of God belongs to such as these. I tell you the truth, anyone who will not receive the kingdom of God like a little child will never enter it." And he took the children in his arms, put his hands on them and blessed them.

Reflect:
Older people often look in the mirror and wonder how they became old. They look at the years gone by and wonder how they arrived where they are. Fifty, seventy, one hundred... these are many years and these are also very few years. Perhaps you are still "young" and don't see life this way. However, even in our twenties and thirties the experience of time can be startling and strange. The hours and days can sometimes drag on while the months and years can fly by. Children tend to live in the present. They don't spend much time on the past or the future. They are at a stage of life where virtually all time is now. Sure they look forward to things that are yet to come and this becomes truer as they age. But the very young live mostly in the right now. Perhaps this is a factor in Kingdom living that correlates to being childlike. We are to be like children in that we are to relearn how to engage the "now" without being overly diverted by the past and the future. Of course, it is childish to not remember the past or to fail to prepare for the future. But is it "childlike" to learn to live more fully in the "now"? The past is beyond our control apart from making amends for our mistakes. The future is outside the realm of our control as well, apart from making necessary preparations for possibilities. The only time we have is now. We can worry about the past, yet it is unchangeable. We can worry about the future, yet it is not ours to control. We can trust in the present by giving God the past and the future. We can learn to walk more closely with God by engaging what he has for us today. Jesus asked, "Who of you by worrying can add a single hour to his life?" (Matthew 6:27). He said that he feeds the birds and clothes the flowers, so stop worrying because you are much more valuable to him than they are. To live in a conversational relationship with God, you must live in the right now of where God has you. Is it challenging? Is it confusing? Is it boring? Okay, but it is where God has you and it is where God wants to meet you. Come to him as a child, today.

Week 32/Day 1
Read:
Ex. 33:11 The LORD would speak to Moses face to face, as a man speaks with his friend.

Reflect:
Moses had a unique relationship with God. He was singled out as a man to whom God spoke "face to face," as friends do.

"Face to face" is a figure of speech. It means "in person" communication, in contrast to more impersonal ways of communicating. Friends don't work through third parties to discuss important matters, because trust is high. When trust is low, face-to-face communication is impossible and so is relationship. The trust relationship Moses had with God included intimate and direct communication. However, later in this same passage God told Moses that no one could see his face and live. There is no contradiction here. In the first instance, "face to face" is a figure of speech indicating personal relationship. In the second instance, "no one may see me and live" is an actual experience. Stop and think about this situation. Moses, who was arguably as close to God as any man has been, could not look directly at God and survive the encounter. It was not because God would kill him, but because the experience would be beyond his physical limits. What would this look like? It is impossible to say. Would his heart stop? Would his brain overload? Would he "fly apart" into basic elements? What is possible to say is that God is awesome, spectacular, and beyond human understanding. Many times in Scripture when people encountered God, they were nearly "undone." Most notably Isaiah: "In the year that King Uzziah died, I saw the Lord seated on a throne, high and exalted, and the train of his robe filled the temple...Woe to me! I cried. I am ruined! For I am a man of unclean lips, and I live among a people of unclean lips, and my eyes have seen the King, the LORD Almighty" (Isaiah 6:1, 5). Isaiah wrote that he "saw the Lord," but he only got a glimpse or a vision of him. This was enough to "wreck" him. Here we get a clue as to what might actually be the real threat to our existence if we were to see God in all his glory. Isaiah became so acutely aware of his own sin and the sins of all humans that he could not bear it. Perhaps the reason we cannot see God and live is because the great distance between his holiness and our sinfulness would be beyond our ability to endure. How different is this vision of God than the one commonly held today where humans take God to task and question his integrity because they don't like the ways he gets things done? Job tried to issue God a subpoena and take him to court, but in the end Job was on his face before God much like Isaiah. If we are to understand the good news of the gospel, we must continually reflect on the bad news of our sin. Our sin does not create a "bit of problem" for us. Rather, it creates an impossible, devastating, and deadly situation for us. The good news is that we, too, can have a "face to face" relationship with God. The bad news is that, apart from the gospel, our sin leaves us "undone" in the presence of God. Remember the bad news so you will rejoice more fully in the good news.

Day 2
Read:
Ex. 33:11-14 The LORD would speak to Moses face to face, as a man speaks with his friend.

Then Moses would return to the camp, but his young aide Joshua son of Nun did not leave the tent. Moses said to the LORD, "You have been telling me, 'Lead these people,' but you have not let me know whom you will send with me. You have said, 'I know you by name and you have found favor with me.' If you are pleased with me, teach me your ways so I may know you and continue to find favor with you. Remember that this nation is your people." The LORD replied, "My Presence will go with you, and I will give you rest."

Reflect:
Does God speak to people? If so, which people? Special ones, such as Moses, or normal ones like you and me? Some believe that God speaks to them about everything and they will wait on him before making virtually any decision. This is not healthy or balanced. Some believe God never speaks to them and, consequently, even if he were to do so they would discount it as other than a message from God. The Bible assumes that God speaks to his people. The primary way he speaks is through the Bible. But he speaks in other ways as well - through other people, through circumstances, and at times directly to us in our "hearts." We say "heart" because we are not quite sure where it is on the "inside" of us that we hear him speak. "Heart" in the Bible is the "thinking, choosing, willing" part of us. It is the center of our being as human beings. So we are to love God with all of our "hearts" and we are to "guard our hearts" above all else. Our hearts are to be wrapped around God in a way that what we most want is what he wants. God spoke to Moses face to face as a man speaks to a friend. Of course, Moses was not perfect so perfection is not a condition for this kind of relationship with God. However, Moses was humble. His humility was a part of his awareness of his great need. His great need made him dependent on God. His dependence on God led him to obey God, even when it was hard and seemed beyond him. Do you want God to speak to you? You must have a heart that is fully is. Not perfection in every action, but perfection in its overall direction. You must continually surrender to his will and ways. This is your part. When you have a heart that is oriented around him, you will have a heart that is prepared to hear him speak. You are prepared to hear God speak when you are prepared to respond to what he might say. In your "heart" what are you saying to God? "Tell me what I want to hear" or "tell me what you want to say and I will hear it"?

Day 3
Read:
Ex. 33:11-14 The LORD would speak to Moses face to face, as a man speaks with his friend. Then Moses would return to the camp, but his young aide Joshua son of Nun did not leave the tent. Moses said to the LORD, "You have been telling me, 'Lead these people,' but you have not let me know whom you will send with me.

You have said, 'I know you by name and you have found favor with me.' If you are pleased with me, teach me your ways so I may know you and continue to find favor with you. Remember that this nation is your people." The LORD replied, "My Presence will go with you, and I will give you rest."

Reflect:

God spoke to Moses "as a man speaks with his friend." This does not mean God and Moses were "buddies." In this same passage, God told Moses that he could not see his face and live. The way in which God communicated with Moses was *similar* to how friends talk to one another, even though it was not a relationship of equals. How does one speak to a friend and how might this apply to a conversational relationship with God? Friends speak about what is on their hearts and minds. God told Moses what he intended to do. God let Moses in on what was important to him and how Moses would be a part of his plans. God told Moses what was most valuable to him and how he wanted Moses to hold to and communicate those values to others. Friends speak honestly about their relationships and even their disappointments, but they do so in a redemptive way. God was direct with Moses in regard to his periodic lack of faith and his overt disobedience. Even so, God did not cast Moses off because, in spite of Moses' shortcomings, he was a "friend of God." Friends deal with each other directly. They do not need an arbitrator or middleman. Moses often served as the spokesman for God to the people, but God spoke directly to him. Of course we are not Moses, but what opportunities do we have to experience God like he did? Because of Jesus, the final mediator, we can go directly to God ourselves. We can communicate with God as friends do, directly, one to one. Because we have the written word of God, we can know what God values and wants done in the world. We do not have to guess. We can read, understand, and join him in what he is doing in and around us. God's way of dealing with each of us in going to be unique in some ways, but in other ways it will be the same. He will not speak to us in a way that is out of sync with what is clearly written in Scripture. If you want to know the will and ways of God, then know the Bible. Do not look for some "mystical, emotional" direction as you read it. Read it in order to understand and apply it to your life. Read it to see who God is, how he works, and what he wants. You have what even Moses did not have - the completed Word of God. Friends do the "work" to understand each other. God has spoken to you already. Now do the work to understand what he has said. Know his word for yourself.

Day 4
Read:
Ex. 33:11 The LORD would speak to Moses face to face, as a man speaks with his friend.

Reflect:
You can have many kinds of relationships such as business, family, volunteer organizations, military, teammates, and others. You can have relationships without having friendships. You can be a biological brother or sister without being a friend. You can share an office or a locker room and have the same goals, but not be friends. A friendship is a special category of relationship. There are many levels of friendship, but in general a friend is someone you trust. If you do not trust them, they are not your friends. God spoke to Moses as a friend. Moses trusted God, but more importantly God trusted Moses. God knew Moses' limitations and was very aware of his failings...past, present and future. But God trusted Moses. He trusted Moses to lead his people. God trusted Moses with his very word. He trusted Moses to represent him. Of course, the selection of Moses was due to God's sovereignty, but at the same time it is not always helpful to just end there in our thinking. If we only look at the role of God's sovereignty in the lives of people he uses, it can lead to passivity in our own lives. Of course, God's sovereignty is of vital importance and should lead us to act and think with humility. At the same time, Moses' response to God is important as well. We must not believe we can wait for God's sovereignty to "fall on us" before we proactively move towards him in faith and towards others in love. God wants to use us in the world. A part of him using us is our "usefulness." That usefulness is not primarily about skill or gifting, but humility. Humility is a character quality. It is a result of making a series of choices over time, choices that reflect both mental attitudes and physical actions. Look at what God's word says about Moses: "Now Moses was a very humble man, more humble than anyone else on the face of the earth" (Numbers 12:3). Was God sovereign in the selection of Moses? Of course he was. Did the choices Moses make, particularly in regard to his humility, matter in how God used him? Of course they did. Do you want to be a friend of God? Walk humbly with God. He can trust those who trust him. Humility is the foundational quality for a trust relationship with God. "He has showed you, O man, what is good. And what does the LORD require of you? To act justly and to love mercy and to walk humbly with your God" (Micah 6:8).

Day 5
Read: Ex. 33:11-20 The LORD would speak to Moses face to face, as a man speaks with his friend. Then Moses would return to the camp, but his young aide Joshua son of Nun did not leave the tent. Moses said to the LORD, "You have been telling me, 'Lead these people,' but you have not let me know whom you will send with me. You have said, 'I know you by name and you have found favor with me.' If you are pleased with me, teach me your ways so I may know you and continue to find favor with you. Remember that this nation is your people." The LORD replied, "My Presence will go with you, and I will give you rest."

146

Then Moses said to him, "If your Presence does not go with us, do not send us up from here. How will anyone know that you are pleased with me and with your people unless you go with us? What else will distinguish me and your people from all the other people on the face of the earth?" And the LORD said to Moses, "I will do the very thing you have asked, because I am pleased with you and I know you by name." Then Moses said, "Now show me your glory." And the LORD said, "I will cause all my goodness to pass in front of you, and I will proclaim my name, the LORD, in your presence. I will have mercy on whom I will have mercy, and I will have compassion on whom I will have compassion. But," he said, "you cannot see my face, for no one may see me and live."

Reflect:

Reflect on Moses waking up drowsy and discouraged one morning. Think of his actual back feeling sore and his mind dreading the day in front of him. See him in your mind's eye bending over to put on his footwear and brushing back his "bed head". Think of him sitting and eating breakfast and spending time talking to God. It is important that you think about Moses and other biblical figures as actual people who lived real lives. It is important because we can turn all kinds of famous people into more than, or other than, human. When we do this, we miss the opportunity to really learn from their lives. When you read of Moses having a "face to face" conversation with God, consider what it might have looked like. Certainly God could have caused Moses' eardrums to vibrate and create signals to his brain that sounded like a person talking. But God doesn't have physical lips or lungs, so it wasn't "talking" like we think of it. Perhaps God skipped Moses' eardrums and just created the words directly in his mind. All communication ends up there anyway and God can skip the other parts of the process quite easily. Go back and read the passage that you have been reading all week and read it like it happened to a real person. Read it like you would if you read it in a newspaper and it was validated as a factual event. What questions would you have in your mind? Train yourself to read Scripture this way. Train yourself to move through life thinking of God in this way. He is the same God now that he was then. He has the same goals and desires now as then. Of course his work in human history is a part of a long plan, so it changes in terms of his processes. But God himself does not change. Clearly he desires friendship with you. Do you desire this kind of friendship with him? If so, what might it look like in your life as you move into today? As you brush your hair and your teeth, as you deal with drowsiness and discouragement...consider the possibility and the reality of friendship with God.

Week 33/Day 1

Read:

Eph. 6:10-18 Finally, be strong in the Lord and in his mighty power. Put on the full armor of God so that you can take your stand against the devil's schemes. For our struggle is not against flesh and blood, but against the rulers, against the authorities, against the powers of this dark world and against the spiritual forces of evil in the heavenly realms. Therefore put on the full armor of God, so that when the day of evil comes, you may be able to stand your ground, and after you have done everything, to stand. Stand firm then, with the belt of truth buckled around your waist, with the breastplate of righteousness in place, and with your feet fitted with the readiness that comes from the gospel of peace. In addition to all this, take up the shield of faith, with which you can extinguish all the flaming arrows of the evil one. Take the helmet of salvation and the sword of the Spirit, which is the word of God. And pray in the Spirit on all occasions with all kinds of prayers and requests. With this in mind, be alert and always keep on praying for all the saints.

Reflect:

A life of faith is a friendship and it is also a war. It is important to keep both realities in mind. Soldiers cannot live in a constant state of battle. There comes a point when, if they remain in combat conditions for too long, they are unable to continue the fight. We cannot live in an ongoing state of "fight or flight." That is why God has given the command for a Sabbath and has offered us his peace and rest in the midst of the war. All that being said, we must not lose sight of the reality of the war in and around us. Even if a soldier is withdrawn from the front lines for a time, that soldier has not left the war. In times of respite and in times of direct spiritual combat, there is a phrase in this passage that is critical to remember. "Be strong in the Lord and in his mighty power." This is a not a call to passivity, but rather to active faith. You must move into the battles and you must endure the conflicts that will come, but you must do so by putting your fullest confidence in the Lord and relying on his power, not your own. This should not lead to a diminished personal effort, but rather it should invigorate your efforts because success does not finally depend on your strength but on the Lord's. Again, we find this mystery of God's sovereignty and our responsibility. As you move into the various battles that rage in your life, you must remember that God ultimately will prevail _and_ that you must choose to be strong in his power, not your own. You must give all of yourself to the battle - heart, soul, mind, and strength. There is no part of you that you can hold back in fear or laziness. But, then, you must remember that in this battle you give yourself in _love_ to God - heart, soul, mind, and strength. And in giving yourself to him in love, you will find him to be all you need in order to win the battles as they come. Here is where the friendship and the combat come together.

Love God with every part of your being and then you will see God, who is your friend, reveal his mighty power in your life.

Day 2

Read: Eph. 6:10-18 Finally, be strong in the Lord and in his mighty power. Put on the full armor of God so that you can take your stand against the devil's schemes. For our struggle is not against flesh and blood, but against the rulers, against the authorities, against the powers of this dark world and against the spiritual forces of evil in the heavenly realms. Therefore put on the full armor of God, so that when the day of evil comes, you may be able to stand your ground, and after you have done everything, to stand. Stand firm then, with the belt of truth buckled around your waist, with the breastplate of righteousness in place, and with your feet fitted with the readiness that comes from the gospel of peace. In addition to all this, take up the shield of faith, with which you can extinguish all the flaming arrows of the evil one. Take the helmet of salvation and the sword of the Spirit, which is the word of God. And pray in the Spirit on all occasions with all kinds of prayers and requests. With this in mind, be alert and always keep on praying for all the saints.

Reflect:

Some people are under the impression that "putting on the armor of God" is merely verbalizing the process. They might say, "I buckle truth around my waist and I take up the shield of faith right now." This may be fine if they are actually doing those things and not just saying words. In a real battle, soldiers don't talk about their armor and weapons, they use them. They don't prepare for battle by saying they are putting on their body armor; they prepare by actually putting it on. Do not turn this into a magic incantation. The battle is real and so are the protections and weapons that we use in the battle. You put on the full armor of God by the lifestyle choices you make. You must know and apply the truth of God to your circumstances. You must live in the realm of God's righteousness in the actual decisions of your day. You must be prepared to share the good news with others and you must live fully in the gospel yourself. This is not spiritual "mumbo jumbo." This is reality. The protections are real, the weapon is real, and the battle is real. Do not go through the motions of preparation for your day. Prepare! Don't merely "say your prayers and have your quiet time." Prepare in real ways for a real war. If you heard bullets and bombs outside your home right now, you would have a heightened sense of awareness. In fact, many do hear those sounds right now and they do not casually and sleepily prepare for another "*yawn*" day. They are in a real fight and they know it. You are as well, but do you know it? Rouse yourself. Sit up. Be prepared. Put on the full armor of God. How? Are you surrendered to him? Is there any part of your life you are holding back for yourself? Surrender is primary. Are you in a position of a "ready yes"?

149

Soldiers thrive and survive in combat conditions by obeying the orders of those in authority over them. In a battle there is no discussion with your commander, because victory requires ready submission. It is likely you won't hear the sounds of war in your day, but nevertheless you will be in a war today. It is very important that are you prepared. Surrender. Say to God right now: "The answer is 'yes', whatever you ask from me." Don't play at this. If your heart is not actually there, cry out to God to help you get there. Close the gap today between your perception of the battle and the reality of the battle.

Day 3
Read:
Eph. 6:10-18 Finally, be strong in the Lord and in his mighty power. Put on the full armor of God so that you can take your stand against the devil's schemes. For our struggle is not against flesh and blood, but against the rulers, against the authorities, against the powers of this dark world and against the spiritual forces of evil in the heavenly realms. Therefore put on the full armor of God, so that when the day of evil comes, you may be able to stand your ground, and after you have done everything, to stand. Stand firm then, with the belt of truth buckled around your waist, with the breastplate of righteousness in place, and with your feet fitted with the readiness that comes from the gospel of peace. In addition to all this, take up the shield of faith, with which you can extinguish all the flaming arrows of the evil one. Take the helmet of salvation and the sword of the Spirit, which is the word of God. And pray in the Spirit on all occasions with all kinds of prayers and requests. With this in mind, be alert and always keep on praying for all the saints.

Reflect:
Once again, this passage demonstrates the balance of both full reliance on God's power and, also, full personal effort and discipline. God's grace need not be at odds with human effort. It is his grace that empowers our efforts to follow him. We are to "be strong in the Lord and in his power." We are to "put on his armor." We are to "stand firm." We are to "take up the shield of faith" and the "helmet of salvation" and the "sword of the Spirit." We are to pray all kinds of prayers and stay alert. All of these instructions indicate activity, not passivity. It shows that a relationship with God, like other relationships, requires proactivity from both parties. God is ever-active in his pursuit of us and we must be the same in our pursuit of him. In anything that requires balance, there are two ways to "fall off the wall." In this spiritual battle we are engaged in, we can fail through believing God's operational power in our lives doesn't require anything from us. It is true that justification is all God's work in us, but it is not true that growth in Christlikeness and engagement in the battle requires nothing from us. If we fail to understand the need for full engagement with God and the battle using all of our heart, soul, mind, and strength, then we will fail in the battle.

On the other hand, if we come to believe ongoing victory depends on our efforts and fail to rely fully on God's power, then we will also fail in the battle. Our strength will never be enough. Do not try to make this into a math problem. It does not and will not work that way. It is 100 percent the grace and power of God. It is 100 percent full effort and engagement on our part. What doesn't work on paper does work in the real world. You must learn to lean into the wind that blows in your life. Do you find yourself overreliant on your own efforts? Reflect deeply on his grace and power and put your full confidence in him. Do you find yourself living passively, waiting for God to do for you what he has told you to do? Rouse yourself! Be strong in his mighty power and stand firm.

Day 4

Read: Eph. 6:10-17 Finally, be strong in the Lord and in his mighty power. Put on the full armor of God so that you can take your stand against the devil's schemes. For our struggle is not against flesh and blood, but against the rulers, against the authorities, against the powers of this dark world and against the spiritual forces of evil in the heavenly realms. Therefore put on the full armor of God, so that when the day of evil comes, you may be able to stand your ground, and after you have done everything, to stand. Stand firm then, with the belt of truth buckled around your waist, with the breastplate of righteousness in place, and with your feet fitted with the readiness that comes from the gospel of peace. In addition to all this, take up the shield of faith, with which you can extinguish all the flaming arrows of the evil one. Take the helmet of salvation and the sword of the Spirit, which is the word of God.

Reflect:

How can he say that our struggle is not against flesh and blood? It is real people who want to destroy people's lives in physical warfare. It is real people who make your life difficult at work, school, and home. It is real flesh and blood people that we struggle to forgive and love and relate to. For that matter, you are real flesh and blood and your largest struggle is most often within yourself. He is not saying that these physical struggles are illusion or irrelevant. He is telling us that behind the struggles we can see, there are also struggles that we do not see. Do not turn this into something weird. Do not overspeculate on what this might mean. Take it at face value. There is a spiritual war that is supernatural in nature and it is real, not weird. It is weird, though, to look at what has happened and is happening in the world and fail to understand there is much more going on than what we can see with our physical eyes. In this fight, like any real fight, words are not enough. There must be real faith and real follow-through behind any words that we try to use in the battle. You might read a verse where Paul or Jesus merely spoke words and demons had to flee. But those words had power because of much more than just vocal chords vibrating air and sending sounds out.

151

Look at what happened when some people who did not have relationship with Jesus tried to use his name in the spiritual battle. "Some Jews who went around driving out evil spirits tried to invoke the name of the Lord Jesus over those who were demon-possessed. They would say, "In the name of Jesus, whom Paul preaches, I command you to come out." Seven sons of Sceva, a Jewish chief priest, were doing this. [One day] the evil spirit answered them, "Jesus I know, and I know about Paul, but who are you?" Then the man who had the evil spirit jumped on them and overpowered them all. He gave them such a beating that they ran out of the house naked and bleeding." (Acts 19:13-16) You see, it's not the words that bring power, it is relationship with Jesus and in that relationship we are able to act on his authority. Your time in prayer, your time in God's word, your choice to continually surrender your heart, and your life of obedience...these are all essential to your ability to effectively engage the real war you are in today. The demons should know **who** you are because they know **whose** you are. "For the kingdom of God is not a matter of talk but of power" (1 Corinthians 4:20).

Day 5
Read:
Eph. 6:18 And pray in the Spirit on all occasions with all kinds of prayers and requests. With this in mind, be alert and always keep on praying for all the saints.

Reflect:
Now you can understand what it means to "pray in the Spirit." It is not mere words. It is not some emotional state you work yourself into you. It is to pray in the realm of the Holy Spirit's power and will. This is a function of being "within" the realm of his power and his will in your life. The realm of God's power in and through your life is the realm of his will for your life. A life of ongoing surrender is essential to a life of praying in the Spirit. Every prayer should originate from a heart that is oriented fully to God. Not that our hearts are ever going to be fully surrendered or fully in sync with him, but our hearts can and should be oriented his direction. A life of perfection in direction, not perfection in every action is the life of conversational relationship with God. This is not merely clever words, it is intentional actions that flow from a life of faith. When we "mess up," we must learn to quickly "fess up" and then move on. We must not deny our sins or avoid facing them. Neither can we allow our sins to compound by staying on the ground after we have fallen. God has said that if you will confess your sins, he is faithful and will forgive you and cleanse you from them (1 John 1:9). It is essential that you take him up on his offer: "if you confess." And you must believe him when he says you "will be cleansed." Do you have important things in your life that you are pouring out to God in prayer? Have you considered your heart? Is it surrendered to him?

Are you harboring unconfessed sin? Do you understand that our sin can hinder our prayers? It's not because God is petty; it is because he is great. How would we expect such a God to continually support and empower our lives if they are going in a direction away from him? How could he possibly be good and do such a thing? This is imminently practical; it shows up in the most basic of relationships, like a marriage. "Husbands, in the same way be considerate as you live with your wives, and treat them with respect as the weaker partner and as heirs with you of the gracious gift of life, so that nothing will hinder your prayers" (1 Peter 3:7). Do you know that if a husband is inconsiderate to his spouse, it can hinder his prayers? This is but one example, there are many more. God desires to empower a life lived in his direction. He loves us too much to do otherwise. "Pray in the spirit on all occasions" by living in the realm of the Spirit's power and will on all occasions. Close the gap, continually. Mess up, fess up, and then move on.

Week 34/Day 1
Read:
2 Tim. 2:2-7 You then, my son, be strong in the grace that is in Christ Jesus. And the things you have heard me say in the presence of many witnesses entrust to reliable men who will also be qualified to teach others.

Reflect:
It is common for people as they near the end of their working careers to begin to look for a way to "play" for a living. The end of a life of working and learning and producing is thought to begin a life of playing and resting and self-indulgence. It is not wrong to rest or to retire. It is wrong for an adult to play for a living. A young child's life is largely about play. To see a child playing is sweet, natural, and beautiful. When a child does not have the opportunity to play, but is forced to "grow up" too fast it can stunt their development. An adult's life need not be devoid of play and fun. In fact, a healthy life must have some times of enjoyment and play. But an adult's life is not designed to be mostly about play and fun. As you grow into adulthood there are many investments that have been made into your life. For most people, other adults have given time, encouragement, training, and teaching to help them along the way. Adults have paid for your food, lodging, and other needs as you grew up because you were unable to do so yourself. Behind all of this investment in your life by other people, God was investing in you. Even if your childhood was difficult, the fact that you are reading this and are interested in spiritual things at all indicates that God has continued to pursue you and invest in you. The longer you live, the more God has invested in your life. The more he has invested the more he wants you to pass that investment on to others. "Now it is required that those who have been given a trust must prove faithful" (1 Cor. 4:2). In 1 Timothy, Paul is speaking to his "son in the faith", Timothy.

He is investing in Timothy's life and challenging Timothy to pass the investment on to others. Are you young? Be invested in. Seek it out from older Christ followers. Begin now to develop a lifelong perspective as a learner and as a mentor. You are the currently the "next" generation. If you live long enough, you will be required to help prepare the "next after next" generation. Embrace this opportunity and challenge. Are you "older"? Are you looking for a place to "sit down" or a way to serve yourself in your last years? No! You can rest some and you can play some, but you must not see your life as being about rest and play. You must invest in the next generation. If you are unprepared for that task, then you must become prepared. If you are unconnected from others who need your help, you must connect. If you believe the next generation does not want your investment, it is not because they are unwilling. It may be because you are unapproachable. If so, change. Learn to listen and understand so you can invest. Do what it takes to be faithful in your stewardship. Start today. See yourself as one whose life is to be about investing in others. Invest for the good of others, for the glory of God, and for the joy of being found faithful.

Day 2
Read:
2 Tim. 2:1-7 You then, my son, be strong in the grace that is in Christ Jesus. And the things you have heard me say in the presence of many witnesses entrust to reliable men who will also be qualified to teach others. Endure hardship with us like a good soldier of Christ Jesus. No one serving as a soldier gets involved in civilian affairs—he wants to please his commanding officer. Similarly, if anyone competes as an athlete, he does not receive the victor's crown unless he competes according to the rules. The hardworking farmer should be the first to receive a share of the crops. Reflect on what I am saying, for the Lord will give you insight into all this.

Reflect:
The first thing to be passed on to the next generation is the primacy of grace. Youth is strength. Strong bodies. Strong wills. Strong desires. Strong opinions. Age teaches weakness. Bodies begin to fail. Experience has demonstrated time and again that strong opinions and desires do not guarantee outcomes. The lessons of youth can lead to foolish and unwarranted self-trust. The lessons of age can lead to cynicism or to grace. The Word of God is leading us to Jesus. Away from both self-trust and cynicism. "Be strong my son, my daughter...in the grace of Christ." Be strong, but in his unmerited favor in your life and not in all you can do and earn and become and obtain. Be strong in his power in your life. Do not think that you can shape your life by the force of your will alone. Be strong in his grace. This is the opposite of passivism and cynicism.

To be strong in the grace of Jesus Christ is to endure anything and everything that comes our way with confidence, with faith. It is to remain an ultimate optimist. All things will, in the end, work together for my good since I love him. This is what must be experienced by every generation and then passed down to each "next" generation. The "normal" way of understanding strength is wrong; this is the right way to understand what it means to be strong. There is strength to survive and to thrive. It is the strength that flows from the grace of Christ. Nothing lasts, except the grace of God by which you are saved in Christ Jesus. All that is weak and passing will fail you, but he will never fail. You are weak and passing, so do not put your final confidence in yourself. Do not pass the folly of full confidence in yourself to the next generation. If you are old, you ought to know better by now. You know you do not have what it takes, so don't pretend that you do. If you are young, you can skip some of the lessons taught by experience and learn directly from God himself. He is telling you now that your strength, your confidence, your arrogance will fail you. Be strong in the grace that is in Christ Jesus. By all means venture boldly into the life God has for you, but do so putting your final confidence in Christ and not in self.

Day 3
Read:
2 Tim. 2:1-7 You then, my son, be strong in the grace that is in Christ Jesus. And the things you have heard me say in the presence of many witnesses entrust to reliable men who will also be qualified to teach others. Endure hardship with us like a good soldier of Christ Jesus. No one serving as a soldier gets involved in civilian affairs—he wants to please his commanding officer. Similarly, if anyone competes as an athlete, he does not receive the victor's crown unless he competes according to the rules. The hardworking farmer should be the first to receive a share of the crops. Reflect on what I am saying, for the Lord will give you insight into all this.

Reflect:
You were made for multi-generational impact. It is not for a select few; it is for all who claim the name of Jesus. In this passage, Paul is telling Timothy to pass on what he has learned to men who will then teach other men. Of course, the same principle holds true for women teaching other women. The things that are to be passed on are specifically related to the gospel, but the gospel has implications for all of life. The truth of the message that is passed on is independent of the messenger. You do not have to live the message perfectly in order to pass it on faithfully. However, you can make the message more accessible to the next generation if you live it more faithfully. They are listening and they are watching. If what they are seeing does not match what they are hearing, it will be difficult for them to believe what they are hearing.

The fact that you are made for multi-generational impact is both a privilege and a responsibility. It is a privilege in that God has included you in his activity in the world. You do not have to wonder if you have purpose or if your life can count. You do have purpose and your life must count. It is a privilege because the fact that you have a stewardship can and should be a built-in incentive for holy living. It is not a curse that others are watching your life; it is a blessing. To have accountability for living the best possible life is a good thing, so embrace it as such. It is a responsibility in that your life is not to be about you. It is to be about the glory of God and the good of others. This responsibility is also not merely a burden, but also a great opportunity. When you live for the glory of God and the good of others, you will in turn maximize your own joy in life. You were made for multi-generational impact and, when you live in line with your design, then clearly life is going to be much more fulfilling and meaningful. "This is love for God: to obey his commands. And his commands are not burdensome" (1 John 5:3). Indeed, his commands are not a burden, rather they are an opportunity. His commands for our lives demonstrate his design for our lives. Live your design and invest in the next generation. Perhaps you do not feel up to the task. Maybe your life does not match the gospel message. Nevertheless, the task is on you. Because if not you, then who? Take up the challenge and close the gap on aligning your life with the gospel message. Then, in spite of your imperfections, give yourself to investing in others.

Day 4
Read:
2 Tim. 2:1-7 You then, my son, be strong in the grace that is in Christ Jesus. And the things you have heard me say in the presence of many witnesses entrust to reliable men who will also be qualified to teach others. Endure hardship with us like a good soldier of Christ Jesus. No one serving as a soldier gets involved in civilian affairs—he wants to please his commanding officer. Similarly, if anyone competes as an athlete, he does not receive the victor's crown unless he competes according to the rules. The hardworking farmer should be the first to receive a share of the crops. Reflect on what I am saying, for the Lord will give you insight into all this.

Reflect:
There are three analogies here that help us understand what a life of investment in others looks like: a soldier, an athlete, and a farmer. A soldier avoids civilian entanglements because his controlling ambition is to please his commanding officer. The soldier does what civilians do. He eats, sleeps, washes clothes, and enjoys when possible some entertainment. However, unlike his civilian counterparts, he doesn't live for any of these. He lives with a singleness of mind and purpose to please his commander. The athlete also has a controlling goal, which is to win the race.

However, no matter how much he trains if he does not stay within the boundaries of the rules of the race, he will be disqualified and fail in his ultimate quest. Therefore, he does not run to obey rules, but he cannot run if he does not stay within the rules of the race. Finally, the farmer whose ultimate goal is a harvest. The few seeds that are sown will hopefully become many seeds in the harvest. The farmer cannot make the seeds grow. Only God in his providence does that. Then does the farmer just pray for seeds to grow and leave it at that? No, he prepares the soil, plants the seed, waters and weeds, and then watches and waits. He has machinery to keep in working condition and multiple other things to attend to that do not directly look like they are a part of the harvest, but they are. So you must be part soldier, part athlete, and part farmer. You must live with a singleness of purpose that can be described in different ways. You live to please God and not for secondary things. You live your life towards a final goal. You train for that purpose. You also desire and expect a harvest, a multiplied return on your investment. You have been given the opportunity to have a multi-generational impact. This doesn't mean your goal is to "change the world." It is not. Your goal is to be found faithful. Your ambition is to please God, to run faithfully the race he has marked out for you, and to do whatever you do with all of your might because you are working for the Lord and, thus, your labor is never in vain. To impact others towards the King and the Kingdom, begin with your own life by making it your ambition to be found faithful. Make this your controlling goal. When you do, others will be drawn to your life. Then through your life they will be drawn to Jesus.

Day 5
Read:
2 Tim. 2:1-7 You then, my son, be strong in the grace that is in Christ Jesus. And the things you have heard me say in the presence of many witnesses entrust to reliable men who will also be qualified to teach others. Endure hardship with us like a good soldier of Christ Jesus. No one serving as a soldier gets involved in civilian affairs—he wants to please his commanding officer. Similarly, if anyone competes as an athlete, he does not receive the victor's crown unless he competes according to the rules. The hardworking farmer should be the first to receive a share of the crops. Reflect on what I am saying, for the Lord will give you insight into all this

Reflect:
"Reflect on what I am saying, for the Lord will give you insight into all this." Cursory is a word that means, "hurried, superficial." A cursory reading of Scripture will lead to a cursory life, a life marked by hurry and superficiality. The antidote to this is the discipline of reflection. To reflect means to think deeply and personally about something. If we want the Lord to give insight into his word and our lives, then we must do the hard work of reflection.

The challenge of reflection is to see what is actually there and not impose what is in our minds back on the passage. To reflect on Scripture is to "read out" what is there, not to "read in" what is not there. We tend to have undue confidence in ourselves and in our own humility. So, of course, we would never "read in to" Scripture. We believe that we sincerely want to know what is true about our lives and how we can close the gap in key areas. While this is no doubt true to a point, it is also true that we are all prone to self-protective ideas and a self-serving bias. Do not think yourself beyond seeing in Scripture and in your own life what you want to see there, rather than what you need to see there. If you are to be a mentor for the next generation, you must be an honest one. If you serve as a "trail guide" for those who are following, you must guide with integrity. You can know what is behind you and pass on that vital experience. You can use that experience guided by wisdom to understand what might be in front of you. But you must never become too busy or too proud for reflection, regardless of how much experience you have gained. Reflect deeply and consistently on what God has said and whether your life is aligning with the truth. You have time for reflection because you are already reflecting all day, every day. Even when your mind is occupied with the work you are doing, there is still "space" in your mind for various kinds of reflections. It is important that, as you live your life, you learn to reflect on truth as it applies to both what you are doing at the moment and what you are doing on the whole. As you live as a soldier, an athlete, and a farmer, reflect. Think deeply and the Lord will give you insight. That insight is not just for you; it is also for you to pass on to others. Not in a proud way or domineering way, but in a humble, helpful way. Be a reflective trail guide, for the glory of God and for the good of others.

Week 35/Day 1
Read:
Gen. 3:17-19 To Adam he said, "Because you listened to your wife and ate from the tree about which I commanded you, 'You must not eat of it,' "Cursed is the ground because of you; through painful toil you will eat of it all the days of your life. It will produce thorns and thistles for you, and you will eat the plants of the field. By the sweat of your brow you will eat your food until you return to the ground, since from it you were taken; for dust you are and to dust you will return."

Reflect:
Work became toil when mankind rebelled against God. The gospel reverses the effect of the curse in our lives, including the effects of our rebellion on our work. However, this reversal, is "already, not yet." We experience some of the fruit of the "curse reversal" now, but the fullness of that experience will not occur in this life. What does that mean for our work?

It means that as we walk with Jesus and as we embrace a theology of "faithful presence" in our homes and work places, we will experience in growing fashion a sense of calling and purpose in all aspects of our lives. This sense of calling doesn't require that you "make a difference" at work. It doesn't mean you have to start Bible studies or share the gospel at work in order for work to be significant. That utilitarian approach to life and ministry misses the mark on the larger purpose of life. Your purpose is not to "change the world" or "make a difference," but rather to be found faithful. You exist for the glory of God. Of course, the person who is committed to being faithful and who has a growing passion for the glory of God will make a difference wherever they go, but that is a result of pursuing the larger goal of the glory of God. If you seek to do good work in your vocation, whether it is outside the home or not, you are positioned to bring glory to God. You may or may not "enjoy" your work, but you can find joy in your work if you will see it as part of a life of faithfulness. If we can learn to rejoice in our sufferings (Romans 5:3), surely we can learn to rejoice in our vocations. Even if they do not always feel as satisfying as we would prefer. You may hope for a sense of purpose, impact, and meaning in your vocation and you may very well have it. But your final sense of purpose and meaning is grounded on your relationship with God and a theology of faithfulness. If you look for and find your purpose in your work, what will you do if you lose the ability to do that work? What will you do if you "out live" your vocation and are faced with years with no such work to give your life meaning? Whether you live or die, work at a job in which you find meaning or not, you live for the Lord. When you labor in him, nothing you do is ever in vain (1 Cor. 15:58). However, if you do not do what you do "in the Lord," then all you do is in vain. "Unless the LORD builds the house, its builders labor in vain" (Ps. 127:1). It's not wrong to enjoy or to want to enjoy what you do vocationally. However, it is important that you seek to find your joy in the Lord, no matter what you do vocationally. This is a heart issue and as it takes root on the inside of you, it will bear fruit on the outside.

Day 2
Read: 1 Cor. 15:58 Therefore, my dear brothers, stand firm. Let nothing move you. Always give yourselves fully to the work of the Lord, because you know that your labor in the Lord is not in vain.

Reflect: Just prior to this verse, Paul writes of the surety of the resurrection from the dead and the final victory of Christ over death. It is the context for the "therefore." Therefore, since as a follower of Christ your death will not destroy the works of your life, stand firm! Be immovable! Give yourself fully to the work God has for you to do. You can be confident that this work will not be in vain. Solomon feared that all he did would be left to a foolish heir who would squander his work.

His fears proved to be valid, because that is exactly what happened. The problem with Solomon's fear is that it did not lead him to labor in the Lord, but rather it led him to cynicism about the ultimate value of a life's work. As an old man, Solomon did come to see that what matters most at the end is what matters most all along the day. By that time, he had squandered a good bit of his life and labors. You do not have to fear that your life's work will vanish into the dust of death, not if you "labor in the Lord." What exactly does that mean anyway? Does it only mean "evangelism, preaching, missions"? Paul writes elsewhere what this means: "And whatever you do, whether in word or deed, do it all in the name of the Lord Jesus, giving thanks to God the Father through him" (Col. 3:17). It means that all we do and all we say is to be done and said in the "name of" Jesus. Which means that we do and say these things under the great family name of Jesus, as his children, as his representatives, and for his glory. This is single story living. There is no "spiritual, eternal" work that belongs "upstairs" and "physical, temporal" work that belongs "downstairs." The two story approach to life believes that upstairs living is meaningful because it is praying, preaching, going to church, and giving to missions. Meanwhile, downstairs is viewed as not meaningful in the end because it involves a job, cleaning house, changing diapers, and mowing grass. Your life is to be a single story dwelling. All you do is to be done as a member of the family of Jesus. The implication for this is that you must "close the gap" on doing whatever you are doing with full assurance that it does have lasting value and impact. If you feel like your day "mattered" because you helped someone in a way that seems significant to you, then rejoice. If you do not feel like your day had any lasting significance because it was quite ordinary, devoid of any obvious "eternal" impact, then perhaps you need to change your perspective. Every day, no matter what the content of that day, is to be lived for the glory of God and for the good others. It is possible to live a day of vanity. It is possible that we live entirely for self and waste our day or days living apart from the will and ways of God. But this need not be true and the difference between a day lived in vain and a day lived for Christ begins in the heart, not in what activities are on the calendar. Start your day and end your day by remembering and reflecting on what matters most at the end. Then remember that what matters most then is what matters most now. What will matter most then will be the glory of Christ and the good of others. Keep that perspective close by. Pull it out and consider it frequently, as you navigate your days. Stand firm, let nothing move you.

Day 3
Read:
Col. 3:17 And whatever you do, whether in word or deed, do it all in the name of the Lord Jesus, giving thanks to God the Father through him.

Reflect:

"Whatever you do, word or action" is absolutely comprehensive. But is it a realistic expectation? Realistic or not, it is the command, the objective, the target for our lives. On the one hand it may be an unreasonable goal, but on the other hand it is the only reasonable thing for a believer to aim for. How can it not be? You were purchased at the price of the Cross and so you belong to Christ. "You were bought at a price. Therefore honor God with your body" (1 Cor. 6:20). Since you belong to Christ you are to honor him with your body. Body? What about mind, Spirit, and heart? This is practical and actionable. Your body is where your "soul" interacts with the world. Your hands do things, your feet take you places, your eyes absorb photons that form images that shape you, and your ears do the same with sound waves. Your lips form words in collaboration with your vocal chords. Your body is like a little "planet" where everything is to give glory to the God who has made it. The rest of the physical world cannot help but praise God. Animals, oceans, rocks, and stars do not and cannot rebel against his glory, they can only manifest it. Humans alone in the physical creation have the capacity to rebel against their design purpose. But you, if you are believer, have been purchased for Christ. Now then, whatever you do, every action and every word, do it all in the great family name of Jesus. You are his son, you are his daughter...reflect him and show the family resemblance. No part of your life is to be empty of purpose and meaning. All that you give your life to doing - whether at home, at work or at play - do it as one who has been purchased and redeemed. Not purchased into slavery, but purchased from it. And the cost was not silver and gold. It was blood. "For you know that it was not with perishable things such as silver or gold that you were redeemed from the empty way of life handed down to you from your forefathers, but with the precious blood of Christ, a lamb without blemish or defect" (1 Peter 1:18-19). Whatever you do, do it for his glory.

Day 4
Read:

1 Thess. 4:11-12 Make it your ambition to lead a quiet life, to mind your own business and to work with your hands, just as we told you, so that your daily life may win the respect of outsiders and so that you will not be dependent on anybody.

Reflect:

Does this admonition sound compelling or boring to you? If your life is hectic and the pace is beyond what you feel you can compete with or if you are a natural introvert and love to "mind your own business" then this may sound wonderful. If you long for adventure and more activity and action and you are an extrovert, it might sound painful. The context of these statements involved a church that was focused on the Lord's return.

Their focus was leading them in exactly the wrong direction. Instead of their perspective on the "end" leading to increased faithfulness in the "now," it led them to be restless and inattentive to their day-to-day duties. They became idle and "meddlers." They were not fully engaged with life themselves, so they spent their time illegitimately worrying about the lives of others. The result was that those outside the church did not find their lives compelling. Who would find restless, idle, and meddlesome people's lives compelling? Throughout the history of the church the eschatological vision (return of Christ in the future) has led to decreased faithfulness in the present. This is a tragedy of epic proportions. An eternal vision should empower a temporal vision. The fact that your health, your life, your job, your possessions, and your status will all come to an end someday should lead to a passion to be found faithful with all of it. We should not become cynical and agree with what Solomon foolishly thought: "All is vanity!" Instead, we should be people who understand that, in Christ, "Nothing is vanity!" Don't see this as "make it your ambition to have no ambition." Rather, this is "make it your ambition to be faithful." Have a compelling and controlling passion for faithfulness. In every sphere of influence where God places you, be found faithful there.

Day 5
Read:
Ps. 127:1 Unless the LORD builds the house, its builders labor in vain. Unless the LORD watches over the city, the watchmen stand guard in vain.

Reflect:
All of your work matters. None of your work matters. Which is true? It depends on how and why the work was done. The Psalmist said that unless the Lord builds the house, its builders labor in vain. Isn't this a nonsensical saying? Is the Lord building the house or are the builders building the house? This is a picture of the balance or lack of balance that is evident in every human life. Every human being endeavors to "build a life." Some do so by entirely relying on their own ideas of what is real and valuable to build a life with. They labor in vain because, in the end, all they built in their life has no final value. When they die, what they gave their lives for is gone and their labor was in vain. Others build their lives based on what God has revealed as being finally real and valuable. Their labor is not vain, because in reality it was the Lord who built the life. The balanced approach to "life building" is to labor in the Lord. This may sound mystical and even hard to know how to apply in real life, but it really means to live life the Lord's way. His way is to believe what he says is real and ultimately valuable and then choose to build those values and behaviors into your life. "Therefore, my dear brothers, stand firm. Let nothing move you.

Always give yourselves fully to the work of the Lord, because you know that your labor in the Lord is not in vain" (1 Cor. 15:58). The imbalanced approach to "life building" is to give your life (time, talents, and treasures) for things that ultimately do not matter in the end. Does your current "labor" feel full of meaning to you? Perhaps your vocational and relational efforts are "paying off" nicely right now. That could be very good or it could be deceiving you. Your current "success" could be hiding a potentially disastrous crack in your life foundation. Many people have seen all they built in the lives crumble in a terrible crash as the foundation gave way because it could not hold. You need not live in fear, but you must live in wisdom. Examine your life now. If you are not living in line with God's will and ways, then you are building on a fault line. In that case, it is not a matter of if but, rather, when the foundation will fail. Reflect today on whether it is truly the Lord who is building your life. Your life is not something on which you want to labor in vain. You are literally betting your life on this.

Week 36/Day 1
Read:
John 3:1 Now there was a man of the Pharisees named Nicodemus, a member of the Jewish ruling council. 2 He came to Jesus at night and said, "Rabbi, we know you are a teacher who has come from God. For no one could perform the miraculous signs you are doing if God were not with him."

Reflect:
The Lord spoke through Jeremiah and told his people who were living their lives as captives of their enemies, "You will seek me and find me when you seek me with all your heart" (Jer. 29:13). They would be in dire circumstances, but God would be found by them if they would seek him. It is a great comfort to know that those who seek God will find God. However, there is an important qualification given in Jeremiah. You must be an authentic seeker who seeks "with all your heart." Nicodemus appeared to be an authentic seeker. He would later defend Jesus before other religious leaders and bring expensive burial supplies to Jesus' tomb. In his encounter with Jesus, Nicodemus was simultaneously drawn to Jesus and confused by him. He could see that Jesus was clearly from God, but he was puzzled by what exactly Jesus was all about. Here was Nicodemus, a man who was trained in "religious" matters, but he was unable to pinpoint exactly who Jesus really was. He was a seeker who came to Jesus at night. We don't know if this was because he was afraid of what his peers might think or just because it was when access to Jesus was more readily available. In any case, it was not just a matter of him having a spur-of-the-moment question for Jesus. He was intentional in going to the Lord to try and find out who he really was. You have seekers all around you. In many cases, the fact that they are seeking will not be readily apparent to you or even to them.

They may know they are empty and feel their need, but not even know that they are really searching for God. You may look at their lives and see people who are hard, who have things together, or who seem disinterested, but you cannot judge based on externals. Many people who are close to the kingdom on the "inside" look far away from it on the "outside." Think for a moment about the people God has placed in your life. Who have you written off as being unreachable, uninterested? Do you need to ask God to open your eyes to what might really be happening in their lives? Seek the seeker. Pray for eyes to see them as they truly are. God is seeking them and they are seeking him. Even if they don't always know that he is what they are searching for.

Day 2

Read: John 3:3 In reply Jesus declared, "I tell you the truth, no one can see the kingdom of God unless he is born again." 4 "How can a man be born when he is old?" Nicodemus asked. "Surely he cannot enter a second time into his mother's womb to be born!" 5 Jesus answered, "I tell you the truth, no one can enter the kingdom of God unless he is born of water and the Spirit. 6 Flesh gives birth to flesh, but the Spirit gives birth to spirit. 7 You should not be surprised at my saying, 'You must be born again.' 8 The wind blows wherever it pleases. You hear its sound, but you cannot tell where it comes from or where it is going. So it is with everyone born of the Spirit." 9 "How can this be?" Nicodemus asked. 10 "You are Israel's teacher," said Jesus, "and do you not understand these things? 11 I tell you the truth, we speak of what we know, and we testify to what we have seen, but still you people do not accept our testimony.

Reflect Jesus did not equivocate, but replied directly, "No one can see the kingdom of God unless he is born again." "Born again" is a phrase that Jesus coined. It is not a concept that came out of modern, western Christianity. This is a bold and revolutionary idea. In order for a person to live in the "kingdom of God," he or she must experience new birth. The kingdom of God is the reign or rule of God. It is universal in its scope since God is the rightful ruler of the universe. But in terms of individual experiences of the kingdom, it comes one heart at a time as people submit their lives to Jesus as the king. To enter this kingdom you must undergo a radical change. It is not just a transfer of loyalty or a change of citizenship; you must be born again in order to gain citizenship in the kingdom of God. Nicodemus was understandably confused, this is not something that comes naturally to the human mind. It is something that must be revealed, not reasoned out. What hope is there then, if we cannot figure it out? We can understand it. We just can't discover it or make full sense of it through unaided human reason. We can understand it because God can empower our understanding. He is not vague or trying to be difficult. He doesn't play "hide and seek" with people.

Jesus is using a very common analogy, one that is, in fact, universal in its experience. Everyone has been born so everyone can relate to this experience. However, the experience is mysterious. We were all "there" when it happened, but we neither remember it nor did we have a choice in the matter. We all do know that when we were born, we entered into life. When someone is born again, they likewise enter into the experience of the new life, which is life in the kingdom of God. This birth you do remember and you do have a choice, but just like physical birth, this life is not the result of effort on your part. As you consider the people who live and work and play in your sphere of influence, do not forget to remind yourself that they also must be born again in order to enter the kingdom of God. They cannot make it happen, but they must choose Christ for it to happen. It is easy to forget that people need new birth, so we must be diligent to remember. You must also remember that God is seeking your friends and family members and he is not hiding himself from them. You can have confidence that he is making himself known, and it is no small part of him making *himself* known to them that he has made *you* known to them. Keep this in mind as you close the gap on loving God and loving others.

Day 3
Read:
John 3:14 Just as Moses lifted up the snake in the desert, so the Son of Man must be lifted up, 15 that everyone who believes in him may have eternal life.

Reflect:
Israel complained about their captivity in Egypt. Then they complained about the conditions of their journey to the Promised Land. They complained about the leadership God had provided for them. And they complained about the perceived threats of entering the Promised Land once they arrived there. At one point, their complaining brought the judgment of a large number of venomous snakes that bit and killed many of them. This is the stuff of nightmares, terrifying to consider. Imagine walking through open wilderness and suddenly finding yourself in a huge den of poisonous snakes. The judgment may seem harsh, but the stakes were high. These people were carrying the light of the truth of God to the nations. If they lost the light, then far worse would befall humanity than some dying by snakebite. Keep this fact in mind when reading the Old Testament accounts of God's dealings with Israel. God provided a cure for them in their suffering. Moses fabricated a bronze snake and put it on a pole that was raised up for anyone to see. If a snake bit someone, they could look to the bronze snake and live. This may sound like so much "hocus pocus," but God was not playing games with them through the whole "snake on a stick" story. Israel continually forgot their great need for God.

Their demanding and complaining showed how in their hearts they believed that they deserved good from God rather than judgment for their sins. This plague of snakes, like other forms of judgment, reminded them of their need. The bronze snake on the pole, on the other hand, reminded them that their salvation was not in their own efforts, but only in looking in faith to God. Then when Jesus the Messiah came, he linked his own death on a cross to the cure in the wilderness. When he was lifted up in crucifixion, he said that all who look to him in faith would be saved. Some of the people God has placed in your life no doubt fail to understand their need for God. The constant complaining you hear in media, in your workplace, and in the places you shop all serve to remind you that people believe they deserve more than they have. The demands that life (God) be more generous, more fair, and more attuned to our needs and wants, demonstrate how far we are from understanding our great dependence on God. All we have is a grace gift. Do not join in the chorus of complaining. Instead, be set apart as one whose words point to the one who was lifted up for our sins. "Do everything without complaining or arguing, so that you may become blameless and pure, children of God without fault in a crooked and depraved generation, in which you shine like stars in the universe as you hold out the word of life" (Phil. 2:14-16).

Day 4
Read:
John 3:16 "For God so loved the world that he gave his one and only Son, that whoever believes in him shall not perish but have eternal life. 17 For God did not send his Son into the world to condemn the world, but to save the world through him. 18 Whoever believes in him is not condemned, but whoever does not believe stands condemned already because he has not believed in the name of God's one and only Son.

Reflect:
John 3:16 is arguably the most famous verse in the Bible. It is seen as a sort of universal "feel good" verse, "For God so loved...he gave." However, what is often missed is the conditional nature of the promise and the dire outcome for not fulfilling the condition. The condition is "whoever believes." You see this prerequisite several times in these three verses. "Believe" is not merely acknowledging the existence of Jesus; it is the act of placing one's faith (confidence) in him. It is the transferring of trust from self to Christ alone for salvation. The outcome for the one who does trust Christ is a restored relationship with God. The outcome for this restored relationship with God has both temporal and eternal implications. The one who truly believes enters now into a different kind of life which also extends past this life into eternity. This different kind of life is a life as God has designed it to be lived. It is a life in the kingdom which Christ often referred to that involves all the benefits of living under a good, loving, and powerful king.

The outcome for one who rejects Christ's offer is that person will remain where they are in relationship to the king and his kingdom. They will live and die outside the reign of the king and outside the realm of his kind of life. This condemnation, Jesus said, is something they are already experiencing, but which they can escape if they will trust him. How do you reconcile "God so loved the world" with "whoever does not believe stands condemned already"? How can God love the world (people) and not save them all? Consider also the reality that God clearly values choice and personal belief. There is no real relationship, if there is no real choice. Jesus said that God did not send him to condemn the world, but to save it. The purpose of God in Christ is to save, but in order to access that salvation, people must believe. There are many questions that we have and some have answers now and some will remain a mystery. But what we do know now is what Christ has said and what he has done. He has said people must believe and he has died in order that people might be saved. Now it remains for us to take him at his word and deed and faithfully make what he has said and done known to others. Do not let your questions keep you sidelined. You know enough to make the gospel known, now will you do so?

Day 5
Read:
John 3:16 "For God so loved the world that he gave his one and only Son, that whoever believes in him shall not perish but have eternal life. 17 For God did not send his Son into the world to condemn the world, but to save the world through him. 18 Whoever believes in him is not condemned, but whoever does not believe stands condemned already because he has not believed in the name of God's one and only Son.

Reflect:
It is not hard to believe that "some" people need the gospel. Their lives are an obvious mess or they are ruthless and cruel. The challenge is to believe that the "normal and nice" unbeliever needs the gospel. Do people really need to be "saved"? Even to say this will be construed as arrogant, narrow minded, and judgmental. To take action, as in actually sharing the gospel with the goal of someone moving from unbelief to belief, can been seen as terrible or even criminal. Once again, this demonstrates the reality of the two-story construct. There are thought to be things that are "really real" like gravity and calories and fire, and then other things that are not really real, like faith. No one would be considered unkind to warn a person to keep them from falling from a height or getting to close to the fire, but to warn a person in regard to ultimate realities is put in a different category. But gravity and faith are not in two categories; they both are about real things. Either gravity is real and people can be hurt or killed if they disregard it or it is not.

Either the gospel is real or it is not and people's lives temporally and eternally are impacted by their decision regarding its reality or not. It has never been "popular" to take stands regarding truth that others do not agree with. The only way to remain popular among all people is to go all along with whatever others believe to be true. But, of course, this is impossible in practice. How could you agree with everyone? Why would you try? You must decide to do what is right by how you relate to others, regardless of how they perceive you. Do not be arrogant, or hardheaded, or judgmental, but do not have a failure of nerve in regard to the gospel either. Do you believe the gospel is true? Do you believe Jesus is the savior of the world? You are not left with the choice of either believing the gospel is true *or* being accepting and kind to others. The gospel is not at odds with accepting all people *and* loving them where they are. It is at odds with failing to speak and live what you believe is true. "For God so loved the world that he gave his one and only Son, that whoever believes in him shall not perish but have eternal life."

Week 37/Day 1
Read:
2 Thess. 1:8-9 He will punish those who do not know God and do not obey the gospel of our Lord Jesus. They will be punished with everlasting destruction and shut out from the presence of the Lord and from the majesty of his power.

Reflect:
The context for this verse was a suffering and persecuted church. Those who opposed the gospel were brutally attacking the church. This reminder that God is the final judge was not intended to be a celebration of the destruction of non-believers, but rather an encouragement to not become embittered and to leave justice in the hands of God. This does not reverse the Lord's commands to love those who persecute you. They were not to delight in final destruction or to harbor anger and rage at those who opposed them. Instead, they were to pray for them to turn to Christ and to love them as they had opportunity to do so in practical ways. Yet, in the face of their terrible suffering and the severe injustice they experienced, they were to keep the end in view. God is just. Injustice will not finally win the day. If the unjust do not turn to Christ, they will finally and fully experience the fruits of their choices. Even though they may control the legal system or live in a privileged state in the present, no one escapes justice in the end. Either they obey the gospel and Christ takes the weight of their sin on himself, thus satisfying God's justice, or they refuse to obey the gospel and they take the weight of their sins on themselves. This is a comforting truth. This is a terrifying truth. It is comforting as you look around at the vast amount of injustice that is seemingly going unpunished in the world.

168

When the powerful prey on the weak and the wicked destroy the lives of the righteous, it can cause one to question the justice of God. But we can be comforted by the fact that justice will finally win the day. Not comforted in the destruction of the unjust, but comforted in the victory of the just God. There are few things that cause more anger and anxiety than to see and experience injustice. The sense of helplessness and hopelessness can be profound. But God is our help and our hope and he will bring justice. He intends for us to work for and pray for justice now, but we do not have to become hopeless when, in spite of our efforts, injustice seems to prevail. This comforting truth is also a terrifying truth. Christ our Savior will return as the judge of all the earth. Those who do not obey the gospel will experience his justice personally. It is easy to think about the legendary "unjust" getting their due, such as the Hitlers of history. But it is more difficult to imagine the more "normal" people around us who reject the gospel experiencing the justice of God in their lives. But if we are to take the Scriptures and the Gospel seriously, we must imagine just that.

Day 2
Read:

2 Thess. 1:8-9 He will punish those who do not know God and do not obey the gospel of our Lord Jesus. They will be punished with everlasting destruction and shut out from the presence of the Lord and from the majesty of his power.

Reflect:

"There are only two kinds of people in the end: those who say to God, "Thy will be done," and those to whom God says, in the end, "Thy will be done." All that are in Hell, choose it. Without that self-choice there could be no Hell. No soul that seriously and constantly desires joy will ever miss it. Those who seek find. Those who knock it is opened." (C.S. Lewis, *The Great Divorce*). Have you let questions immobilize you? Questions about God's sovereignty, human responsibility, heaven, hell, suffering...? If you have, will you ask God to mobilize you into action again? To be mobilized into action to love him and to love others? You will have questions throughout your life and you will also have questions when this life is over. Only God is and ever will be all-knowing, but you can have knowledge that is "enough." Enough to have confidence that what you believe is true, in spite of the things you don't yet know. You can have confidence that is enough to take decisive action. You can have knowledge enough to live with assurance that you are not wasting your life on the gospel, but rather recognize any other life would be a waste. Will you move with humility and confidence into the lives of those God has given you to love with the message of the gospel? Will you live it and tell it today? Will you leave to God the things that belong to him and also assume responsibility for the things he has given to you? You have been given the responsibility and the privilege to know God and to make God known. There is no mystery in this. As you move faithfully into what God has given you, he will give you more. More knowledge, more power, more influence, more intimacy with him. Make Jesus known today, as you go, wherever you go. Don't see this as pressure or burden. See this as opportunity and privilege. You personally know the source of joy that the world is stumbling in the dark trying desperately to discover.

Day 3
Read:
2 Thess. 1:8-9 He will punish those who do not know God and do not obey the gospel of our Lord Jesus. They will be punished with everlasting destruction and shut out from the presence of the Lord and from the majesty of his power.

Reflect:
The exclusivity of the claims of Christ can be troubling for some and infuriating for others. Who is Jesus to believe that he is the only way? Who are Christians to believe that many sincere people are wrong? However, everyone is exclusive in their view of truth. Those who believe there is no absolute in terms of religious truth are absolute in that belief. That is, they would believe the person who does believe in absolutes is wrong. If they believe they are right (no absolutes) and others are wrong, then what do you have but a person who is absolute in their disbelief of absolutes. The fact is everyone believes something is true and something is not true. Those who believe Jesus is not the only way believe that He and his followers are wrong. They believe they are right about Jesus being wrong. It is important as you consider verses such as the one for today and struggle with the exclusive and harsh nature of its claims that you keep in mind that either this verse is true or it is not. It is not important how you or anyone else "feels" about it. However, it is very important that we believe what is real and align our lives with that reality. If this verse is not real, then we should disregard it along with all the rest of Scripture that makes gospel truth claims. If this verse is real, then it has very real bearing on our beliefs and behaviors today. So, we are *not* left with the choice of not having to choose. We are not able to "keep our options" open and just accept all views of reality as equally valid or equally invalid. We have to decide because the stakes are just too high. What will you believe about Jesus? Is he who he said he was? Is he a reliable source for understanding what is ultimately real? How does he "stack up" against others who propose to speak about what is real? You would do well to trust Jesus; he is unique in all of human history. To live with perpetually "open options" is not wise and generous. In fact, it is unwise and ruinous. It's not really even possible. You have to decide everyday how you will live and those decisions require conclusions about what is and is not true.

In the real world, you will either live as if the gospel is true and real or you will live as if it is not. You cannot live as if the gospel is both true and not true. Decide, and then go live decided.

Day 4
Read:

2 Thess. 1:8-9 He will punish those who do not know God and do not obey the gospel of our Lord Jesus. They will be punished with everlasting destruction and shut out from the presence of the Lord and from the majesty of his power.

Reflect:

Why would God bring lasting justice to those who do not know and obey him? Many simple cannot believe that God would do such a thing. They believe that in the end all will be saved and none will finally be shut out from God's presence. In order to believe that, they must disbelieve what is written here and elsewhere in Scripture. It may appear to be mean-spirited to say and to believe such things are true, but what if these things were true? Would it not, instead, be mean-spirited to not say and believe these things if they actually are true? Imagine someone is walking toward a chasm and is in danger of falling to their death. Perhaps they are really enjoying the walk and, in fact, are convinced that the way they are walking is going to bring them great joy if they just continue in the same direction. If you interfered with their enjoyment by telling them of the grave danger ahead, you would likely be accused of being mean and arrogant. Who are you to tell someone where they should or shouldn't walk? Who are you to ruin someone's enjoyment of a path they have freely chosen? The question, once again, must always be "is this true?" If it is true, then what others think of your warnings is not as important as the very real danger they are in. You could be someone who is considered to be a nice, open-minded, and "good person," when in fact you would be far from any of that. If you know the path others are walking is a dangerous one and fail to tell them in appropriate ways, then there would be nothing "good" about that. This doesn't change the fact that we are responsible to tell others the truth in ways that makes the truth look compelling. The urgency of the message does not take us off the hook to be compelling messengers. You must be willing to be disliked if you are going to love. But you must not be intentionally dislikeable, because there is nothing loving about that.

Day 5
Read:

2 Thess. 1:8-9 He will punish those who do not know God and do not obey the gospel of our Lord Jesus.

They will be punished with everlasting destruction and shut out from the presence of the Lord and from the majesty of his power.

Reflect:
How much of what can be known do you think we know? One percent? Of course not, we are not anywhere near that much knowledge. We cannot know how much we know, because we cannot know what we don't know. The truth about the human condition is that we are specks on a speck in space, living for a brief moment in an incredibly small part of the universe. This truth, the truth of our extreme limitations, can lead one to become cynical about all knowledge. It should not make us cynics, but it should certainly make us humble, much more humble than we normally are. When it comes to the things that we most need to know, we cannot possibly discover them on our own. These things must be revealed to us by God. The fact of our sin-separation from God is evident in human history and individual human behavior, including yours and mine. But the truth of what this means temporally and eternally had to be revealed. The hopelessness of trying to change ourselves and make ourselves acceptable to God is likewise self-evident, if we have honest eyes to see it. But what is not self-evident is the need for a Savior, a sinless sacrifice who can bring us peace with God. The greatest "knowledge-needs" of humanity are inaccessible to unaided human reason. These things must be revealed to us and, thanks be to God, they have been. This passage, though a hard one, is a revealed truth of God. It will not do for us to sit in judgment on it; we must let it sit in judgment on us. Will we be fully challenged to give our lives to making Christ known? Will we live in time in the light of eternity? What God has revealed to us because of his great mercy, let us never doubt. Let us believe, value, and do his revealed will for us.

Week 38/Day 1
Read:
Matt. 28:18-20 Then Jesus came to them and said, "All authority in heaven and on earth has been given to me. Therefore go and make disciples of all nations, baptizing them in the name of the Father and of the Son and of the Holy Spirit, and teaching them to obey everything I have commanded you. And surely I am with you always, to the very end of the age."

Reflect:
Jesus began his "Great Commission" with a declaration of his authority. This is important to note because what he is telling his people to do is going to be widely misunderstood and disagreed with. This was true then, it is also true today. He is instructing his friends to go and tell people to obey Jesus and to follow him with their lives. What this means is that all other beliefs that have shaped their lives were wrong.

He didn't say, "Go tell everyone who doesn't follow me how wrong they are." He told them to proclaim the good news of the gospel. But clearly many who heard this good news were going to hear it as the bad news of "you are wrong!" Now you can see why Jesus started with his absolute authority. "All authority, everywhere has been given me," he declared. Absolute authority has been given by God the Father to God the Son. When a source of legitimate authority makes a declaration that falls under that authority's jurisdiction or scope of power, then that declaration is true and legitimate. Jesus' scope of power is all heaven and earth. That covers everything and everywhere. His commission to go and make disciples has legitimacy because of who he is. Other human founders of religions have made bold claims, but they lacked the legitimacy to make those claims. They had not been given all authority; they had simply tried to assume authority on themselves. These religious founders did not demonstrate by the quality and power of their lives that they had absolute authority, but Jesus did. They did not rise from the dead. They are still in the graves, so their claims to authority over ultimate matters of life and death are not valid. The starting point for making the good news known to others is the absolute authority of Jesus to make truth claims that apply to everyone, everywhere. Think about the authority of Jesus, consider what the implications of his authority are for your life today. What are the implications of his authority for those you interact with today, and what are the implications for ignoring his legitimate authority? Since he knows what is real, what is valuable, and what is lasting... what, then, are the implications for those who disregard him? What are the benefits of those who obey him?

Day 2
Read:
Matt. 28:18-20 Then Jesus came to them and said, "All authority in heaven and on earth has been given to me. Therefore go and make disciples of all nations, baptizing them in the name of the Father and of the Son and of the Holy Spirit, and teaching them to obey everything I have commanded you. And surely I am with you always, to the very end of the age."

Reflect:
In light of the absolute authority of Jesus, those who know him are to make him known as they go about their lives. "Therefore go" is intentional in several ways. It is intentional in that there are times when we "go" to others with the objective of sharing the gospel with them. It is also intentional in that as we go about our normal affairs of life we are to pray for, look for, and take advantage of opportunities to make Jesus known. This is both "go" and "as you go." It is a life of intentionally sharing the good news of the gospel. But what does this look like in a "regular" life. Missionaries "go" to share the gospel and "as they go" it is their "job" to share the good news.

But what of the rest of us? We go to our jobs, our kids' programs, our hobbies, our doctors... we don't "go" to share for a living. There should be times for all followers of Christ when we do go specifically with the goal of sharing the gospel with others. It may be going to talk to strangers on the streets or it may be going to dinner with a friend in order to share the good news as a friend. But, for the most part, this life of intentional "going" will be "as you go." As you go out into your life, you will interact with a host of people who need to hear the good news. Knowing when and how and what to share will take wisdom and sensitivity to the Holy Spirit. Two main imbalances plague believers as they seek to make the good news known in their "going." First, simply failing to pray for, look for, and take the opportunities as they come. This may be because of fear or lack of confidence in the gospel, but often it is simply a component of not being aware of what God is doing around us. We forget to remember that the gospel is real and that people do need to hear it. The second imbalance is to share in ways that alienate and drive people away. To clumsily toss out spiritual "jabs" void of situational awareness and relational connectedness is normally not helpful. This "as you go" intentional lifestyle requires an ongoing connection with the Spirit of God. This "requirement" is a great opportunity and privilege. The opportunity is that you will get to see where God is moving in your everyday life and join him there. The great privilege is that you will get to be a part of what God is doing in the world around you. The Great Commission should feel more like privilege and opportunity than task and duty. Close the gap on seeing it as such.

Day 3
Read:
Matt. 28:18-20 Then Jesus came to them and said, "All authority in heaven and on earth has been given to me. Therefore go and make disciples of all nations, baptizing them in the name of the Father and of the Son and of the Holy Spirit, and teaching them to obey everything I have commanded you. And surely I am with you always, to the very end of the age."

Reflect:
To become a "disciple" is to come into a relationship with Jesus where he is the authority, the "boss" of your life. You accept what he says is right because he has said it. You value what he values because he knows what is valuable and you also do what he has said to do because he knows how life is to be lived. All people, everywhere, at all times are to be taught what it means to obey what Jesus has commanded. He summed up all of his commands in these words: "Love God with all of your heart, soul, mind and strength" and "Love your neighbor as yourself." There is no time limit on these commands; his authority has no term limits. His teachings are relevant to the "very end of the age." There are many teachings that become outdated.

They lose relevance and cease to apply as human history marches on. The teachings of Jesus will never fail to be what humanity most needs to hear. His teachings are timeless because he is timeless. His teachings are universally authoritative because his authority is universal. His teachings are always practical because he designed us and he knows what our design parameters are. When you invite someone to become a follower of Christ, you are not trying to convince them to join your "religion" rather you are inviting them to live fully in reality as it. If this seems arrogant, then you need to read this passage again, carefully. Jesus is the one declaring his supreme authority. Some can call him arrogant, but there was nothing about his life that demonstrated he was anything but humble. In addition, it is not arrogant for God to declare his own authority. This is exactly what God the Son, Jesus, is doing here. Invite others into a relationship with Jesus. There is no hubris in this invitation because the gospel is about the wisdom of Christ, not our own. "For we do not preach ourselves, but Jesus Christ as Lord, and ourselves as your servants for Jesus' sake" (2 Cor. 4:5).

Day 4
Read:
Matt. 28:18-20 Then Jesus came to them and said, "All authority in heaven and on earth has been given to me. Therefore go and make disciples of all nations, baptizing them in the name of the Father and of the Son and of the Holy Spirit, and teaching them to obey everything I have commanded you. And surely I am with you always, to the very end of the age."

Reflect:
To be baptized in the name of the triune God indicates that repentance has come. Repentance does not merely mean to feel sorry for sin; it is a change of mind that leads to a changed life. A changed mind in regard to the gospel means that one experiences a transformed mind, a mind that now understands that what God wants is good and best. If I am committed to walking a down a path and I am told it is not a good path, in fact it is a very bad one, I will not turn from that path with my feet unless I first turn from that path in my mind. I must believe there is a better path to walk. Gospel repentance impacts the mind as a person comes to see God's way as "*the* way." This repentance shows up in a life lived God's way. However, although through conversion the mind and heart are transformed and we want to walk the better way, we don't automatically know how to walk that better way. We need to be taught. So, the Great Commission is to go and make disciples who will "repent" and become committed "learners." These are not multiple different things; they are single parts of a whole. When a person becomes a follower of Christ, they are "justified." To be justified means to be declared legally righteous by God through faith in Christ.

A person repents of their sin and is given new desires and new power to go God's way. Then, over a lifetime, they are "sanctified." Being sanctified means someone becomes increasingly righteous in their thoughts, will, and actions. This process requires knowledge. They must be taught, but knowledge is never enough for transformation. There must also be ongoing motivation and power. This power comes from the Spirit of God at work in us. The motivation comes primarily through our relationships with other believers who are walking "the way" with us. As you contemplate the good news and your part in making it known to others, you will be challenged in your own transformation. Others will certainly benefit as you share the gospel, but you will as well. You will constantly be reminded of all the good God has brought into your life in the gospel and you will be encouraged to travel God's good path more faithfully. "I pray that you may be active in sharing your faith, so that you will have a full understanding of every good thing we have in Christ" (Philemon 1:6). Close the gap on your understanding of the good you have in Christ by making Christ known to others.

Day 5
Read:
Matt. 28:18-20 Then Jesus came to them and said, "All authority in heaven and on earth has been given to me. Therefore go and make disciples of all nations, baptizing them in the name of the Father and of the Son and of the Holy Spirit, and teaching them to obey everything I have commanded you. And surely I am with you always, to the very end of the age."

Reflect:
Many dying leaders have given final words of exhortation and instruction. Only one leader in human history has given post-mortem instructions, the Lord Jesus. He died, resurrected, and then gave his followers some additional life-instructions. Someone might say a deceased loved one is always "with them" meaning in their memory, or indirectly impacting their lives through former example, but in fact that loved one is not with them in terms of being able to interact and communicate and help them. Jesus, on the other hand, is actually alive. He doesn't exist in the same mortal existence that we do, but he exists and interacts with us nonetheless. This may sound strange, or impossible, but even those people who disbelieve in the supernatural world still believe in more dimensions than what our physical senses can experience. So when Jesus said, "surely, I am with you to the very end of the age" this was no hyperbole. It was a declaration of fact. "Surely" can also mean "look here!" or "pay attention!" Jesus was putting an exclamation mark on his instructions. This is no dead leader saying, "Carry on without me." This is a risen Lord saying, "Carry on with me." Jesus is at work in the lives of people around us. Are you looking for him there?

Jesus is moving in your office, classroom, and home. He is at work in hospitals, battlefields, courtrooms, playgrounds... everywhere people are, he is at work there. Do you see him there? Will you join him there? You don't have to "sell" the good news; you only need to "tell" it. There is no pressure to produce results, there is only the opportunity to join him in what he is doing in the lives of people. It is important that you "pay attention" to what he is doing because "surely he is with you" to the end of the age and to the end of this day. Look for him today... join him today.

Week 39/Day 1
Read:

Acts 1:8-11 But you will receive power when the Holy Spirit comes on you; and you will be my witnesses in Jerusalem, and in all Judea and Samaria, and to the ends of the earth." After he said this, he was taken up before their very eyes, and a cloud hid him from their sight. They were looking intently up into the sky as he was going, when suddenly two men dressed in white stood beside them. "Men of Galilee," they said, "why do you stand here looking into the sky? This same Jesus, who has been taken from you into heaven, will come back in the same way you have seen him go into heaven."

Reflect:

Power is ability. If a drill has power it is able to function as a tool to drill holes. The sun has power. It is able to warm the earth to maintain life on earth. When a person becomes a follower of Christ, they have received the Holy Spirit who permanently resides in them. When the Holy Spirit comes he brings latent power. Latent power is real, but not yet released. The drill has latent power, but the power must be released in order for it to accomplish its purpose. The sun continually releases photons into space toward our planet. The power has to be released in order to enable life. In the same way, if you are a believer you have latent power in you. Power that is real and ready to be released, but it must be released. The power that is at issue here is the power to be witnesses to the gospel of Christ. Is that power operational or latent in your life? Do you belong to him? Have you believed and received the gospel? If so, then the Holy Spirit has taken up residence in you and brought with him power. That power is meant to be released into gospel-centered relationships and a gospel-centered lifestyle. Is it? If not, do you know why? There are several reasons why the power of gospel witness might not be operational in your life. It could be that apathy has taken over your heart and mind. Apathy is a power drain. It runs in the background of our lives, removing motivation and ability to proactively make Christ known to others. It could be disbelief. Disbelief disconnects us from the available power source. Perhaps you believe, but you are praying at the same time, "Lord, help my unbelief." Unbelief often takes the form of "I *sort of* believe."

This means that we believe enough to "hang on" personally to the gospel lifestyle, but we don't believe enough to actively and passionately and consistently make Christ known to others. Unreleased power is the same as no power at all, but perhaps worse. Where there is no power available, there is no accountability. Where the power is available but unreleased, there is responsibility and there will be accountability. On the positive side, where there is power available, there is also opportunity. The Holy Spirit's power in you is great and your opportunity is as well.

Day 2
Read: Acts 1:8 But you will receive power when the Holy Spirit comes on you; and you will be my witnesses in Jerusalem, and in all Judea and Samaria, and to the ends of the earth."

Reflect:
This passage serves as the outline of the rest of the book of Acts. The Holy Spirit did indeed come on them and the gospel spread out geographically from Jerusalem to Judea onto Samaria, and then beyond. The gospel continues to spread across the globe. In many places it has ebbed and flowed over the years. There have been times when it appears that the gospel light is going to be snuffed out, but then like an ember blown alive by the wind, the fire breaks out again. The gospel spread out from Jerusalem because of persecution. Trouble has often been a catalyst for the spread of the gospel, both on a macro scale as large populations experience hardship and also on a micro scale as individuals suffer and in their suffering they began to fully rely on God. Why does it take trouble for us to see what is valuable? John wrote in Revelation to seven churches; he had different things to say about each of them. To the church at Laodicea he rebuked them for being "lukewarm." They were never completely cold toward God nor were they hot toward him. You would think "lukewarm" would be preferable to God over cold, but that is not the case. Perhaps because spiritual "coldness" is clearly distinguishable from being spiritually "on fire." But lukewarm could pass for cold, or hot, or neither. It is confusing for people to look at a church that claims to follow the Messiah who died for the sins of all people and yet it is sitting idle, void of passion for the claims of Christ. Spiritual coldness is not confusing. Being spiritually on fire is not confusing. But being spiritually lukewarm is confusing. Worse than confusing, it is disgusting to God. Part of what made the church at Laodicea lukewarm was their wealth. Listen to part of the rebuke they received. "You say, 'I am rich; I have acquired wealth and do not need a thing.' But you do not realize that you are wretched, pitiful, poor, blind and naked" (Rev. 3:17). Most people in America have ready access to food, water, shelter, protection, and entertainment and would be considered as rich as kings when compared to people who lived in the first century or to people who live in most places in the world today.

We may not consider ourselves to be wealthy and feel like we do need many things, but nevertheless our relative wealth can blind us to our great need for God. As a result, our hunger for Christ is muted and, therefore, our passion for the gospel is as well. If we fail to understand our deep need for Christ, then we are unlikely to understand the need others have for him as well. The Lord went on to speak these words to all the churches and he speaks them to us still. "Those whom I love I rebuke and discipline. So be earnest, and repent" (Rev. 3:19). God, help us repent and be people with fire in our hearts for him.

Day 3
Read:
Acts 1:8-11 But you will receive power when the Holy Spirit comes on you; and you will be my witnesses in Jerusalem, and in all Judea and Samaria, and to the ends of the earth." After he said this, he was taken up before their very eyes, and a cloud hid him from their sight. They were looking intently up into the sky as he was going, when suddenly two men dressed in white stood beside them. "Men of Galilee," they said, "why do you stand here looking into the sky? This same Jesus, who has been taken from you into heaven, will come back in the same way you have seen him go into heaven."

Reflect:
Is evangelism religious bigotry? To tell someone they "need" Jesus is to indirectly tell them that if they believe something other than the gospel is true, then they are wrong. The fact is, all people believe that what they believe is true. Otherwise, they would believe something else. If they believe their belief is true, then by default they must believe other beliefs are not true. But what of those who are more "generous" in their beliefs? What of those who believe that all beliefs are equally valid; don't they escape the "trap" of religious bigotry? Not really. If they believe all beliefs are equally valid, then the first problem they have is what to do with the fact that many beliefs are mutually exclusive. To be mutually exclusive means that you cannot hold them all to be true at the same time. The other problem is that if you believe all beliefs are equally valid, then what do you do with the belief that says there is only one valid belief? The dilemma here is that the view that all beliefs are valid cannot accept the opposing view that all beliefs are not valid. Therefore, no one is truly completely inclusive in their beliefs. Something is ultimately true and other beliefs that are at odds with this truth are wrong. You can be mean and bigoted whether you are right or wrong about something, but to believe you are right and others are wrong does not automatically make you mean and bigoted. Followers of Christ are to approach all people with kindness and gentleness. They are to listen and seek to understand, not merely talk and seek to be understood.

179

They are to accept and love people where they are and pray and encourage them to become who God wants them to be. If you seek to make Christ known to those who do not know him, you may well be misunderstood and criticized. You may be accused of being mean-spirited and judgmental. Just be sure that you are not mean and judgmental. Make sure the accusations are false. Love God. Love people. Love God and people by making God's love known to people. "This is how we know what love is: Jesus Christ laid down his life for us. And we ought to lay down our lives for our brothers" (1 John 3:16).

Day 4
Read:
Acts 1:8-11 But you will receive power when the Holy Spirit comes on you; and you will be my witnesses in Jerusalem, and in all Judea and Samaria, and to the ends of the earth." After he said this, he was taken up before their very eyes, and a cloud hid him from their sight. They were looking intently up into the sky as he was going, when suddenly two men dressed in white stood beside them. "Men of Galilee," they said, "why do you stand here looking into the sky? This same Jesus, who has been taken from you into heaven, will come back in the same way you have seen him go into heaven."

Reflect:
A witness is someone who claims personal knowledge and experience of something. You don't have to have seen something with your physical eyes to qualify as a witness. The disciples were eyewitnesses to the life, death, and resurrection of Christ. As followers of Christ, we are not eyewitnesses to Christ's physical life on earth. However, we are "ear witnesses" to the truth of the gospel, "heart witnesses" to the impact of the gospel, and eyewitnesses to the change the gospel brings in our lives. It does not make you less of a qualified witness because you have not seen the Lord with your physical eyes. In fact, Jesus says it makes you more of a "blessed" witness that you have believed without seeing. "Then Jesus told him, 'Because you have seen me, you have believed; blessed are those who have not seen and yet have believed' "(John 20:29). It is not irrational or unreasonable to give your life for a Savior you have not seen with your eyes. Peter did see the Lord Jesus with his physical eyes, but he did not consider that to be a qualification for experiencing Jesus personally. He wrote, "Though you have not seen him, you love him; and even though you do not see him now, you believe in him and are filled with an inexpressible and glorious joy, for you are receiving the goal of your faith, the salvation of your souls" (1 Peter 1:8-9). Notice that Peter did not make salvation an entirely future tense experience. He said that salvation is ongoing, in this life, for those who believe and love the Lord. If you have put your confidence in Jesus and have surrendered your life to him, you are a qualified witness.

This is not presumption; this is something he has given to you as both a privilege and a responsibility. You should not say "I believe" as in "I think" or "I believe but can't prove or know for certain." Instead, you should say "I believe" as in I am certain and I am currently experiencing the reality of new life in Christ. I have not seen him, but I am a qualified and confident witness to his life.

Day 5
Read:
Acts 1:8-11 But you will receive power when the Holy Spirit comes on you; and you will be my witnesses in Jerusalem, and in all Judea and Samaria, and to the ends of the earth." After he said this, he was taken up before their very eyes, and a cloud hid him from their sight. They were looking intently up into the sky as he was going, when suddenly two men dressed in white stood beside them. "Men of Galilee," they said, "why do you stand here looking into the sky? This same Jesus, who has been taken from you into heaven, will come back in the same way you have seen him go into heaven."

Reflect:
Is this a command or merely a statement of fact? Is Jesus saying, "you must be my witnesses" or that "you will be my witnesses"? It is no minor distinction. You do not have to tell an apple tree to produce fruit. If you plant it in the earth and if it receives light and moisture and grows to maturity, fruit will happen. The apple tree is not commanded to bear fruit. It has the "power" to do so by virtue of how God has designed it. Of course, in Matthew chapter twenty-eight Jesus did command his followers to go make disciples and to teach them to obey him. But here, in Acts 1, it seems the result of the Holy Spirit coming in power into their lives was that they would witness to the reality of Jesus. If we are not faithful witnesses, does it mean that the Holy Spirit is not resident in us? Not necessarily, but it does indicate that the Holy Spirit is not released in and through us. If the apple tree bears no fruit, it does not cease to be an apple tree and the latent power in it has not ceased to exist. The power to produce apples remains in it by virtue of it being a true apple tree, but that power is unreleased and so it is fruitless. There are many reasons why an apple tree doesn't bear fruit and there are many reasons why a Christian might not bear fruit as well. None of the reasons why a Christian doesn't bear fruit are irreparable; the cause of the fruitlessness can be fixed. If you look at your life and see no gospel witness over a long period of time, then understand that this is evidence of a problem to be addressed. Do not wallow in guilt and despair, instead simply ask God to help you see why the Holy Spirit who lives in you is not empowering your life as a witness to the gospel. He will show you if you ask him. It might be apathy, or unbelief, or you may have wrapped your heart around some idol, or any other number of reasons.

181

Whatever the reason, he will reveal it to you if you ask him. But if you ask him to reveal the reason, be prepared to repent of that reason. Repent and release the power of God that lies dormant and is ready to touch the lives of people who are far from God but close to you.

Week 40/Day 1
Read:
1 Pet. 4:10-11 Each one should use whatever gift he has received to serve others, faithfully administering God's grace in its various forms. If anyone speaks, he should do it as one speaking the very words of God. If anyone serves, he should do it with the strength God provides, so that in all things God may be praised through Jesus Christ. To him be the glory and the power for ever and ever. Amen.

Reflect:
When a child receives a gift, he is not prone to want to share it. Perhaps when he has grown tired of it or if it is replaced with another gift that is more interesting, he might let other children have access to the gift. But the child normally sees a gift as being entirely for his own pleasure, not for the enjoyment of others. As we mature we come to see the reality that our enjoyment of gifts is multiplied when we share them with others. As we put childish ways behind us we learn to use whatever gifts we receive to serve others not self. God gives his people spiritual gifts and these gifts are sources of great joy for the recipient, but only as they are used to serve others. We are really conduits or pipelines of God's gifts. His grace flows into us in the form of certain capabilities and opportunities and then it flows through us to others as they are blessed by our expression of his gifts. If our hearts turn into reservoirs rather than pipelines we are not able to "hoard" more joy and satisfaction. His life "in" us is meant to be his life "through" us. If we shut off the outflow, then we are also shutting off the inflow. This is part of what Paul meant in his prayer for Philemon: "I pray that you may be active in sharing your faith, so that you will have a full understanding of every good thing we have in Christ" (Phm. 1:6). It was to be Philemon's sharing of the gift of faith that would lead to a fuller understanding and enjoyment of all that was his in Christ. The principle is clear; you have been gifted by God to serve others. When you serve others you are in a real sense "serving self" because your own joy and life satisfaction is multiplied. Selfishness is a universally failed method for personal happiness; it has never worked and it will never work. Serving others is a universally successful method for personal happiness. How much more so when your service is a conduit of the grace of God to others!

Day 2
Read:

1 Pet. 4:10-11 Each one should use whatever gift he has received to serve others, faithfully administering God's grace in its various forms. If anyone speaks, he should do it as one speaking the very words of God. If anyone serves, he should do it with the strength God provides, so that in all things God may be praised through Jesus Christ. To him be the glory and the power for ever and ever. Amen.

Reflect:

In regard to personal gifting it's possible that we might fall into one of two errors. One error is to believe you are more and better than you actually are. This attitude fails to take into account the fact that gifts are received and not earned. Paul declares this to be true with his rhetorical question: "For who makes you different from anyone else? What do you have that you did not receive? And if you did receive it, why do you boast as though you did not?" (1 Cor. 4:7). Clearly, boasting about a gift is wrong, but on the other hand to fall into the opposite error is equally harmful. The second error occurs when someone from a misguided sense of humility, or maybe pride-based shame, downplays their gifting. Paul combines both of these errors in his letter to the church at Galatia. "If anyone thinks he is something when he is nothing, he deceives himself. Each one should test his own actions. Then he can take pride in himself, without comparing himself to somebody else" (Gal. 6:3-4). We must learn to lean into the wind that blows in our lives. Does the wind of pride in your gifting blow strong in your life? If so, then lean hard into it by continually remembering that your gifts are from God, for the good of the others, for the glory of God. If, instead, the wind of insecurity or false humility blows hard, then lean into it by remembering that God has indeed gifted you and he intends for you to use those gifts to serve him by serving others. Do not put up with pride or insecurity, neither have anything at all to do with using gifts. Both pride and insecurity result from making life about us. Close the gap on faith and love by seeing how God has gifted you and by getting busy using that gifting to serve others. If you wish that God had gifted you otherwise, quickly and consistently put those thoughts away. Do not compare your gifting with that of someone else. There is no joy and no benefit in that. Their gift came from God, as did yours. In the end, no one will care a whit about who had what gift, all that will remain is faithfulness. Be found faithful with what God has given you today.

Day 3
Read:

1 Pet. 4:10-11 Each one should use whatever gift he has received to serve others, faithfully administering God's grace in its various forms. If anyone speaks, he should do it as one speaking the very words of God.

If anyone serves, he should do it with the strength God provides, so that in all things God may be praised through Jesus Christ. To him be the glory and the power for ever and ever. Amen.

Reflect:
To use (or administer) your gifts to serve others is to be a good steward of God's grace in your life. The words "various forms" mean multifaceted or multi-colored. Think of this in terms of God's grace being a beautiful diamond that is held up to the light and as you turn the diamond the various colors of the light spectrum are reflected to the eyes revealing more fully its beauty. The church (individual believers living life together) reflect the manifold glory of the Lord through the faithful expression of the gifts God has given. This fuller expression of his grace to us leads to a fuller experience of his grace in us. We become more like Christ over time as we serve others with the gifts he has given us. "And we, who with unveiled faces all reflect the Lord's glory, are being transformed into his likeness with ever-increasing glory, which comes from the Lord, who is the Spirit" (2 Cor. 3:18). A life of serving others is the only possible way to experience and enjoy life as God has designed it. Whenever something is used in a way that defies its original design and purpose the result is frustration and eventually brokenness. This is true of tools and machines as well as people. You were designed by a master designer for his purposes. Ultimately, his purpose is that you would bring him joy and glory by loving him and loving others. To this end he gives unique gifts and opportunities. When these gifts and opportunities are not used to their proper end, then frustration and emptiness will always result. Do you feel frequent frustration, emptiness or lack of purpose in your day to day life? Then take a hard look at your actions, your attitudes, or both. Take a look at your actions, are you "using your life" to serve others or mostly to serve self? Take a look at your attitudes, perhaps you are serving but you are doing so grudgingly, not joyfully. Close the gap on actions and attitudes. See service as your privilege and your responsibility. See it as your purpose and your opportunity to live life as God has designed it to be lived.

Day 4
Read:
1 Pet. 4:10-11 Each one should use whatever gift he has received to serve others, faithfully administering God's grace in its various forms. If anyone speaks, he should do it as one speaking the very words of God. If anyone serves, he should do it with the strength God provides, so that in all things God may be praised through Jesus Christ. To him be the glory and the power for ever and ever. Amen.

Reflect:

"Husbands, love your wives, just as Christ loved the church and gave himself up for her" (Eph. 5:25). It is always good for husbands to be challenged to love their wives, but the application of that verse for today is that "Christ loved the church and gave himself up for her." If we love Christ, we will love the church. Some see the church as irrelevant in regard to a "personal" relationship with Christ. The Bible, and therefore God himself, would not agree with that assessment. The church was and is and will be God's plan for his people to live in relationship with him. By "personal" relationship, if one means that each person must choose individually to follow Christ, then that is correct. However, often it means that my relationship with God is entirely "my own business" and it has little or nothing to do with others. It is this kind of thinking that Paul addressed in 1 Corinthians 12. He uses the analogy of a physical body to describe how the church, a spiritual body, is made up of individual parts. Each part needs the others. An unattached physical arm, or eye, or leg, is a horrific thought, a tragedy. Likewise, an unattached and uncommitted member of Christ's body, the church, is a tragic and horrific thing. It simply ought not to be. Peter, of course, agrees with Paul on this matter. The only way each individual can use their gifts to serve one another is to live in connected relationship in a local body. Of course, the "Church" is made up of all Christ followers of all time periods and in every place. However; for the most part, in order to use your gifts to serve one another you must live in the same time and place with them. In your physical body, your arm doesn't live in jealousy of your leg and your eye doesn't hold a grudge against your ears. Your body is many parts, but they form a single whole and they work together for the common good. When this is not true, there is disease and dysfunction in the body. Lay aside jealousy and pettiness. The people who are busy using their gifts to serve others are the very people who are enjoying the most meaningful and satisfying lives. What might be keeping you from consistently enjoying this kind of life?

Day 5
Read:

1 Pet. 4:10-11 Each one should use whatever gift he has received to serve others, faithfully administering God's grace in its various forms. If anyone speaks, he should do it as one speaking the very words of God. If anyone serves, he should do it with the strength God provides, so that in all things God may be praised through Jesus Christ. To him be the glory and the power for ever and ever. Amen.

Reflect:

This might on the surface seem presumptuous - to speak for God and to act as if God were acting through you. However, clearly it is the opposite of presumption; it is obedience.

We have been commissioned, sent to speak and to serve for God. In fact, what this verse tells us is that we "must" see ourselves as directly speaking for God. This means we must have a working knowledge of what God has said to us in his word. Then we are to use those words to serve one another by speaking that truth to them. How are we to serve one another with the strength God provides? This can mean a number of things, but at the very least it means that we will often find ourselves using the gifts he has given us to serve others in ways that seem way beyond our own strength and ability. To serve with the strength God provides has, as its ultimate aim, that God is praised. He is the sole "celebrity" in the universe. He alone is worthy of worship and praise. How do we ensure that he receives the praise for our service to others? It's not by merely mouthing humble sounding words. If someone says to you, "Thank you for your service, it was meaningful to me," there is no real humility in saying, "Oh, it was nothing." It was obviously not "nothing" to them! Better to say, "You are welcome. I was happy to do it." Then be sure your heart is becoming more and more truly happy to serve. God receives praise through our service when we serve with willing hearts because of love for God and others. He is glorified when we serve with the strength he provides. This strength is revealed when we feel too tired, too selfish, too lazy, or too passive to serve, but we do it anyway. It is no mere cliché to say that we are most likely to see God's power when we come to end of our own. Do not stop serving others when you are out of strength, this could be the point where you actually serve them out of God's strength. Of course, this can be taken too far because rest is good and necessary, but the point remains, serve others out of his strength not just your own.

Week 41/Day 1
Read:
1 John 1:5-11 This is the message we have heard from him and declare to you: God is light; in him there is no darkness at all. If we claim to have fellowship with him yet walk in the darkness, we lie and do not live by the truth. But if we walk in the light, as he is in the light, we have fellowship with one another, and the blood of Jesus, his Son, purifies us from all sin. If we claim to be without sin, we deceive ourselves and the truth is not in us. If we confess our sins, he is faithful and just and will forgive us our sins and purify us from all unrighteousness. If we claim we have not sinned, we make him out to be a liar and his word has no place in our lives.

Reflect:
Darkness is the absence of light. When light is low or absent altogether the human eye is unable to perceive color. Everything becomes shades of grey until finally all becomes black. Light is essential to seeing.

Even in the darkest night the trees, flowers, and lakes retain the properties that give them "greenness" or "redness" or "blueness," but in the dark of night their beauty is unrevealed to our eyes. Likewise, dangers are hidden in the dark. One could stumble off a cliff on a dark trail because the eye cannot perceive the break in the trail. Light is essential for beauty and also for safety. God is said to be "light" or "*photos*" in the Greek. That, of course, is the word from which we get photon. Photons are the packets or particles of light that bounce off objects and then strike our retinas creating images that we can see. God is essential for "seeing" things as they are. In him there is no darkness, there is never a time or circumstance in which he does not clearly see what actually is and even what actually should be. His "light" extends into the past and the future; he sees all time and all events as an eternal "now." He also "sees" into our hearts. He has perfect clarity on our motives and desires. He sees through our words and our emotions and our attempts to hide from the truth that is inside us. He sees exactly what is real and true about us. This can be terrifying or this can be, and should be, a great relief. We really don't have to expend the energy to pretend or to hide anymore. God sees everything anyway. He can see you better than you can see yourself. Yet, he has accepted you in Christ Jesus. Therefore, you can rest in his light. We normally prefer to physically rest or sleep in darkness, but for spiritual rest we need light. We need to understand that there is no dark to him. There is no hiding our deeds, our thoughts, or our motives from him. All is laid bare before him and, yet, he does not despise us. He loves us. Rest now, but don't sleep, in the light. Be honest with who you really are and what is really going on inside of you with God. He sees it...talk to him about it.

Day 2
Read:
1 John 1:5-11 This is the message we have heard from him and declare to you: God is light; in him there is no darkness at all. If we claim to have fellowship with him yet walk in the darkness, we lie and do not live by the truth. But if we walk in the light, as he is in the light, we have fellowship with one another, and the blood of Jesus, his Son, purifies us from all sin. If we claim to be without sin, we deceive ourselves and the truth is not in us. If we confess our sins, he is faithful and just and will forgive us our sins and purify us from all unrighteousness. If we claim we have not sinned, we make him out to be a liar and his word has no place in our lives.

Reflect:
To say God is light is another way of saying he is "truth." The light reveals what is actually there. If it becomes dark enough, visual perception goes away completely. Consequently, John wrote that if we walk in the dark, then we are not living in the truth. There are many ways to live in this "lie-dark" rather than the "truth-light."

It could be denying the truth of the gospel itself. It could be denying that we are sinful and need the gospel personally. It could be claiming to have close relationship with God and yet having broken relationships with the people around us. Clearly, there are times when having a relationship with others is beyond our control. But, when it is within our ability to have fellowship with others and we do not because of our own hardness or selfishness or even because we are hiding the true "us" from others, then we are not able to live in fellowship with God. It seems like this is stating the obvious, that we cannot walk in the "lie-dark" and the "truth-light" at the same time. However, one of the many terrible things of the "lie-dark" is that it tricks us into thinking it is the light. We can, instead, believe that this grey world around us is the way things really are. We can think that a world of colors and safety and beauty in relationships with God and others is all a myth. It is all a beautiful lie. The real world is shades of grey and ultimately just a monolithic blackness. War is normal, divorce is normal, hate is normal, division is normal, brokenness is normal, darkness is the norm. But what is "normal" is not what is "natural". God has designed us to live in the light and in the light we have fellowship with him. When we have fellowship with him, then we have fellowship with one another. Fellowship means partnership or communion. It means we have significant, honest friendship with others. We see each other and we love each other. Even as he sees us and loves us. He is the sun that gives the light that allows us to see each other in all of our imperfections and our uniqueness. If we walk in his light, then we have fellowship with one another. Enter this day without the shades of grey that can take us over. See people today in full color. See them as God sees them.

Day 3
Read:
1 John 1:5-11 This is the message we have heard from him and declare to you: God is light; in him there is no darkness at all. If we claim to have fellowship with him yet walk in the darkness, we lie and do not live by the truth. But if we walk in the light, as he is in the light, we have fellowship with one another, and the blood of Jesus, his Son, purifies us from all sin. If we claim to be without sin, we deceive ourselves and the truth is not in us. If we confess our sins, he is faithful and just and will forgive us our sins and purify us from all unrighteousness. If we claim we have not sinned, we make him out to be a liar and his word has no place in our lives.

Reflect:
Who would ever claim to be without sin? Surely, nobody is that "self-unaware"! There are those who claim to live a sinless life and there are those who don't believe sin is even a real thing at all. It's not likely that we would believe we are sinless or that sin doesn't exist. It is more likely that we will sin and then deny that we did.

We tend to see sin more easily in others than in ourselves. We also tend to "weigh" sin on a scale and to do so in our own favor. So, we may see that we have sinned, but believe that our own sin is not as bad (or heavy) as someone else's. We can easily deceive ourselves and fail to live in the full light of truth. To live in the light requires openness and honesty about our own sins and failures. This life in the light begins with honesty with God, but it does not end there. We must also practice living open and honest lives with one another. Confessing our sins to one another is important for maintaining clear relationships, but it is also vital for experiencing victory over sin. As we live openly and honestly with one another about our personal struggles, we are positioned to get help and encouragement from each other. In addition, the humbling process of confessing our sins opens up pathways of God's grace into our lives that can translate into victory over sin patterns. We will either humble ourselves or sin will humiliate us. Humiliation is not required, but humility is. An open and honest lifestyle is a life in the light of truth. If you have practiced hiding parts of your life in the shadows, this idea can be a frightening thing to consider. But the light of truth will set you free. You must make the "faith-choice" to step into it and the ongoing choice to stay in the light. You don't have to tell everyone your struggles, nor should you. However, you must have someone you can tell them to. You must drag your sins into the light so they will not drag you further into the dark. You can do this. God stands ready to provide his grace.

Day 4
Read:

1 John 1:5-11 This is the message we have heard from him and declare to you: God is light; in him there is no darkness at all. If we claim to have fellowship with him yet walk in the darkness, we lie and do not live by the truth. But if we walk in the light, as he is in the light, we have fellowship with one another, and the blood of Jesus, his Son, purifies us from all sin. If we claim to be without sin, we deceive ourselves and the truth is not in us. If we confess our sins, he is faithful and just and will forgive us our sins and purify us from all unrighteousness. If we claim we have not sinned, we make him out to be a liar and his word has no place in our lives.

Reflect:

1 John 1:9 has been called "spiritual breathing." When we sin we "exhale confession and inhale forgiveness." This truth does not imply "cheap grace" or that the confession of sin is a small, insignificant thing. What it means is that we can and we should move through life keeping short accounts with God. We do not have to try and pay for sin by "feeling bad" or by hiding from God in shame until we believe we have "suffered adequately." We can move through life constantly "breathing" God's grace. We cannot pay for our sins and we must not try.

Repentance is the process whereby we see our sins as God does, then we turn around and go his direction. This process begins in our minds, but shows up ultimately in our actions. Since God stands so ready to forgive, we should both stand ready to forgive one another and also to quickly and completely confess our sins to one another. This lifestyle of "spiritual breathing" can empower us to live more open and honest lives because we don't have to hide from one another in shame. We don't have to pretend we are doing better than we actually are. As we comprehend that we are fully accepted and forgiven by God, then we can take greater risks to forgive and accept one another. A person whose foundational relationship is secure is able to venture out into other less secure relationships. The foundational relationship for all of humanity is with God, who is the creator and Father of us all. In the gospel, that relationship has been restored and permanently secured. Now, from that secure foundation we can love, forgive, and live appropriately open lives with one another. This secure foundation doesn't mean we will never suffer difficulty in relationships or that we cannot be hurt by others. It does mean that we will increasingly be able to approach one another in ways that seek to give life rather than take it. This fact alone increases the overall health of our relationships. Our relationships can now reflect his abundance rather than merely our own need because he is continually meeting our deepest need.

Day 5
Read:
1 John 1:5-11 This is the message we have heard from him and declare to you: God is light; in him there is no darkness at all. If we claim to have fellowship with him yet walk in the darkness, we lie and do not live by the truth. But if we walk in the light, as he is in the light, we have fellowship with one another, and the blood of Jesus, his Son, purifies us from all sin. If we claim to be without sin, we deceive ourselves and the truth is not in us. If we confess our sins, he is faithful and just and will forgive us our sins and purify us from all unrighteousness. If we claim we have not sinned, we make him out to be a liar and his word has no place in our lives.

Reflect:
When two people (or more) walk together in the light, then they have fellowship with one another and they experience the ongoing beauty of continually renewed relationships with one another. In all human relationships two things are necessary. One is that they are going in a common direction. You cannot "walk" with someone if you are going one way and they are going another. Of course, you can still be friends with people who do not share your life purpose. These friendships can be deep and meaningful, but in the end, if they do not ultimately value what you hold most valuable, the friendship will have something of a hollow core.

The other necessary factor is that as the two walk together on a common path they will need to continually forgive and be forgiven. There is just no way for people to live life together and not sin against one another. So, the common denominator in this common life is Jesus. He is the purpose for our lives; he is our common path. He is also the reason we can continually forgive and be forgiven. Jesus is the light and the path we walk and it his blood that cleanses us from all sin. Open and honest lives are not about demonstrating perfection in every action, but rather perfection in overall direction. We walk with him together and we give and receive his grace together when we fail him and one another. The light is terror to those who do not want to live in open and honest relationships. The light exposes what has been hidden and what wants to remain in the dark. The light is pure joy to those who desire open and honest relationships. It exposes what is a threat to relationship so that it can be dealt with and not hidden away. If you have a subtle or not so subtle fear of being exposed, will you ask God to help you love the light? Will you trust God enough to trust others to truly know you? You are as healthy as your secrets. Bring the light into the dark places so that, over time, there are no more dark places in your heart and life.

Week 42/Day 1
Read:
Matt. 5:23-24 Therefore, if you are offering your gift at the altar and there remember that your brother has something against you, leave your gift there in front of the altar. First go and be reconciled to your brother; then come and offer your gift.

Reflect:
The Lord gives an example in action of what John gives us in principle. "If anyone says, 'I love God,' yet hates his brother, he is a liar. For anyone who does not love his brother, whom he has seen, cannot love God, whom he has not seen" (1 John 4:20). Jesus describes a situation where someone has gone to worship and while in the act of worship remembers, or the Lord brings to mind, someone they have sinned against. The intuitive thing would be to finish what you are doing, complete your time of worship, and then go make things right with the other person. But the Lord frequently gives direction that is counter-intuitive. We are prone to trust our "intuition" but that is often a mistake. We must learn to trust the Lord and to do as he says. The principle in practice here is that it is not possible to be in right relationship with God if we are not in right relationship with others. We must continually do all we can to maintain clear relationships with others. There are, of course, times when this is not possible because others refuse to have relationship of any kind with us. But when it is up to us and as far as possible, we must live at peace with all people (Romans 12:18). Maintaining clear relationships is an ongoing, lifelong process.

This should not be a surprise because virtually everything about our lives requires ongoing maintenance. Your home, your physical health, your clothes, your car. All these things and more require regular attention and energy. If we do not maintain them, they will fall into disrepair and become even greater burdens. Passivity is one enemy of clear relationships with others. If we believe that relationships can run on "auto-pilot" and that we do not have to devote regular efforts to keeping them healthy, then they will stop "running" at all and they will become "sick." The regular efforts required to maintain good relationships with others is nothing at all compared with the enormous cost of having broken relationships, especially when those relationships are the ones who are supposed to be the closest to you. You see how important clear relationships are to God; they must become as important to you as well. God does not hold you to account for the choices of others, only for your own. If others do not respond well to your efforts, leave them to God. But you must put forth appropriate and consistent effort. Does this sound hard and tiring? Again, it is a very small price to pay for a great treasure, a life of clear relationships and a clear conscience before God and others.

Day 2
Read:
Matt. 5:23-24 Therefore, if you are offering your gift at the altar and there remember that your brother has something against you, leave your gift there in front of the altar. First go and be reconciled to your brother; then come and offer your gift.

Reflect:
We are so different. We see things so differently. How is it possible to maintain constantly clear relationships with one another? How different do you suppose we are than God? How differently (and correctly, I might add) does he see the world than we do? Yet, he is willing to take the initiative in relationship with us. It is from his absolute spiritual "maturity" that he moves towards us in grace. As we close the gap on spiritual maturity ourselves, we will more and more move towards each other in grace. We will not focus on the petty differences, instead we will focus on the priority of faith expressing itself in love. The heart behind the action outlined by the Lord in today's passage is one of love for God expressed in obedience to God. This obedience is revealed in moving towards others in love and so the circle of "love to faith to love" is complete. If you will think clearly and correctly about this matter of "maintaining clear relationships," you will find yourself enjoying more and more people and thriving on the very differences that used to annoy and divide. You will find that God himself will choose friends for you that you would never choose for yourself. These friends will become very dear and precious to you and you will know that your life would have been less if God had not brought them into it.

192

It is important that you understand that if you will experience God like this, you must actually let him select your friends. It doesn't mean you have no say in the matter, but it does mean you must not "pre-decide" whom you can learn to love. If you do, you will frequently get it wrong; there are many more people that we can love than we now imagine. Open wide your heart and your mind. Grace is a spacious place with room for so many, but judgment is a small and cramped space with room only for self. Eventually judgment will run out of room even for self and you will find yourself unhappy everywhere, all the time. Grace continually grows in its capacity for happiness, as more and more people are welcomed into our lives. Who is God trying to bring into your heart and life? Will you let them in?

Day 3
Read:
Matt. 5:23-24 Therefore, if you are offering your gift at the altar and there remember that your brother has something against you, leave your gift there in front of the altar. First go and be reconciled to your brother; then come and offer your gift.

Reflect:
The Lord said we must not proceed in worship until we have made things right with one another. Paul said we should not proceed to another day holding on to bitterness towards one another. " 'In your anger do not sin': Do not let the sun go down while you are still angry, and do not give the devil a foothold" (Eph. 4:26-27). It is interesting that Paul separates anger and sin. This doesn't mean that you should harbor or hold on to anger, because his point is not that there are times when anger is okay. Rather, his point is that we must not let anger take hold in our hearts, because if we do, then we are allowing the enemy to set up camp in our hearts as well. If he establishes a foothold, then it is not long before he can establish a stronghold. From that stronghold he can carry out all kinds of attacks in many different areas our lives. Of course, there are things that we can legitimately become angry about, but again, the principle here is that we must not let anger dominate to the point that we carry it over from one day to the next. If we become angry with one another and then we sleep on that anger and wake up angry the next day, we have potentially embedded that anger in our hearts. Do this often enough and you will not merely be a person who gets angry, you will become an angry person. This is when the devil has set up an encampment in your heart. Our hearts are the home of the Holy Spirit and though we will become angry, we must not become angry people. Love, not anger, must define us. To maintain clear relationships with one another means we will act consistently and resolutely against fostering anger towards one another. We can experience and express it appropriately, but then we must give it to God and not allow it to become our constant companion.

193

Anger loves to unlock "heart-doors" to the devil. Grace and love will lock those doors to the enemy of your soul as they unlock them to God and others.

Day 4
Read:
Matt. 5:23-24 Therefore, if you are offering your gift at the altar and there remember that your brother has something against you, leave your gift there in front of the altar. First go and be reconciled to your brother; then come and offer your gift.

Reflect:
Divorce is common. Broken relationships are common. Division and separation are common. What is common is not what should be the norm. People living in long-term harmonious relationships is uncommon, but it should be normative. We were designed to live in community and ongoing harmony, but sin has reordered relationships where disharmony has become normal. The gospel is God's intrusion into the disorder of what has become normative in order to bring back the order of his original, intended norm. How can we say what should be normative? Some believe that whatever is, is right. But, if anyone is honest, they know that the psalmist was right when he wrote, "How good and pleasant it is when brothers live together in unity!"(Psalm 133:1) Of course, it is good and pleasing to see two people living in harmony. There is nothing pleasant or good about people who are at odds with one another. There can be no doubt that when two people purpose to live in unity, they can and they will. If one remains undetermined, then there is no guarantee of peace and harmony. But when both sides of a relationship are equally committed to the good of the relationship, then that relationship will be good and pleasant for them, for others, and for God himself. This is not naïve thinking, this is simple fact. What is uncommon and, therefore, rarely good and pleasant for many, should still be the bottom line norm in relationships for those who claim the name of Christ. You may believe you have good reason to hold a grudge or to not forgive. But if it is at all possible to regain a relationship, then you must do so because you have better reason to do it. You belong to Jesus; your life's purpose is to bring him glory and joy. It is good and pleasant for him when you live in unity with others. What is good and pleasant for him would be the same for us if our hearts were properly ordered. If you trust him enough to obey him by doing all you can to live in unity with others, then you will see him prove himself faithful. You will enjoy what he enjoys and you will experience in your life what is ultimately most valuable.

Day 5
Read:

Matt. 5:23-24 Therefore, if you are offering your gift at the altar and there remember that your brother has something against you, leave your gift there in front of the altar. First go and be reconciled to your brother; then come and offer your gift.

Reflect:

The Lord's demand that we maintain clear relationships is not a burden; it is an opportunity and a privilege. Ongoing strive, unconfessed and unforgiven sin, broken relationships...these things are a burden and a curse. When Jesus told the worshipper to stop his worship and go make things right with his brother, this was Jesus inviting the worshipper to experience life as it has been designed. It was Jesus inviting the worshipper into the Lord's quality of life. The Triune God had lived in unbroken fellowship since eternity past. The only time Jesus would experience anything resembling disunity would be when he bore our sins on the cross. There on the cross, in a way that is a mystery, God the Father turned his face away from God the Son. On the cross Jesus cried, "Why have you forsaken me?" This cry of despair was not a real question in that Jesus did not know why. It was a cry of pain, the pain of bearing our sin leading to relational separation he had not previously experienced. Jesus knew why God had to forsake him, but the pain of that experience was great indeed. Jesus bore our sins and willingly experienced the loss of fellowship with God the Father. He did this for us. We, on the other hand, experience the loss of fellowship with one another because of our sins and it need not be and it should not be. The gospel transforms our relationship with God and with one another. We do not have to experience separation from God and we do not have to experience separation from one another. There is simply no good reason for two Christ followers to live in ongoing disunity. So Jesus said, "Stop...I'll be ready for your worship when you return, now go to your friend, your brother, your sister, your son, your daughter, your parent. Make things right with them and then come back to me and we will truly enjoy our relationship." This is not Jesus laying a heavy burden on us; this is part of the gospel removing a heavy burden from us. Maintain clear relationships with others to whatever extent you possibly can. This is a benefit of the gospel gift that is yours to experience. Jesus experienced separation so that you can experience unity both with God and with one another. Do not despise this great gift; enjoy it.

Read:
Phil. 2:3-8 Do nothing out of selfish ambition or vain conceit, but in humility consider others better than yourselves. Each of you should look not only to your own interests, but also to the interests of others. Your attitude should be the same as that of Christ Jesus: Who, being in very nature God, did not consider equality with God something to be grasped, but made himself nothing, taking the very nature of a servant, being made in human likeness. And being found in appearance as a man, he humbled himself and became obedient to death — even death on a cross!

John 13:14-17 Now that I, your Lord and Teacher, have washed your feet, you also should wash one another's feet. I have set you an example that you should do as I have done for you. I tell you the truth, no servant is greater than his master, nor is a messenger greater than the one who sent him. Now that you know these things, you will be blessed if you do them.

Reflect:
We must pursue nothing. A life of nothing done from selfish ambition is our goal. Doing nothing out of selfish ambition seems like a high bar to clear. Nothing? Not a thing? This, of course, is not a New Testament grade card where you must get 100% in order to get an "A." It's not about grades; it's about hearts. Of course, perfection is the direction we are to head, where else would we go? Can you imagine if Paul wrote, "Don't do everything out of selfish ambition, try for fifty-fifty." This is how man-made religion would approach putting the interests of others ahead of your own. It would turn into a scorecard. Somewhere around 70% would be a passing grade. But it would be graded on a scale, so if you look around and see people who are much more selfish than you are, then you could turn that 70% into a perfect score. Or you could go well below 50% and still pass. But if this is the approach, then what has happened to the heart? It has become a scorekeeper, not a lover of God and others. This kind of heart tends to give itself more credit than it deserves and others less than they do. This kind of heart can and does even make serving others about self. Do you see, then? The standard is "nothing out of selfish ambition," because that is the heart of Jesus. To aim for something less than this would be to aim for something less than Jesus. Of course, we will never reach perfection in every action and attitude, but we must have as our goal to become like Christ. In addition, we must believe this is actually possible and then pursue every means available to ensure that it does happen in increasing fashion. "See to it, brothers, that none of you has a sinful, unbelieving heart that turns away from the living God" (Heb. 3:12). We must "see to it" that we do not turn away from God in disbelief. This proactive belief in God is to be manifest in real life choices.

We do not just hope that what God has called us to actually happen some day; we are to see that it does. Pursue "nothing"...this is the only realistic goal.

Day 2
Read:
Phil. 2:3-8 Do nothing out of selfish ambition or vain conceit, but in humility consider others better than yourselves. Each of you should look not only to your own interests, but also to the interests of others. Your attitude should be the same as that of Christ Jesus: Who, being in very nature God, did not consider equality with God something to be grasped, but made himself nothing, taking the very nature of a servant, being made in human likeness. And being found in appearance as a man, he humbled himself and became obedient to death — even death on a cross!

John 13:14-17 Now that I, your Lord and Teacher, have washed your feet, you also should wash one another's feet. I have set you an example that you should do as I have done for you. I tell you the truth, no servant is greater than his master, nor is a messenger greater than the one who sent him. Now that you know these things, you will be blessed if you do them.

Reflect:
"Beyond all question, the mystery of godliness is great: He appeared in a body, was vindicated by the Spirit, was seen by angels, was preached among the nations, was believed on in the world, was taken up in glory" (1 Tim. 3:16). Clearly, the incarnation is beyond our full comprehension. Paul outlines for Timothy the facts of the gospel, while at the same time confessing how this is all a great mystery. Yet, although it is a mystery, it is one that has been revealed in such ways that we can experience its power and change. We will never fully grasp what it means that "the Word became flesh and dwelt among us," but we can certainly understand the key implications for this great reality. First among them, of course, is that we can have relationship with God through the Son. But, in addition, we can have a different kind of life with one another as well. We can live similarly to the way Jesus lived; we can experience the joy he had as we seek to put the interests of others ahead of our own. We all do what makes sense to us. Sometimes what makes sense to us is foolish and, therefore, we do things that are foolish. For instance, very often it makes sense to us to make selfish choices, so we act selfishly. Then we find, over and over, that these selfish choices did not deliver what they had promised. We are not happier or more content. In fact, we are more dissatisfied and we are less content. Jesus always did what made sense to him as well. The difference is that what made sense to him was always right, it was always the best possible way to live.

Embed this thought in your mind...water it, fertilize it, let its roots grow deep into your brain so that it becomes a tree whose fruit falls out into all of your life...put the interests of others ahead of your own. This made sense to Jesus, therefore, it must consistently make sense to us.

Day 3
Read:
Phil. 2:3-8 Do nothing out of selfish ambition or vain conceit, but in humility consider others better than yourselves. Each of you should look not only to your own interests, but also to the interests of others. Your attitude should be the same as that of Christ Jesus: Who, being in very nature God, did not consider equality with God something to be grasped, but made himself nothing, taking the very nature of a servant, being made in human likeness. And being found in appearance as a man, he humbled himself and became obedient to death — even death on a cross!

Reflect:
If I put the interests of others ahead of my own who will look out for my interests? Won't I come up short? How will this principle work if I practice it, but others around me do not? First of all, it "works" because it is the right way to live. Many people, probably most people in human history, have put their own interests first and the outcomes of their lives have not been good. It has simply not worked. Those who have lived others-centered lives have been the ones whose lives have "worked" well in terms of the various measurements of human well-being, such as satisfaction, contentment, healthy relationships, and purpose. But the principle is not intended to be, "I scratch your back and you scratch mine." It is a sort of "risk" of faith. I may very well put the interests of others first and they may be self-serving. They may put their own interests ahead of mine and I may be cheated or taken for granted. The guarantee here is that you will be living life in a God-pleasing way. There is no promise that others will reciprocate. However, all that being said, it is very likely that if you live this "put others first" lifestyle in a joyful, consistent, and faith-filled way, then the people around you will eventually join you in that lifestyle. Individuals who lead with lifestyles that are healthy and relational often reset their cultures. This includes family, work, church, and even larger societal cultures. First, we must learn to lead ourselves and then we will have the capacity to lead others in this. Self-leadership in this area is continually making choices to serve and bless others and not to give in to self-pity, selfish desires, and self-exaltation. We lead ourselves by taking our thoughts, words, attitudes and actions captive to the truth of Christ. He is our Lord and he has given us the ability to exercise leadership over ourselves. This "self-control" is both a fruit of the Spirit and also a result of choice and training over time.

As we lead ourselves to follow God by putting others first, others will be drawn to the fruit of this lifestyle as well as to the source of this fruit, which is the Holy Spirit at work in us. This is how the world changes. Follow Christ by leading yourself to put others first. Many around you may not follow you in this, but over time it is very likely that many will.

Day 4
Read:
Phil. 2:3-8 Do nothing out of selfish ambition or vain conceit, but in humility consider others better than yourselves. Each of you should look not only to your own interests, but also to the interests of others. Your attitude should be the same as that of Christ Jesus: Who, being in very nature God, did not consider equality with God something to be grasped, but made himself nothing, taking the very nature of a servant, being made in human likeness. And being found in appearance as a man, he humbled himself and became obedient to death — even death on a cross!

John 13:14-17 Now that I, your Lord and Teacher, have washed your feet, you also should wash one another's feet. I have set you an example that you should do as I have done for you. I tell you the truth, no servant is greater than his master, nor is a messenger greater than the one who sent him. Now that you know these things, you will be blessed if you do them.

Reflect:
Often we look for the great opportunities to put others first. We are ready to make the great sacrifice and to put forth the heroic effort, but rarely do those opportunities come. What is most often needed are simple, small, barely noticeable acts of kindness. Someone may stand ready to give their life to save another life, but be unwilling to serve others in ways that seem insignificant. Most of the time putting the interests of others first will be unspectacular. It will be listening to someone talk about what interests them, but maybe doesn't interest you and doing so in way where you "choose" to be interested...for their good. It will be helping with some banal task that you feel someone else could easily do, but yet here you are and now you must choose to embrace this small thing with a large heart. Putting the needs of others ahead of our own will necessitate developing better situational awareness of others. We must learn to "see" them and not just ourselves. When most people are shown a group photograph, the first thing they look for is how they look in the photograph. This is normal, but it demonstrates how most people move through life as a whole. We enter rooms, situations, and relationships thinking first and foremost about ourselves. To grow in this important quality of the Christ-life, we must grow in "seeing" others and not just self. You can train to have better awareness of others.

You can pray as you go to work, or a store, or church, or to an event where people will be present: "Lord, open my eyes to the needs of others, help me to see them as you do." You can make small choices to put others first, to move through life with a growing awareness in every situation of the opportunities to represent Christ by loving and serving others. There is great joy and great adventure in this kind of life. The lifestyle of "self-first" is void of joy, always needing more and never finding contentment. There is no adventure in a life spent putting yourself first; it is, instead, the way of an animal in the woods...wandering, foraging with no sense of a greater purpose than survival today. You were not made for this. You were made for greatness and greatness is washing the feet of others.

Day 5
Read:
Phil. 2:3-8 Do nothing out of selfish ambition or vain conceit, but in humility consider others better than yourselves. Each of you should look not only to your own interests, but also to the interests of others. Your attitude should be the same as that of Christ Jesus: Who, being in very nature God, did not consider equality with God something to be grasped, but made himself nothing, taking the very nature of a servant, being made in human likeness. And being found in appearance as a man, he humbled himself and became obedient to death — even death on a cross!

John 13:14-17 Now that I, your Lord and Teacher, have washed your feet, you also should wash one another's feet. I have set you an example that you should do as I have done for you. I tell you the truth, no servant is greater than his master, nor is a messenger greater than the one who sent him. Now that you know these things, you will be blessed if you do them.

Reflect:
What if someone demands that you put him or her first? What if they are not grateful, but expectant...you are supposed to serve them. Does this irk you? Do you feel pride rise up inside saying, "How dare you expect me to serve you! I will serve you on my term, not yours. I will put your needs ahead of mine because I am so noble and so Christlike, not because you demand and expect it!" Do you see the irony in this thinking? We tend to put others first as long as we are in control of the situation. As soon as someone dare treat us as a servant then the true nature of service becomes clear. If we are to serve as Christ serves and as we are meant to serve, then we do not expect applause, or appreciation, or to serve on our terms. We put others first because this is the life God has for us, not because we want to appear to be "spiritual" people. What if you put someone else's needs ahead of your own and they don't even notice? What if they personally benefit from your sacrifice and service, but give you no credit or recognition.

200

What if they give someone else credit for what you did for them? All these questions are "gut checks." It is important that as we serve and put the interests of others first we do so in ways that are actually moving us towards becoming like Christ in our character. This requires that we do make the choice to serve, even when our motives are not perfect and, in addition, we continually check our motives so that they are yielded to Christ. Does all of this sound complex? It's really not complex, but it is difficult. When we are treated like servants, we must yield our pride to Christ. When we are not recognized for our service, we remain quiet and yield our reputation to Christ. When we serve and someone is ungrateful, we remember that we ultimately serve Christ by serving others. His pleasure is our reward. Train your mind to remember that always.

Week 44/Day 1
Read:
1 Thess. 5:12-13 Now we ask you, brothers, to respect those who work hard among you, who are over you in the Lord and who admonish you. Hold them in the highest regard in love because of their work. Live in peace with each other.
Heb. 13:17 Obey your leaders and submit to their authority. They keep watch over you as men who must give an account. Obey them so that their work will be a joy, not a burden, for that would be of no advantage to you.

Reflect:
Everyone leads. Not everyone leads well, but everyone leads. At the very least, everyone leads himself or herself. This leadership is called self-control. Again, not everyone leads themselves well. In addition, most people will at some point in their lives have the opportunity and the responsibility to lead others; if not in their vocation or ministry, then in their homes. It would seem that since most people have experienced the role of "leader" they would know how challenging leadership is and, therefore, readily and willingly support those God has placed in leadership over them. But, it is often a fact of human nature that we tend to want others to give us respect and grace and, yet, are slow to give the same to others. This often proves true for those whose stewardship is to follow a God-appointed leader. Just as all people will lead, all people will also follow. Everyone will operate under God-appointed leadership whether it is familial, government, ministry, or work. Wherever God has placed you under a leader, he has given you the responsibility to be found faithful there. You are to submit to leadership as if you were submitting to the Lord. This does not mean you blindly follow or do things that are illegal, immoral, or unbiblical. You are to submit first and foremost to the leadership of God, and then to submit to human leaders he places over you unless they demand that you disobey the leadership of God.

It is extremely rare that you will be asked to obey a human leader by disobeying God. If this does happen, then of course you must obey God. But outside of this extreme set of circumstances, you obey God by obeying those in leadership over you. Do this in the same manner and spirit that you would want those who God places under your leadership to follow you. Truly in leadership and "followership" the golden rule applies. "Do to others as you would have them do to you." How do you want to be followed when God tasks you with leading? Now go and follow in that manner.

Day 2
Read:
1 Thess. 5:12-13 Now we ask you, brothers, to respect those who work hard among you, who are over you in the Lord and who admonish you. Hold them in the highest regard in love because of their work. Live in peace with each other.
Heb. 13:17 Obey your leaders and submit to their authority. They keep watch over you as men who must give an account. Obey them so that their work will be a joy, not a burden, for that would be of no advantage to you.

Reflect:
Leadership is the immune system of a family, church, or any organized human culture. When leadership is compromised, the system is or will soon become ill. There are many ways leaders can compromise their own leadership. Legal and moral violations top the list of the things that lead to leadership "suicide." But it's also possible for followers to compromise leadership. A well-differentiated and disciplined leader is impossible to stop, but that leader's impact on your own life certainly can be stopped. If you are a complainer, a demander, or if you believe it is a leader's job to "fix" your life, then you will perpetually act against healthy leadership and healthy leaders in your life. To act against the leaders God has placed in your life is to work against your own best interests. Why would anyone do this? For some, it is because they are "wise in their own eyes." Leaders who fail to meet a follower's own standard (that they themselves do not meet) are seen as being unworthy of their loyalty. They are looking for perfection in a leader and will work against any leader who falls short of this impossible standard. This also leads to perpetual disillusionment as people live in search of a leader "worthy" of their loyalty, but when this leader, like all others, proves to be less than perfect the follower then turns elsewhere feeling angry and betrayed. It is likely all the leader did to bring this kind of displeasure is try to lead, but their crime was really a lack of perfection. By all means, look for a settled and Christ-like direction in a leader, but by all means do not look for a life of perfection in a leader. Follow in a way that empowers the leaders God has placed in your life; this will be an advantage to them and to you.

Day 3
Read:

1 Thess. 5:12-13 Now we ask you, brothers, to respect those who work hard among you, who are over you in the Lord and who admonish you. Hold them in the highest regard in love because of their work. Live in peace with each other.

Heb. 13:17 Obey your leaders and submit to their authority. They keep watch over you as men who must give an account. Obey them so that their work will be a joy, not a burden, for that would be of no advantage to you.

Reflect:

Moses was one of history's greatest and most reluctant leaders. God spoke to him face-to-face as a man speaks to a friend (Exodus 33:11). He led an entire nation out of bondage on a perilous journey over 40 years. He had moral courage, wisdom, a clear vision, and he was a spiritually deep man. Yet, he failed in a way that might have seemed subtle, but was in fact quite significant. He added to what God had said and in so doing he got in the way of God's glory revealed to the people. In spite of this costly failure by Moses, his overall pattern of leadership was a good one. He sacrificed for his people and he only led because obedience required it of him; he would have preferred for someone else to do it. The people of Israel, like all people, had an imperfect leader. But unlike many people they had a man who knew, loved, and (for the vast majority of the time) obeyed God. It was not Moses' occasional failures that made their lives so hard, it was their own failures to follow him that did. It is sadly true that: "A man's own folly ruins his life, yet his heart rages against the LORD" (Pr. 19:3). In the case of Israel, their folly was often seen in their refusal to follow God's appointed leader and then they would complain to God when things didn't go well as a result. It is never wise to blindly follow a leader. It is never good to put a leader on a pedestal, but it is certainly never wise or good to make a leader's God-given calling more difficult than it needs to be. Israel loved to complain. They had short "gratitude memory" and it led to a childish approach to life and leadership, namely, "But what have you done for me today?" This is the language and the heart of a child. We are not to be children, but spiritual adults. Spiritual adults operate well under God-ordained leaders and God-ordained leaders operate well over spiritual adults. What is an advantage to one is an advantage to another.

Day 4
Read:

1 Thess. 5:12-13 Now we ask you, brothers, to respect those who work hard among you, who are over you in the Lord and who admonish you. Hold them in the highest regard in love because of their work. Live in peace with each other.

Heb. 13:17 Obey your leaders and submit to their authority. They keep watch over you as men who must give an account. Obey them so that their work will be a joy, not a burden, for that would be of no advantage to you.

Reflect:
Jesus was asked a number of times about the source of his authority. "'By what authority are you doing these things?' they asked. 'And who gave you authority to do this?'" (Mark 11:28). After his resurrection he gave the definitive answer regarding the source and scope of his authority. "Then Jesus came to them and said, 'All authority in heaven and on earth has been given to me'" (Matt. 28:18). The source of his authority is that it had been "given" by God the Father and the scope of his authority was "all." Authority has many meanings; some synonyms include: power, ability, jurisdiction, privilege, and prerogative. To have authority means you have legal or rightful ability to oversee or rule over. All rightful human authority is derived. The authority of government in a nation ruled by laws is the law itself. The authority of a boss over his or her employees is derived from a position determined by the owner or shareholders. Ultimately, all authority is derived from God. He sets up and deposes kings and kingdoms. He gives life, breath, and everything else. The authority of a spiritual leader in the church is derived from the authority of God. These leaders can, and sometimes do, misuse this authority and when they do they must be set aside. But short of a misuse or abuse of authority, these leaders are to be treated and followed as authorized representatives of God. This does not mean they are more "loved" by God or that they are unable to make mistakes. It simply means that they have been given a role and often with that role comes a gift or gifts that enables them to serve the church well. Leadership is a stewardship given to certain people in the church to serve the church. It is no more "special" than the stewardship of service or any of the other gifts that God gives his people so they may serve one another. The gift and responsibility of leadership must not be misused by the leader or despised by the follower. All the gifts and all authority are given by God for his own glory and for his people's good. We must think and live with clarity about this.

Day 5
Read:
1 Thess. 5:12-13 Now we ask you, brothers, to respect those who work hard among you, who are over you in the Lord and who admonish you. Hold them in the highest regard in love because of their work. Live in peace with each other.
Heb. 13:17 Obey your leaders and submit to their authority. They keep watch over you as men who must give an account. Obey them so that their work will be a joy, not a burden, for that would be of no advantage to you.

Reflect:

Everyone follows and everyone answers to someone. If you own a business, you answer to your customers. A four-star general has a civilian boss. The work of the follower is to follow well. When followers do their work, they make the work of the leader a joy. When followers fail to do their work well, they make the work of a leader a burden. When the leader's life becomes all or mostly burden, then the follower has undermined his or her own life. It is common to complain and second-guess leadership, but this approach is the equivalent of punching yourself in the face as an attempt to hurt someone else. God has placed you under human authorities, so to undermine them is to attempt to undermine him. This is not to say that you should blindly and unquestionably follow all human leaders, you should not and you must not. But unless those God has placed over you ask you to do something illegal, immoral, or unbiblical, you should be very slow to disregard them. If you want to have a voice to speak into the life of a leader, you must first demonstrate a heart that understands the difficult work of leading and also a life that shows solidarity with the leader. Those who shout criticism from the sidelines are unlikely to get a hearing from a leader who is in the middle of actually leading. Good leaders listen, but they listen most carefully to the people who are clearly with them in the action. "Obeying and submitting" to leaders is not mindless activity. It is intentional actions designed to work together with a team that is able to accomplish much more than you can by yourself. These actions make the life of a leader a joy and they enable you to multiply the impact of your own life as well. Even if you decided to act selfishly in regards to leadership, you would still "obey and submit" because this is how you will personally prosper as well. But if you follow Christ, you have multiple reasons to make the leader's life a joy. You have your own self-interests and you also have the higher purpose of the glory of God to attend to. God is glorified when you live under his authority by living well under the authority he has placed in your life.

Week 45/Day 1
Read:

2 Cor. 9:6-8 Remember this: Whoever sows sparingly will also reap sparingly, and whoever sows generously will also reap generously. Each man should give what he has decided in his heart to give, not reluctantly or under compulsion, for God loves a cheerful giver. And God is able to make all grace abound to you, so that in all things at all times, having all that you need, you will abound in every good work.

Reflect:

We often get anxious, angry, or defensive when we are pushed to give attention in an area in which we are struggling. We tend to enjoy it when we read or hear about important life issues that we are currently doing well in,

205

but not so much if we feel we are failing in those areas. Praying, sharing the gospel, diet, exercise, forgiveness, and money, these are examples of areas in which we can feel "pushed." Instead of anxiety, anger, or defensiveness, when we are challenged to do better or do something other than what we are doing, it would be good and wise to take a calm and honest look at the issue. If the anxiety or anger is unwarranted, because we are not actually falling short, then disregard it. You ultimately answer to God and if he is "okay" with what you are doing or not doing, then that is all that matters. If the issue is legitimate and you are actually falling short in an important area of faith and life, then anxiety and anger are unwarranted once again. What we want is to obey God, to know his pleasure, and to bring him pleasure. If, in his mercy, he helps us see how we can better align our will with his and our lives with his, then we have to change our thinking and our feeling and embrace his good for us. Anxiety, anger, and defensive postures are warning lights. They are not the real issue, but they do indicate that there is an issue. So, when it comes to the stewardship of your money, how are you doing? Are you generous, obedient, and joyful in your giving? If so, then rejoice in the freedom you know in this area. If you are not, why not? It is never a matter of can you afford to give, of course you can. Is God not able to make you abound so that will have all you need? Giving money is not, at its root, about money. It is about confidence in God. What do you feel as you read about the opportunity and responsibility to give generously and cheerfully? Anxiety, anger, defensiveness? Joy, freedom, peace? Maybe somewhere in between? If you want clarity, wisdom, and freedom on this or on any issue, the place to start is with a settled "yes!" "Lord, the answer is 'yes' to whatever you want, now help me understand what it is you want." From that starting point, you are positioned to move more fully and freely into the center of his will for your life. Where do you want to live?

Day 2
Read:
2 Cor. 9:6-8 Remember this: Whoever sows sparingly will also reap sparingly, and whoever sows generously will also reap generously. Each man should give what he has decided in his heart to give, not reluctantly or under compulsion, for God loves a cheerful giver. And God is able to make all grace abound to you, so that in all things at all times, having all that you need, you will abound in every good work.

Reflect:
Giving is not a law; it is an opportunity. It is an opportunity for freedom from misguided loves and commitments. The love of money, Paul told Timothy, is the root of all kinds of evil (1 Tim. 6:10). In fact, this love has caused some people to lose their love for God.

The writer of Hebrews wrote, "Keep your lives free from the love of money and be content with what you have, because God has said, 'Never will I leave you; never will I forsake you'" (Heb. 13:5). The love of money is a form of bondage because it robs us of contentment and of faith. Look at the "because" in that verse. We are to stay free of the love of money and be content "because" God has promised to never leave or forsake us. The love of money, which is in effect a "faith" in money, is a threat to faith in God. Money will leave us, (you can't take it with you) but God will not. We were designed with infinite desire, a desire that was meant to be directed towards God. Sin has warped this desire and now we experience an insatiable desire for any number of things that will not and cannot satisfy. Money is often one of the more common of these things people pursue. Lest you think that if only you had enough money you would not "love it so much," listen to what Solomon, who was very wealthy, wrote from personal experience: "Whoever loves money never has money enough; whoever loves wealth is never satisfied with his income. This too is meaningless" (Eccl. 5:10). The very poor, the very rich, and everyone in between, can fall into the trap of loving money rather than loving God. Give as God leads you to give, generously, joyfully, and consistently. Give when you think you can afford to give and also when you do not think you can. Give so that God, not money, will hold your heart and capture your affections. Give because God has said to give and it's not because he needs your money, but because he wants your heart.

Day 3
Read:

2 Cor. 9:6-8 Remember this: Whoever sows sparingly will also reap sparingly, and whoever sows generously will also reap generously. Each man should give what he has decided in his heart to give, not reluctantly or under compulsion, for God loves a cheerful giver. And God is able to make all grace abound to you, so that in all things at all times, having all that you need, you will abound in every good work.

Reflect:

What do people spend their money on? Cars, clothes, food, housing, entertainment? Yes, but also no. They most often spend their money on their hearts. "Above all else, guard your heart, for it is the wellspring of life" (Pr. 4:23). The heart is the "real you." It is the thinking, choosing, feeling, believing you. From this "inside" place flow all of our "outside" choices. So, we must carefully guard, keep watch, and protect this place because it shapes our lives. Everything else flows from there. So then, how do we spend our money on our hearts? The heart is the wellspring of life, thus it is what drives our spending or, if we are out of money, our desire to be able to spend. When the heart is full of faith in Jesus and love for people, then spending patterns flow from there.

When the heart is full of need and want and discontentment, then the spending patterns (or desire to spend) flows from there. Some people, maybe many people, have trained their hearts to find joy and meaning in buying things. Of course, buying doesn't work very well or very long as a source of joy and meaning, so it is more of a temporary "buzz" than a real source of meaning. This is why spending can become an addiction, because people will look for the next "buzz" from the next purchase. Some have trained their hearts to find security and significance in saving money. They do not need to actually spend to find meaning; instead, they need to hoard the ability to spend in order to feel safe and powerful. There are many ways money can hold central place in a human heart. These are just two of those ways. We must act continually and decisively against money going from its rightful place as a neutral "tool" to a non-neutral god in our lives. It is not money, but the "love" of money that is the root of all kinds of evil. Give your money away faithfully and generously as an act of faith, obedience, and heart training. As you do, keep this important truth in the center of your mind: "God is able to make all grace abound to you, so that in all things at all times, having all that you need, you will abound in every good work" (2 Cor. 9:8). Giving and living in God's sufficiency go hand in hand or "hand in heart."

Day 4
Read:
2 Cor. 9:6-8 Remember this: Whoever sows sparingly will also reap sparingly, and whoever sows generously will also reap generously. Each man should give what he has decided in his heart to give, not reluctantly or under compulsion, for God loves a cheerful giver. And God is able to make all grace abound to you, so that in all things at all times, having all that you need, you will abound in every good work.

Reflect:
There is no promise here, or elsewhere in Scripture, that if you give money away God will replace that money in multiples. God does bless the cheerful, generous giver by "making all grace abound." As we demonstrate with our practical choices, such as giving, that we trust God above all else, we will have all we need and then some. It doesn't mean we will have all we desire, if our desires are off track. We will have all we desire, if our desires are properly ordered. Many wealthy people would trade all of their wealth for peace, love, purpose, hope, and deep relationships. Christ provides all of this to those who trust him with their lives and live within the bounds of his will and his ways. "I tell you the truth," Jesus replied, "no one who has left home or brothers or sisters or mother or father or children or fields for me and the gospel will fail to receive a hundred times as much in this present age (homes, brothers, sisters, mothers, children and fields — and with them, persecutions) and in the age to come, eternal life" (Mark 10:29-30).

Obviously, he is not saying that literally you will have hundreds of biological parents and siblings, but rather when you give away what you have for the sake of the gospel, God's provision more than makes up for the loss. You will have a huge family of believers, closer than biological family often is. You will have resources that are multiplied as you live in Christ's community. But take note, along with the provision Jesus promised there is also persecution. Who would possibly want such a deal? Anyone who God has revealed himself to would. When we understand who God is and what he has actually promised us, then we will be eager to want the life he offers for us. There will be sacrifice, but there is also abundant provision. There will be persecution, but there is also purpose. Many live to acquire, spend, and save, only to lose, squander, and fail to save their very lives. Jim Elliott, a missionary who lost his life, famously said, "He is no fool who gives what he cannot keep, to gain what he cannot lose."

Day 5
Read:
2 Cor. 9:6-8 Remember this: Whoever sows sparingly will also reap sparingly, and whoever sows generously will also reap generously. Each man should give what he has decided in his heart to give, not reluctantly or under compulsion, for God loves a cheerful giver. And God is able to make all grace abound to you, so that in all things at all times, having all that you need, you will abound in every good work.

Reflect:
If each person should give what he has decided to give and if God loves a cheerful giver, then can I give a meager sum if that is what I decide to give and what I can cheerfully give? If God has given you a meager sum of grace in your heart, if your love for Christ is meager, and if you are okay with having a meager amount of joy in the gospel, then yes, give a meager amount. But if God has blessed you immeasurably, if he has put the love of Christ in your heart, and if you want to increase your joy in the gospel, then give generously by faith and watch your heart become more cheerful. This is no "sales job" here, because Paul is not selling anything. Instead, this is a "tells job," as Paul is simply telling the truth of how the world actually works. God blesses cheerful and generous givers. How this blessing will manifest is going to be different from person to person and situation to situation, but whether it will manifest is not in doubt. Paul is not saying, "If you cannot give cheerfully, then don't give at all." He is saying, "Learn to have a heart that can and does give cheerfully." Will you trust God with your money? If you will not, then you cannot trust him with your life. If you want to experience the life God has for you, it will require that you give your life away. You can experience abundant life, but it is found in daily dying to self.

Then Jesus said to his disciples, "If anyone would come after me, he must deny himself and take up his cross and follow me. For whoever wants to save his life will lose it, but whoever loses his life for me will find it. What good will it be for a man if he gains the whole world, yet forfeits his soul? Or what can a man give in exchange for his soul? For the Son of Man is going to come in his Father's glory with his angels, and then he will reward each person according to what he has done" (Matt. 16:24-27). Dying to self is the pathway to the fullness of life. "Yes, Lord, what good is it to gain the world and lose the soul? It is a terrible thing to contemplate and a more terrible thing to experience. Deliver us from all that would take our hearts away from you. Deliver to all the good of the life you have purchased for us. We were bought with a great price, all we have, all we are...is yours."

Week 46/Day 1
Read:
Matt. 18:15 If your brother sins against you, go and show him his fault, just between the two of you. If he listens to you, you have won your brother over.
Prov. 27:6 Wounds from a friend can be trusted, but an enemy multiplies kisses.
Prov. 19:8 He who gets wisdom loves his own soul; he who cherishes understanding prospers.

Reflect:
It is common to "feel" loved when others tell us what we want them to tell us. The truth is, we are "being" loved when others tell us what we need them to tell us. Jesus *is* love and he often told people things that might not be considered loving, but of course they always were. Even a strong rebuke or harsh critique from the Lord was an attempt to turn people away from the very attitudes and actions that were going to destroy them. Giving and receiving correction is essential to a life well lived. Even if a person was completely self-serving and cared nothing about God or others, that person - if they had all the facts - would live in line with God's will and ways. Because God's ways work. Of course, it would not be possible to live in line with God's will and ways without a heart change, but even if one were to apply the "brute facts" of the truth to life, they would still fare better than one who did not. The person who has learned to lean into correction, to stay open to improvement and direction from others, will prosper in many ways. The one who is proud, insecure, unwilling to be corrected, will not prosper – whether spiritually, vocationally, or relationally. We are all a work in progress. No one has "arrived." Since we are all "arriving," we must learn to literally love correction. The sad fact is, we most often have learned to hate it. We hate it because it shows us where we are wrong. But if we are wrong, shouldn't we want to be right? We hate it because it shows us we are not perfect. But don't we know that already?

Why would we so persistently run from that obvious reality? We hate it because it shows us we are weak and needy. But since we are weak and needy, wouldn't it be wise to embrace that which will develop us and make us stronger? To get wisdom, even in the form of correction, is to love your own soul. It is good for you, immediately and eternally good for you. It is the friend of your soul who offers you words that may feel unloving, but are in fact like the careful cuts of a surgeon's knife. They are wounds that serve, heal, and show love. He is no friend of your soul who offers you flattering and sugary words that confirm what is not good or true in your life. This "friend" who throws "kisses" your way is self-serving. They need you to like them more than they want to show you love. Be kind to the flatterer, but do not embrace their flattering ways. Learn to respect and appreciate those God has put in your life who are willing to show you love with "faithful wounds." Not because they are foolish and randomly brandish a "word-knife," but because they love you and even though they would rather not do so, they are willing to tell you the hard truth when it is in your best interests. This is the person to respect, embrace, and treasure. This person is showing you real love.

Day 2
Read:
Heb. 3:12-13 See to it, brothers, that none of you has a sinful, unbelieving heart that turns away from the living God. But encourage one another daily, as long as it is called Today, so that none of you may be hardened by sin's deceitfulness.

Reflect:
"See to it" means that it is your responsibility to do or be something. It is not God's, or the church's, or the government's, or your friend's responsibility, it is yours. You *must* "see to it" and, therefore, you *can* "see to it." What are you to take responsibility for here in this passage? That you do not allow sin and unbelief to shape your heart in such a way that you turn from God in your life. Then you are to "see to it" that you do the exact opposite of that by pouring courage into one another day after day for as many days as God grants you. Sin is like plaque in your artery. It is slow, insidious, building up day-by-day and choice-by-choice until the artery is hardened and blocked to the life-flow of blood. See to it that this doesn't happen to you, because it doesn't have to happen. The preventative action offered here is daily encouragement. To live in this life-saving encouragement will require authentic, day-to-day kinds of relationships. If you do not have these kinds of encouraging relationships, you must not place the blame on others, you must start today and "see to it" that you have them. Others have them, why not you? There is no conspiracy against you; if you do not have them, it is because you have not done the work others have done to obtain them. It is work to have encouraging relationships.

211

It takes initiative, it takes endurance, it takes openness and honesty, and it takes being willing to be corrected, challenged, and wrong. If you have these relationships, do not take them for granted. You are blessed to have these kinds of friends in your life, cherish them by fully taking advantage of what God has given you. He has built a pipeline of encouragement between you and others and through this pipeline flows his courage from you to them and them to you. As you walk with Jesus and your friend(s) walk with Jesus, there is ample courage to flow back and forth to keep you encouraged and to keep sin from hardening your heart against God. "See to it" sounds like work and it is...really, really good work. To have a heart hardened by sin's deceitfulness is much harder work than encouraging and staying encouraged. You will "see to it" either that you do not allow your heart to harden by living in daily encouragement or you will "see to it" that your heart turns away from God. There is no third way. This a strong warning and this is a wonderful opportunity. If you are hard already, it is not too late to change. You are reading these words, so you are alive and breathing, now start today and "see to it."

Day 3
Read:
Prov. 13:18 He who ignores discipline comes to poverty and shame, but whoever heeds correction is honored.

Prov. 15:10 Stern discipline awaits him who leaves the path; he who hates correction will die.

Prov. 15:32 He who ignores discipline despises himself, but whoever heeds **correction** gains understanding.

Reflect:
These are dire warnings for those who ignore correction. So, is this correction from the Lord or from other people? Most likely the answer is both. Of course, God can and does correct and instruct directly and through the Bible, but very often he also speaks to us through others. To ignore correction and direction in whatever form it takes is to "despise yourself." Why is this so? Because of our insecurity and pride we tend to see correction as a threat to our well-being. We would rather be happily wrong, than unhappily right in our thinking and living. The problem is that happily wrong will soon become unhappily wrong and unhappily right will eventually lead to a good place, if we stay the course. To ignore direction and correction is to despise yourself because it is failing to heed God's loving attempts to redirect you off a bad path. Very often, failing to heed repeated warnings leads to irrevocable damage.

212

There is a very stern warning along these lines in the book of Proverbs: "A man who remains stiff-necked after many rebukes will suddenly be destroyed — without remedy" (Pr. 29:1). When the end of the opportunity comes, it is too late to make a difference in the outcome. Of course, as long as we breathe we can repent and turn to God or return to him. However, God's gracious forgiveness does not undo all of the consequences that may have come into our lives as a result of not heeding correction. Perhaps you feel you are nowhere near being this hard-hearted or hardheaded. You would never remain this obstinate after many attempts by God and others to correct you. Hopefully, that is true for you and so the warning given here is not for you. But be careful, even if you are not in danger of some dire consequence, we are often in danger of missing many small opportunities and blessings and escaping many small problems because of our pride and self-trust. Ask God to help you hear from him and others. Ask him for clarity in your understanding and courage in your actions. It is his kindness that leads us to repentance (Rom. 2:4). Is he offering you kindness in the form of a correction now? Will you receive his kindness?

Day 4
Read:
Eph. 4:14-15 Then we will no longer be infants, tossed back and forth by the waves, and blown here and there by every wind of teaching and by the cunning and craftiness of men in their deceitful scheming. Instead, speaking the truth in love, we will in all things grow up into him who is the Head, that is, Christ.

Reflect:
The contrast here is between heresy and the truth of the gospel. Paul is casting a vision for living as spiritual adults who are not blown around by clever sounding words that are, in fact, wrong. It is love that speaks the truth to lies, because lies that are lived out lead to lives that are ruined. James wrote: "Whoever turns a sinner from the error of his way will save him from death and cover over a multitude of sins" (James 5:20). Here again is the loving proclamation of the truth of the gospel that turns sinful men and woman from error. The result is that they are saved from spiritual death and all of their sins are forgiven. The fact that speaking the truth of the gospel to people is an act of love can be missed, and often is, because by and large people do not like to be told that what they are believing or doing is wrong. Let's turn our attention now to the truth "teller." Whether it is telling the truth of the gospel to a person who has never been born again or reminding a believer of the truth of the gospel as a corrective to their rebellion, it can take courage to speak the truth in love. We do not sell the gospel, but to non-believers and believers alike, we must tell the gospel. We must do so from a "mindset" and from a "heart" of love.

213

We must understand that whether people feel loved by our "truth-telling" or not, telling the truth is an act of love. As we tell the truth, we must do all we can to make the truth appealing and "realistic" to others. This involves many important factors, but chief among them is authenticity on our part. Truth does not depend on our ability to defend it or live it. Truth stands by itself whether any human lives it or believes it. However, although truth is inherently beautiful in itself, it can be seen as less so when spoken through the lips of person whose life does not align with it. Of course, this alignment need not be perfect, but it must be authentic. Speak the truth in love to others, for God's glory and for their good. Speak the truth in love to others from a life that is determined to live and to die resolutely headed in the direction of the Lord Jesus who is the Truth. Never mind that you fail. Do not let failure silence you. Let the needs of others drive you to continually mess up, fess up, and move on in your walk with others. People need to hear the truth from authentic lips. If not from you, then from who?

Day 5
Read:
Prov. 12:1 Whoever loves discipline loves knowledge, but he who hates correction is stupid.

Reflect:
"Discipline" here is corrective instruction. Who would love that? The one who has learned to love what is real regardless of what they feel will love it. There is a delicate balance between dealing honestly with the brute facts of my current situation and also holding on to hope regarding what could yet be true. It is common to either deny the truth of what is real about my life and my choices **or** to face that reality honestly and lose hope about ever changing. This is a false dichotomy; it is not an either-or scenario. I must face the facts of my life as they stand **and** I can hold on to a real and living hope for what my life can yet be. A part of this balance is to know that, since I am imperfect in my thinking, feeling, and doing, I will always need corrective instruction. I will always be "arriving," but never having "arrived" in this life. Since this is true, I must love correction because it is the path to knowledge, which is truth. Can a person actually learn to love to be wrong like this? It's not really about learning to love being wrong, rather it's about learning to love the truth no matter what path we must take in order to get to the truth. If I must go through discipline, correction, and humility to get to truth, then I will take that path. You do not have to love everything about the process of getting to the truth. There are parts of discipline that are terribly difficult and no one would choose them if there were another way. This is about the fact that sometimes there is no other way. We need to face the facts squarely in order to embrace being wrong, so that we can move in the direction of the One who is "the way, the truth, and the life" (John 14:6).

The one who "hates" (shuns, avoids) this corrective discipline is said to be "stupid" (Pr. 12:1). The word is not derogatory here, it is descriptive. It was used to describe an animal, a beast that lives in ongoing unawareness of self and, therefore, is never going to actually change. This is normal for a beast, but not for an image bearer. You are like the beasts in that you are created, but you are also made in God's image. You were made to aspire to become like your father in increasing fashion. Live like a child of God, not a beast of the field. Love discipline, love correction, and do so because you love God.

Week 47/Day 1
Read: 1 Thess. 5:16-18 Be joyful always; pray continually; give thanks in all circumstances, for this is God's will for you in Christ Jesus.

Reflect: To be thankful with no one to thank is ultimately an empty thing. Most people feel "something" when they look at their young child at play, see a sunset, or hear a moving piece of music. They feel a need or a desire to give thanks. Some people do not believe there is anyone who is deserving of their ultimate thanks. Perhaps they thank someone for writing and playing the music, but who do they thank for the musician? Perhaps they thank the "universe" for its beauty, but who do they thank for the universe? They feel thankful for their child, but who do they thank for the child? Many do not think this deeply about their "thanksgiving," but everyone should. Being thankful, meaning becoming a person who IS thankful, is essential to closing the gap. We can and should choose to speak and act with gratitude, but the final goal is to be a person who IS actually thankful. It is something that we have become rather than something we choose to occasionally move in and out of like a room or a mood. When bad things happen, people ask "why?" and question God's goodness, power, or reality. They no longer have reason - they believe - to give thanks. When good things happen, people do not ask "why" they simply enjoy the good. They may feel thankful and give thanks, but their thanksgiving is entirely based on their circumstances not their settled state of being. Becoming a thankful person flows from a deep and abiding relationship with God. God is the one behind all that is good, including our very existence. But what of all that is bad, is it "fair" to be thankful for the good and not to be "unthankful" for the bad? How do we avoid turning life into a scorecard where we give God points for the good and deduct points for the bad? When God is seen in this light, we have become the center of our own universe. The result will be that inevitably God will score in the negative because we will have become people who largely see the negatives. Sooner or later we will lose all sense of being thankful because we do not believe God is worthy of our thanks, he is only worthy to be put on trial for the bad. There are many theological and philosophical rabbit trails we could travel at this point, but let's go to our heart's true home instead.

You have a lot of questions and there are answers for those questions, though many answers are beyond our current limits of understanding. But in addition to your questions, you have a heart that wants to thank someone, just like a child who really wants to be angry at her parent, but is also powerfully, emotionally drawn to that very parent. She is unhappy about circumstances and her parents' seeming unwillingness to change their circumstances in her favor. Yet, her little heart loves her parent. In her confusion and disappointment with the parent, she ultimately finds her comfort in her parent's arms. This may feel intellectually dishonest or unsatisfying as an answer, but it is, in fact, a real answer. God is your father and he is a good father. You can be confused, disappointed, and angry with him, but you were made by God, for God. Whether circumstances are favorable or not, he is your father. Regardless of your circumstances the question remains, what will you do with him? If you knew your heart well, you would know that it wants to be thankful, because that is how it was designed. Will you lay aside your disappointment, confusion, and anger for a moment and simply go to your father?

Day 2
Read:
1 Cor. 11:18-22 In the first place, I hear that when you come together as a church, there are divisions among you, and to some extent I believe it. No doubt there have to be differences among you to show which of you have God's approval. When you come together, it is not the Lord's Supper you eat, for as you eat, each of you goes ahead without waiting for anybody else. One remains hungry, another gets drunk. Don't you have homes to eat and drink in? Or do you despise the church of God and humiliate those who have nothing? What shall I say to you? Shall I praise you for this? Certainly not!

Reflect:
Being thankful moves our thoughts away from ourselves and towards God. As our thoughts and the corresponding emotions move away from self, we begin to "see" others around us. Often, without a heart of thanksgiving, we see others as sources of annoyance or as means to our own ends. They are roadblocks to our own desires or pathways, to be walked upon to get what we want. When our hearts are full of gratitude to God, then our lives will more fully move in love towards others. If we are not closing the gap on loving others, then we can be sure we are not closing the gap on moving towards God in faith and thanksgiving. It is not possible to move towards God in faith and thanks and not, at the same time, find our hearts and minds moving towards others in love. Imagine this, you are at a dinner designed by the Lord for the church to help them remember. What are we to remember? We are to remember the ultimate sacrifice Jesus made for us. It is a meal of thanksgiving, remembering to be thankful for what Christ had done.

Now, as you are participating in this meal of remembering, you find people "grouping up." Over there are the ones who take pride in what they have, they are enjoying a potluck made of richer fare and they are not about to share it with those who brought more meager items to what is supposed to be a common meal. Then, there are also those who take pride in their ability, or their knowledge, or their nationality...you get the picture. Everyone has formed factions designed to set themselves apart as unique and special and to keep others out of their inner rings. At what might have been a beautiful meal, the ugliness of selfishness destroys and distracts. All people must eat. If they do not eat, they die. Rich, poor, all nationalities, and all levels of intellect...still, all people eat. In the eating of food we should remember what we have in common. We, all alike, are not self-sufficient; we are needy beings. As the church comes together in community, all the temporal, and ultimately meaningless, distinctions should melt away like the mists that they are. In the bright light of the Son of God we see clearly what is true about us. We are all hungry, needy people who need our daily bread, but yet we do not live on bread alone. We live by the very Word of God. Jesus is the Word of God made flesh. Start with being thankful to the Lord Jesus for what he has given. Then look at your neighbor and respond accordingly. When you find yourself acting without grace towards others, your root issue is that you do not love God. If you love God, if you are nurturing a heart of thanks towards him, you are at the same time nurturing a heart that loves others.

Day 3
Read:
1 Cor. 11:24 "...The Lord Jesus, on the night he was betrayed, took bread, and when he had given thanks, he broke it and said, "This is my body, which is for you; do this in remembrance of me.""

Reflect:
On the night that Jesus was betrayed, he took bread and gave thanks. A man who Jesus had treated as a dear friend traded the relationship for a bag of coins. In addition to this betrayal, his other friends would sleep through his most difficult night, misunderstand his life mission, and deny they even knew him. Then, what also was coming for the Lord (and he knew it) was that his Father would turn his face away from him. He would be forsaken by God. Now, with all this in mind, hear this story again...On the night that Jesus was betrayed, he took bread and gave thanks. He gave thanks as he broke the bread that symbolized his own body that would be broken for the sins of others. He drank a cup that symbolized the blood that would flow for your sins and mine. Jesus was not a man who had died to all passions and desires. He was not a stoic who had trained himself to not care or feel. He was a man who gave full vent to his passion and desires. He felt and cared like no human ever has.

He fully embraced his passions and desires because they were righteous and good and blessed. He always did what he ultimately wanted to do because his heart was such that he always wanted what was good. Yes, he asked his Father for another way than the cross, but he added, "Not my will, but yours be done" (Luke 22:42). This doesn't mean that Jesus had a different will than his Father's; he did not. This simply shows that Jesus was facing the full implications of what was coming. He was showing that he was no "iron man" who felt nothing. He was bearing the full emotional weight of what he was going to experience. His statement, "Not my will, but yours be done" was the Lord communicating the reality of what it looks like to be a surrendered human. Does this mean Jesus had a divided heart? No, it means we can identify with him. His heart was fully surrendered to the Father's will. But his own humanity, understandably, wanted to know if there were other options. There were not. So the Lord settled into what the writer of Hebrews called the "joy set before him" (Heb. 12:2). For Jesus, the ultimate good was always his preference. God incarnate did not come to serve self, but to give his life as a ransom. Serving self is a universally failed method of personal happiness. Why would the one who designed life try something like that? Of course he would not, and he did not. So on the night he was betrayed, with all that was coming to him fully in his mind, he gave thanks. But it was not just a cross that was coming, joy was set before him. You, too, can give thanks. If you have given your life to Christ, there is joy coming your way. It may be on the other side of a cross, in fact, it most certainly will be. But joy is there, set before you. Do you see it? There is part of us that would, at times, prefer a different way than the way set before us by God. But for those with a thankful and surrendered heart, in the end we willingly choose the way God has chosen for us. You are not there yet? Don't be dismayed; close the gap a little more today. Close the gap by giving thanks right now, and again and again as you move through this day.

Day 4
Read:
1 Cor. 11:17-22 In the following directives I have no praise for you, for your meetings do more harm than good. In the first place, I hear that when you come together as a church, there are divisions among you, and to some extent I believe it. No doubt there have to be differences among you to show which of you have God's approval. When you come together, it is not the Lord's Supper you eat, for as you eat, each of you goes ahead without waiting for anybody else. One remains hungry, another gets drunk. Don't you have homes to eat and drink in? Or do you despise the church of God and humiliate those who have nothing? What shall I say to you? Shall I praise you for this? Certainly not!

Reflect:

It is tragic to even consider the fact that a celebration of the Lord's sacrifice could do more harm than good, but that is what Paul said was happening. The goodness of God in Christ displayed in a cross-death was submerged to human posturing, jealousy, and pettiness. How absurd...how could this happen? The cross of Christ as a reality brought us peace with God and with one another. Too soon after the death of Christ, the cross as a celebration of peace, had become another chance for pride and division. By the time Paul penned this letter, the cross as a historical, spiritual reality had already become (for some at least) a cultural artifact. It had been drained of its power to transform their lives. It is both frightening and enlightening to realize how quickly this happened. We all "leak" perspective. It drains from us like water from a bucket with a hole in the bottom. We would like to seal the leak and be able to remain full of perspective, but it is not going to happen. Then what hope do we have? We have the hope of a continual infusion of perspective from God through the Holy Spirit. The fact that we "leak" can help us remain dependent on God. We cannot simply become full and then go away on our own and live lives independently of God. We need him day by day, and hour by hour, to pour living water into our hearts. His grace empowers us to live thankful lives and his grace enlightens our minds to remain grateful for what he has done for us. This grace is his gift, but like all gifts it must be received. In this case, it is a gift that is to be continually received into our lives. The most crucial component of living continually in this "grace-gift" is to practice with our minds and our mouths the discipline of giving thanks. When we become independent, or begin to feel entitled, or like we have somehow been cheated by God, then we shut off the flow of grace into our lives. God has not stopped offering it; we have stopped receiving it. To "give" thanks mean to give something back to someone who has given something to you. This is not "you scratch my back, I'll scratch yours," because God needs nothing from us. This is about giving thanks to the one who needs nothing *from* us, but wants much *for* us. He wants us to be continually full of his life and, therefore, our giving him thanks is part of living in the flow of perspective that keeps us grateful and joyful.

Day 5
Read:

1 Cor. 11:17-26 In the following directives I have no praise for you, for your meetings do more harm than good. In the first place, I hear that when you come together as a church, there are divisions among you, and to some extent I believe it. No doubt there have to be differences among you to show which of you have God's approval. When you come together, it is not the Lord's Supper you eat, for as you eat, each of you goes ahead without waiting for anybody else. One remains hungry, another gets drunk. Don't you have homes to eat and drink in?

Or do you despise the church of God and humiliate those who have nothing? What shall I say to you? Shall I praise you for this? Certainly not! For I received from the Lord what I also passed on to you: The Lord Jesus, on the night he was betrayed, took bread, and when he had given thanks, he broke it and said, "This is my body, which is for you; do this in remembrance of me." In the same way, after supper he took the cup, saying, "This cup is the new covenant in my blood; do this, whenever you drink it, in remembrance of me." For whenever you eat this bread and drink this cup, you proclaim the Lord's death until he comes.

Reflect:
Ideally, in the act of communion you engage all of who you are as a person. You use your mind to remember what Christ has done. Your emotions are activated as you are drawn towards Christ and others in the act of remembering. With your body you touch and taste and smell and see the elements. And you do all of this in community as a choice made to proclaim the reality of the gospel and the relationship with God which it has opened up for you. I say "ideally" because it is possible to simply go through the motions. It is possible to turn the celebration of the Lord's sacrifice into a meaningless ritual, void of the powerful impact that it could make in our lives. The Lord died once, but his death is to be celebrated over and over. The reality of the transformation brought by his death comes into our lives in an instant at the moment of our conversion. But it is the active practice of remembering and engaging the transformation reality that turns the potential of becoming like Christ into the actual experience of Christlikeness. Communion is but one of many means God has given us to close the gap on becoming like Christ. These are means and not the end. The end is to grow in Christlikeness and the many means are ways or paths for you to journey on to that great end. In the celebration of communion, as in other useful means, it is important to fully engage realities, not merely perform rituals. The reality of his death on the cross and all that his death has brought to us should be engaged in communion. The reality of peace with God spilling over into peace with one another should be engaged in our lives together in communion. The reality of God's self-revelation in his word given to us should be engaged as we read, study, and think deeply about the Bible. In these means and many more, we engage the reality of God - not mere religious ritual - in order to become different at our very core. We "do" these things because "doing" is a powerful ally in becoming. However, it is important that that we remember why we do what we do. It is not to impress, or to earn, but to celebrate and to become like our Savior.

Week 48/Day 1
Read:

Ex. 2:23-3:7 During that long period, the king of Egypt died. The Israelites groaned in their slavery and cried out, and their cry for help because of their slavery went up to God.

Reflect:

The etymology of the word "wait" has to do with a "watchman" or a "sentry." We tend to view waiting as largely a passive thing and very often we approach waiting in that spirit. But a "waiter" at a restaurant is not passive but active. The good waiter's activity is "responsive waiting." When the patron needs water the waiter is standing by to fill the cup. When the patron is ready to order the waiter takes the order and ensures the meal is properly prepared and delivered in timely fashion. Waiting, when done well, is very hard work. It is not hard to be busy, to do, to fill your hours with activity. It is very difficult to "stand by" then when called upon, to act decisively and energetically, and then return to waiting. Waiting can be exasperating and it is humbling. Waiting implies that we don't get to decide when and how we act, the one we are waiting on gets to decide that. "Important" humans don't wait on anyone, others wait on them. Military leaders, politicians, leaders of business...they all have a host of "waiters" at their disposal. Their staffs "stand by" continually ready to serve the needs of those they work for. The "important ones" act while others wait. Jesus was a king who came as a waiter. He said of himself: "For even the Son of Man did not come to be served, but to serve, and to give his life as a ransom for many." (Mark 10:45) and "Therefore Jesus told them, "The right time for me has not yet come; for you any time is right." (John 7:6). Human kings do not wait, why should they? The timing of events and actions is theirs to determine and to direct. But Jesus, the King who came to serve and not be served, choose to wait on his Father's timing. He had the power to act when and how he wanted to, but he chose to wait. Waiting is hard work, waiting is humbling work, and waiting is powerful work. "I waited patiently for the LORD; he turned to me and heard my cry." (Psalm 40:1) Are you waiting on God? Are you doing so with passivity or with passion? With grumbling or anticipation?

Day 2
Read: Exodus 1:8-14 Then a new king, who did not know about Joseph, came to power in Egypt. "Look," he said to his people, "the Israelites have become much too numerous for us. Come, we must deal shrewdly with them or they will become even more numerous and, if war breaks out, will join our enemies, fight against us and leave the country." So they put slave masters over them to oppress them with forced labor, and they built Pithom and Rameses as store cities for Pharaoh.

But the more they were oppressed, the more they multiplied and spread; so the Egyptians came to dread the Israelites and worked them ruthlessly. They made their lives bitter with hard labor in brick and mortar and with all kinds of work in the fields; in all their hard labor the Egyptians used them ruthlessly.

Reflect:
Joseph, a celebrity of national and international fame who was used by God to save an entire nation became an irrelevant, unknown to the reigning king. What the former celebrity did for the nation in the past had no bearing on life now. Such is the fate of all humans of great renown. They are soon forgotten. Now the people this hero helped save from famine find themselves living as slaves in a hostile place. A new king, who did not know about Joseph, came to power and the waiting began. The hero who had taken the people of Israel into Egypt had been a waiter himself, as had his father, and his father's father. They had all been trained through waiting on God to know and trust God. Now the people as an entire nation had new vocations, they were all waiters. Their wait would last for centuries. Some of these waiters would die waiting. Some would live to see God's deliverance and the end of their waiting in Egypt only to enter a time of waiting in the wilderness. When God said, "go" they went, when he said, "stop" they stopped. Such is the life of a waiter. Israel was, by and large, not good at waiting. They complained...a lot. They tried to quit and take up other vocations but God convinced them through very direct means that they should stay where he had put them. Israel finally came to the land of promise but the obstinate waiters did not get to go in. Their children did and these children of waiters became warrior waiters. They were trained in a different kind of waiting. Their parents walked (wandered) in the wilderness as God trained them in the grace of waiting. The children, now in the land of promise, lived in a state of near constant combat. Was this the promise they had waited for? Yes, and no. The promise was not a life free from the waiting or walking, or "warrioring" it was a life free to experience God and his life. The various ways God trained his people to wait was part of his larger purposes in training them to trust and to love him. Those who died in Egypt, or in the wilderness, or later in Canaan, all alike, had the same opportunity to experience God's abundant life for them. None of them were cheated; all of them, regardless of their circumstances could experience God if they would. Some did, some did not. Waiting is training. Waiting might feel like you are stuck in Egypt, wandering in the wilderness, or hoping this current battle will finally come to an end. Whatever your situation...your vocation is waiter. Waiting is what waiters do. The only question is what kind of waiter will you choose to be? Whether you will wait is not your choice, what kind of waiter you will be is entirely your choice.

Day 3
Read:

Ex. 2:23-3:7 During that long period, the king of Egypt died. The Israelites groaned in their slavery and cried out, and their cry for help because of their slavery went up to God. God heard their groaning and he remembered his covenant with Abraham, with Isaac and with Jacob. So God looked on the Israelites and was concerned about them. Now Moses was tending the flock of Jethro his father-in-law, the priest of Midian, and he led the flock to the far side of the desert and came to Horeb, the mountain of God.

Reflect:

Moses became a waiter but he was first an "at risk child." He was placed by his mom into a basket and put afloat in the river. This seems like a reckless way of protecting a baby but it was her desperate attempt to keep him from a certain death. God, of course, intervened and Moses then became royalty. Scripture fast forward's Moses early years. In one verse he is being rescued from the River, in the next verse he is all grown up. Those years probably did go by quickly for Moses; they were likely years of ease and privilege. But then the clock slowed down for him. The next approximately forty-years were spent herding sheep. It wasn't that Moses knew he was waiting on God's timing to go and lead the nation out of Egypt, he didn't. But it was true nonetheless that God was teaching him how to wait. Specifically he was teaching him how to wait on sheep. A shepherd leads his sheep but he does a whole lot of waiting on the sheep. He waits for them to eat, and they are never in a hurry to eat. He waits on them to sleep, and protects them through the night watches. God was training Moses to wait on his people, he would shepherd them through forty years of wandering. Waiting can feel like nothing significant is happening. When we are active, doing, working...then it feels like we are actually "living life." Waiting feels like life is slipping away, like we are missing out. But waiting is living and living is waiting. Waiting only feels like a waste when we do so disconnected from God and his larger purposes in our lives. To simply wait for the seasons to turn and then finally for our last breathe, this truly is meaningless waiting. But to wait on God, to serve with our very lives at his pleasure...this is the only meaningful life. If he says to "go, be active, accomplish" then we do so and it matters what we do. If he says "be still, wait" then we do so and it matters what we do. All humans enter life waiting. Waiting to be held, to be fed, and to be changed. We are at the mercy of others. Many humans end this life in the same way they began it; waiting. Frailty or illness removes our ability to act freely; we are once again at the mercy and the timing of others. In between infancy and end of the life...we would do well to remember and to reflect on our lives as waiters of the living God. Working or waiting...living or dying...in Him alone we find purpose.

Day 4
Read:

Ex. 2:23-3:7 There the angel of the LORD appeared to him in flames of fire from within a bush. Moses saw that though the bush was on fire it did not burn up. So Moses thought, "I will go over and see this strange sight—why the bush does not burn up." When the LORD saw that he had gone over to look, God called to him from within the bush, "Moses! Moses!" And Moses said, "Here I am." "Do not come any closer," God said. "Take off your sandals, for the place where you are standing is holy ground."

Reflect:

Imagine you are a slave in Egypt and you hear for the first time of the great promises of God made to Abraham. How exciting that would be! You might, for the first time in your life, have hope. Perhaps your waiting and suffering has purpose. Perhaps your waiting will soon come to and end. Maybe you put a calendar up and began to mark the days until God's promise is fulfilled in your life. The days are long and hard but each night, with joy, you mark off another day. Each day you mark off means the great day of release is getting near. But...the days began to drag on. That initial burst of excitement dissipates into the dust of your daily grind. Days turn to years and to decades. Then your final day on earth dawns, your very last chance to experience God's great promise and then the sun sets on your final day and you die a slave in Egypt. Now for the question...did God rip you off? Were you cheated, lied to and given over to false hopes? Were his promises not for you after all? Let's go back in our narrative, back sometime after the early days of excitement and before the days of despair. In those days of waiting, looking to the future, and anticipation of freedom you find that your heart is becoming more and more drawn to God himself. Gradually your thoughts and feelings of what God might do cause your mind and heart to more and more contemplate God himself. You speak to him and he speaks to you, even as you make bricks for Pharaoh's projects. You still mark your calendar looking to the future but you also began to write on the calendar what God said to you and did in and around you today. You find that you would truly love to see God move among his people in your lifetime and bring about the great rescue...but you have become a person of deep contentment in God. Life has become about God, not what God might or might not do in your life. Whether you die in Egypt or experience the exodus, either way, you are already free. Waiting is work and your labor in the Lord is never in vain. "Therefore, my dear brothers, stand firm. Let nothing move you. Always give yourselves fully to the work of the Lord, because you know that your labor in the Lord is not in vain." (1 Cor. 15:58)

Day 5
Read:

Ex. 2:23-3:7 Then he said, "I am the God of your father, the God of Abraham, the God of Isaac and the God of Jacob." At this, Moses hid his face, because he was afraid to look at God. The LORD said, "I have indeed seen the misery of my people in Egypt. I have heard them crying out because of their slave drivers, and I am concerned about their suffering.

Reflect:

You are waiter. How are you doing with that? Some days and some situations you probably do better than others. If you want to close the gap on faith and love then you must do an honest evaluation of how your waiting is going. If you find that you are responding the same ways in your thoughts, emotions and choices now that you did a year ago, and those choices do not reflect Christ then you are not closing the gap. Do not despair, be honest and take the reality of who you are right now to God. Ask him to help you change, to give you a vision for real change. If you are serious about change...then commit to it. Then go and utilize the many resources he has put at your disposal to actually change. You may think you have no resources or opportunity to change but that is not true. You have God's word, God's Spirit, God's people, and God's promises. Those are tangible resources with practical applications and results...it is important that you see them that way. Now as you employ God's resources in your life you must also fully embrace waiting. Waiting on God is critical to becoming like Christ. Impatience is not a friend of growth. It takes us off the path and into the ditch. Then when have grown tired of living the "ditch life" we get back on the waiting path. We go back into the path of God's will and God's resources. Remember, waiters are never passive they are always vigilant and active in their waiting. Passivity is the opposite of real waiting. Waiting implies something anticipated in the future. People do not wait for nothing; they wait for something. You are to wait on God. As you wait on God you are simultaneously experiencing God. The beauty of being a waiter for the King is that even in the waiting, and maybe especially in the waiting, we experience God's presence, power, and beauty. You are waiting on God. You are not merely waiting on God to "do" something; you are waiting on him. Like the bride waits for the groom, so we wait for God. It is God's full presence in our lives we are waiting for. During the time of waiting we get to experience his presence in part. Therefore even the waiting on God is experiencing God.

Week 49/Day 1
Read:

Is. 9:1-7 Nevertheless, there will be no more gloom for those who were in distress. In the past he humbled the land of Zebulun and the land of Naphtali, but in the future he will honor Galilee of the Gentiles, by the way of the sea, along the Jordan— The people walking in darkness have seen a great light; on those living in the land of the shadow of death a light has dawned.

Reflect:

"On my bed I remember you; I think of you through the watches of the night. "(Psalm 63:6) The Psalmist spoke of remembering God, thinking of him while lying in his sleepless bed throughout the night. The night was divided into three "watches" of four hours. To lie sleepless through the night indicates something was amiss. The Psalmist says that he was worried about his enemies who wanted to take his life. As he waited he remembered and he intentionally chose his thoughts and directed them towards God. Who has not waited for morning to come? Night can be a particularly difficult time to wait. The hours can drag by so slowly, the shadows can be so deep and ominous. When morning breaks and shadows flee it is often true that our spirits lift a bit. The circumstances may not have changed but our perspective has. The same kind of thing happens when a long, dark winter finally gives way to spring. Or a long time of personal darkness breaks into the light. Whatever the nature of the darkness the waiting is long and hard. We cannot choose to make the sun rise or the spring to hasten and we cannot always choose the circumstances that brought darkness to our lives to go away but we can always choose our thoughts. God has given us this. The Psalmist set his thoughts on God through the long night. This was and is a great strategy for waiting. He had plenty to worry about as he waited for the unknowns of the next day but with God as the subject of his thoughts he had even more to rejoice about. He remembered God, as he thought back in time to all that God had done in his life so far. He thought of God's promises as his mind took him forward in time to the future. Our physical bodies are tied to time and place. We cannot take them backwards or forwards in time and we cannot be in two places at a time. But with our thoughts we can move around in both time and space. We can go to where God moved in the past and "see" him being faithful and powerful there. This is not creating mental unrealities this is taking a mental journey to a past reality. In a similar way we can travel in our thoughts to the God's faithfulness in the future. We can rest on his promises ahead of us as surely as we can remember his promises fulfilled behind us. The prophets looked back, looked forward...then looked around. We must do the same. While we wait through the watches of the night...our thoughts must go to the reality of God past, present, and future. This is how we wait in the light through the dark night.

Day 2
Read:

Is. 9:1-7 You have enlarged the nation and increased their joy; they rejoice before you as people rejoice at the harvest, as men rejoice when dividing the plunder. For as in the day of Midian's defeat, you have shattered the yoke that burdens them, the bar across their shoulders, the rod of their oppressor. Every warrior's boot used in battle and every garment rolled in blood will be destined for burning, will be fuel for the fire. For to us a child is born, to us a son is given, and the government will be on his shoulders. And he will be called Wonderful Counselor, Mighty God, Everlasting Father, Prince of Peace. Of the increase of his government and peace there will be no end. He will reign on David's throne and over his kingdom, establishing and upholding it with justice and righteousness from that time on and forever. The zeal of the LORD Almighty will accomplish this.

Reflect:

The prophets kept the vision of God in front of God's waiting people. These "foreseers" and "forth talkers" were God-gifted to live with their feet in the present but their minds-eye in the future. Not just any future, a future where God would reign. Sure often their "intel" regarding the future included coming judgment, they never sugar coated the facts. But after the judgment there was also promise. God would rescue his people. God would restore his people. God would redeem his people. God would return for his people. The people of God have frequently lived for long periods of time in the darkness, the valley of the shadow. When you have lived long in death valley it can seem like this is all there ever has been and this is all there ever will be. So the prophets spoke to those waiting in dark times and spaces. They told them of another time and place when and where the light will dawn. Warrior's boots will be burned in the fire along with the bloody garments of war. The oppressor's shackles will be broken and the government of the peace-prince will be never ending. This bright future can feel like an unreality if you have waited long for it. A dawning light can seem like a distant dream because it has been perpetual night for so long. This may all seem much to gloomy to describe your life right now. Maybe for you, for now...all is well. If so, then thank God but remember to cry out to him to help you set your hope fully on him not on the current "sunny days." The temptation, when all is "light" is to put our confidence in things that will not ultimately hold. If your life is one of dark waiting right now you too can be temped to misplace your hope. Your ultimate hope is not in a financial or relational or physical change for the better. You can pray and work and hope for those things, but you must put your ultimate hope in grace of the Lord Jesus. Lesser hopes can be good and God may grant them but only Jesus can hold as the anchor for your soul. "We have this hope as an anchor for the soul, firm and secure."(Hebrews 6:19)

Day 3

Read:

Is. 9:1-7 Nevertheless, there will be no more gloom for those who were in distress. In the past he humbled the land of Zebulun and the land of Naphtali, but in the future he will honor Galilee of the Gentiles, by the way of the sea, along the Jordan— The people walking in darkness have seen a great light; on those living in the land of the shadow of death a light has dawned. You have enlarged the nation and increased their joy; they rejoice before you as people rejoice at the harvest, as men rejoice when dividing the plunder. For as in the day of Midian's defeat, you have shattered the yoke that burdens them, the bar across their shoulders, the rod of their oppressor. Every warrior's boot used in battle and every garment rolled in blood will be destined for burning, will be fuel for the fire. For to us a child is born, to us a son is given, and the government will be on his shoulders. And he will be called Wonderful Counselor, Mighty God, Everlasting Father, Prince of Peace. Of the increase of his government and peace there will be no end. He will reign on David's throne and over his kingdom, establishing and upholding it with justice and righteousness from that time on and forever. The zeal of the LORD Almighty will accomplish this.

Reflect:

The prophets did a lot of foretelling of future events but much of what they said was directed at their present day. We are told enough about the future to know that it is secure, but not so much that we can attempt to live there. We trust the future to the Lord but we honor the Lord with our lives in the present. Often, perhaps too often, prophecy has been misused as a way of not fully engaging the present time. It has become a source of intellectual curiosity and a mental diversion rather than its intended motivation to live fully in the present time with confidence. The actual present can be hard, or dull, or unhappy and an imagined future can be easier, more exciting, and much better. Be careful that the imagined future is more than wishful thinking. Not that it is wrong or unhelpful to dream of a better day. But if we live perpetually dreaming of a future that we believe will be better but is not really promised by God then we do not live resilient, faith-filled lives in the present. The future we dream of may or may not come if God has not promised it to us. By all means dream, plan, and work for whatever "better" future you hope for. But if your future hope does not lead to full engagement in the present then it is off track. "This is the day the LORD has made; let us rejoice and be glad in it." (Psalm 118:24) Since this is so, God intends for us to fully engage today and to rejoice in the various aspects that make today, today. Of course not every part of today seems good to us. Perhaps much, or all of today seems bad. But this day will not have the final say in our lives. Choose to fix your thoughts on the future God has promised to you.

Let those thoughts shape your feelings and actions today. This is not wishful thinking this is wise living. Ultimate truth must shape today's choices.

Day 4
Read:
Matt. 4:13-17 Leaving Nazareth, he went and lived in Capernaum, which was by the lake in the area of Zebulun and Naphtali — to fulfill what was said through the prophet Isaiah: "Land of Zebulun and land of Naphtali, the way to the sea, along the Jordan, Galilee of the Gentiles — the people living in darkness have seen a great light; on those living in the land of the shadow of death a light has dawned."

Reflect:
Everybody trusts somebody. Maybe they trust an "expert" or an influential peer or perhaps they simply trust self. Who we decide to make our authority determines who will direct what we think and believe. This then determines how we "feel" about our lives and this in turn directs the choices we make. So how important is it that we are wise and careful in deciding how to trust? There have been many through the ages who have been self-proclaimed prophets. They have made predictions of the future that did not come to pass. They have declared certain things to be true about the present that were in fact not true. These prophets, not all of them religious, many have been politicians, professors, and often entertainers have gained a large following. Those who followed the false prophets experienced the bitter fruit of believing what is not true. Often this has led to utter devastation but at times just lives of quiet desperation. This is why James wrote that "Not many of you should presume to be teachers, my brothers, because you know that we who teach will be judged more strictly." (James 3:1) We should be very careful to "teach" what is real and true about God, people, and life because the stakes are very high in the realm of "thoughts". What we think shapes our very lives. We should also be very careful in who we choose to believe. There are a thousand teachers and prophets out there, all declaring diverse views on what you should give your life to. Be careful here, your very life depends on getting this right. Even if you have believed the gospel and have settled that Jesus is Lord of your eternity do not forget that he is Lord of your life now. If you can trust him with the truth of eternity then surely you must trust him with the truth of how you use your time, talents, and treasures now. Jesus is the final prophet and he is the greatest teacher. What he says about your life is said as the supreme, infallible expert. Will you look closely at the ONE the prophets foretold would come as the expert on your life right now? Look to how he thought, felt, and acted to understand how you are to live your life right now. He was more than merely an example, but he is not less than one. Look to Jesus, seek to live today his way.

229

Day 5
Read:

Matt. 4:13-17 Leaving Nazareth, he went and lived in Capernaum, which was by the lake in the area of Zebulun and Naphtali — to fulfill what was said through the prophet Isaiah: "Land of Zebulun and land of Naphtali, the way to the sea, along the Jordan, Galilee of the Gentiles — the people living in darkness have seen a great light; on those living in the land of the shadow of death a light has dawned."

Reflect:

"All these people were still living by faith when they died. They did not receive the things promised; they only saw them and welcomed them from a distance. And they admitted that they were aliens and strangers on earth." (Hebrews 11:13) What good is a promise of the future if you die before it arrives? The people listed in Hebrews 11 believed the promises of God and lived their lives with expectancy however they died before those promises were realized. Was their faith in vain? No, of course not. The promises they "outlived" were partially fulfilled in their lives and will be fully realized in the age to come. They were not "cheated" because they did not experience the fullness of the promises in their life on earth, no one does. They were looking "past" this life to the fuller experience of life that God had planned for them. "People who say such things show that they are looking for a country of their own. If they had been thinking of the country they had left, they would have had opportunity to return. Instead, they were longing for a better country — a heavenly one. Therefore God is not ashamed to be called their God, for he has prepared a city for them." (Hebrews 11:14-16) This doesn't mean that their earthly lives were basically a "throw away." They experienced God personally during their lives of faith on earth. They didn't get to see all he was going to do, but they did get to experience personal relationship with God. Ultimately the promises of God all lead to God himself. The full experience of the promises of God will not be something God "does" or "provides" it will be God himself. We will see him face to face and we will know him as he is. So while these men and women of faith did not live to see the final fulfillment of God's promises they did live knowing and experiencing the God of those promises. They may not have seen the promises fulfilled yet God himself fulfilled them. Today you can experience the God who makes and keeps promises. You may outlive the final fulfillment of his promises in his life but you will not outlive the God who makes those promises. "I have set the LORD always before me. Because he is at my right hand, I will not be shaken." (Psalm 16:8)

Week 50/Day 1
Read:

Luke 2:1-16 In those days Caesar Augustus issued a decree that a census should be taken of the entire Roman world. (This was the first census that took place while Quirinius was governor of Syria.) And everyone went to his own town to register. So Joseph also went up from the town of Nazareth in Galilee to Judea, to Bethlehem the town of David, because he belonged to the house and line of David. He went there to register with Mary, who was pledged to be married to him and was expecting a child. While they were there, the time came for the baby to be born, and she gave birth to her firstborn, a son. She wrapped him in cloths and placed him in a manger, because there was no room for them in the inn.

Reflect:

Hope is a powerful thing. It is a thought based on a thing, event, or person. It is an emotion and it is deeper than a thought and it drives action when "reason" says "give up!" Hope drives people to accomplish what might seem impossible. Hopelessness drives people to give up on what is entirely possible. "Hope deferred makes the heart sick, but a longing fulfilled is a tree of life."(Proverbs 13:12) When the "Living Hope" was born in Bethlehem it was with much heavenly fanfare but with little human attention. What gets "heaven's" attention and what gets "earth's" attention are often two very different things. Jesus said that what is highly valued among men is detestable in God's sight. What people tend to see as valuable is what they have placed their hopes in. One reason God finds what people value as detestable is because of his love for men and women. He knows that misplaced values lead to misplaced hopes. A misplaced hope leads to misplaced lives. Something that is misplaced is lost. Lostness is a component of having misplaced, or wrong hopes. Jesus came to earth in ways that most humans would deem strange. When the Savior of the world would come, his coming would be the most important event in history. Thus the wise men went looking for him in a palace not a stable. They searched for the Savior in line with their own ideas of what is valuable. Christ came to set our values straight in order that we would set our hopes straight. He came not be served, but to serve and to give his life as a ransom for many. Hope is powerful but it must be well placed. It has the power to drive action and to propel our very lives. In the end if the hope was not in Christ then that hope drove life to a dead end. We must value what is valuable and hope for what is certain. Close the gap on faith and love today by examining closely what you holding on to most closely and dearly in your heart.

Day 2
Read:

Luke 2:1-16 In those days Caesar Augustus issued a decree that a census should be taken of the entire Roman world. (This was the first census that took place while Quirinius was governor of Syria.) And everyone went to his own town to register. So Joseph also went up from the town of Nazareth in Galilee to Judea, to Bethlehem the town of David, because he belonged to the house and line of David. He went there to register with Mary, who was pledged to be married to him and was expecting a child. While they were there, the time came for the baby to be born, and she gave birth to her firstborn, a son. She wrapped him in cloths and placed him in a manger, because there was no room for them in the inn.

Reflect:

A virgin birth is a strange thing, but a birth is a strange thing as well. We are used to births. They have happened billions of times. We are not used to virgin births, they have happened one time. If throughout human history people simple suddenly appeared on earth and that was the way it had always happened it would not be strange it would be normal. If people slowly evolved from the mud in ponds and lakes around the world and over months and years eventually became a "person" that would likewise not be strange, it would be normal. What is strange and what is normal is tied to what is and has been. If no one had ever been born from a woman's body and suddenly a person was born in that fashion who would believe it? It would impossible. "People just 'appear' or people come from 'mud' but people don't just 'come out of a woman', why that is absurd." Why have many found the virgin birth absurd? Because it is not normally how people have been born. When you start with "people" and with the idea of "normal" then you find the birth of Jesus ridiculous. But what if you start at the proper place, with God? Then ask the question..."could God do it this way if you wanted to?" The answer is "of course he could." Then the next question is, "is there evidence that God did bring Jesus into the world through a virgin birth?" The answer is, "yes, much evidence." We all become used to what is normal for us, even when what is normal is fantastic. A sunset is normal, but it is fantastic. A baby's birth is normal, but it is fantastic. Human love is normal, but it is fantastic. What is normal for us ceases to be fantastic for us and it also limits our "vision" as to what will yet be true for us. What happened at the birth of Christ was a singularity, a one-time event. It was something that was inconceivable by the human mind. What will happen in the future, the things that God has planned for his people are inconceivable now. We who are trapped in space and time and cannot fully conceive of anything other than what is "normal."

However as we contemplate our ultimate hope and the source of that hope, the living God, we can expand our imaginations to go beyond the "now" and the "normal." We can live in the "now" and "normal" with a fuller vision of our future and fantastic hope.

Day 3
Read:
Luke 2:11-14 Today in the town of David a Savior has been born to you; he is Christ the Lord. This will be a sign to you: You will find a baby wrapped in cloths and lying in a manger." Suddenly a great company of the heavenly host appeared with the angel, praising God and saying, "Glory to God in the highest, and on earth peace to men on whom his favor rests."

Reflect:
The answers to our most important questions cannot be discovered by human exploration or reasoned out by the human mind. We can ponder with our minds the great questions regarding our origins, our purpose, and our destiny but we cannot know the answers unless there is someone who stands outside of space and time who can and will give them to us. These questions and their answers transcend space and time but we cannot. Unless there is a God and unless he speaks to us we cannot know the most important things that can be known. Jesus is the Word of God made flesh. God has come to us so that we can know God. We do not have to guess regarding our purpose, we can know these things. We do not have to live in fear and uncertainty regarding our future destiny we can know. There are many important things that humans have discovered using their God-given reason but why we are here and what is to come are not among those things. "No eye has seen, no ear has heard, no mind has conceived what God has prepared for those who love him." (1 Corinthians 2:9) This verse demonstrates the hopelessness of unaided human reason in discovering purpose and destiny. We cannot with our senses or our minds discover what God has planned, yet we can know these things. The next verse shows us how, "God has revealed it to us by his Spirit." (1 Corinthians 2:10.) We cannot discover or reason out our destiny but we can know them because God has made it known to us. There are some things we can know via our senses and minds. We can know of God's existence and some things regarding his creative power. Paul wrote that, "The wrath of God is being revealed from heaven against all the godlessness and wickedness of men who suppress the truth by their wickedness, since what may be known about God is plain to them, because God has made it plain to them. For since the creation of the world God's invisible qualities — his eternal power and divine nature — have been clearly seen, being understood from what has been made, so that men are without excuse."(Romans 1:18-20) Knowing "about" God is a long way from knowing God in a personal way.

To know God "relationally" requires more than the testimony of the physical universe he has created. It requires the incarnation of his uncreated Son, Jesus. "No one has ever seen God, but God the One and Only, who is at the Father's side, has made him known." (John 1:18) Do you have questions that remain unanswered? Perhaps some of these questions are important and life affecting. Perhaps you are anxious, or sad, or angry that you do not have all the answers you want. Take time today to give thanks to Jesus because has answered the most important question that can be asked in time or in eternity. Will you trust him with the mystery and praise him for what he has revealed?

Day 4
Read:
Luke 2:1-16 But the angel said to them, "Do not be afraid. I bring you good news of great joy that will be for all the people. Today in the town of David a Savior has been born to you; he is Christ the Lord. This will be a sign to you: You will find a baby wrapped in cloths and lying in a manger."

Reflect:
The story of the birth of Jesus evokes strong "cultural emotions." In fact the Christmas season as a whole brings warms feelings to the general population, at least in much of the western world. But sadly these warm feelings are often devoid of sound thoughts. Most people do not believe that the birth of Jesus into the world was the most important event in history in terms of the advancement of "human knowledge." It may seem strange to think of the birth of Jesus this way but we must in fact "think" not just feel regarding the incarnation. The greatest "knowledge" leap forward for humanity was not a scientific discovery but the incarnation. Jesus brought to us the knowledge of God as well as the only way to relationship with God. He brought to us what we could not, in an infinity of time, have discovered on our own. Read the account of Jesus' birth again but do so as if you are reading "real information" not "religious information." Read, as it is, a historical narrative with spiritual implications. Read it as "news" with important facts that concern how you deal with your life today and in the future. Read it as valuable, incredibly valuable information that you desperately need to escape disaster and experience good. Read it again and rouse yourself as you do. Tell yourself the truth about this. If only you could see it as the terrific news that it is you would read it with laughter, or tears, or shouts, or fear...or all of that. Ask God to help you think and feel what is appropriate to think and feel about this news of Jesus entrance into our collective history. If we can think more clearly and accurately and feel more appropriately about the coming of Christ into the world we will be positioned to live more accurately and appropriately in the world. Have warm cultural feelings regarding Christmas season, or not. Some do and some don't. Whether the season evokes warm or terrible feelings it is very important that the truth evokes correct thoughts.

Let the facts of Jesus settle deeply in your mind, so those facts can shape how you feel, and those feelings can power your life to worship him in the totality of your life.

Day 5
Read:
Luke 2:1-16 Suddenly a great company of the heavenly host appeared with the angel, praising God and saying, "Glory to God in the highest, and on earth peace to men on whom his favor rests." When the angels had left them and gone into heaven, the shepherds said to one another, "Let's go to Bethlehem and see this thing that has happened, which the Lord has told us about." So they hurried off and found Mary and Joseph, and the baby, who was lying in the manger.

Reflect:
Gospel means good or joyful news. The angels declared that the birth of Christ was "good news of great joy." The angels declared the gospel of the coming of the Savior. Something that had never happened before in human history was occurring then and there. In fact the pivot point of all human history was that very day. Consider all the momentous events in history, great accomplishments, great tragedies, great births and great deaths. All of these together are nothing compared to the birth and death of the Savior. The birth of the Savior came with some fanfare, angels declared the glory of that day. Yet theirs was a very limited audience; some shepherds in a field. For the most part the day went without notice, the event shrouded in relative obscurity. The glory of that day spread as the gospel spread heart by heart day by day. What is "today" for you? Is it a day of great accomplishment or great sorrow? A day of personal history making or a day to soon be forgotten? How do see today? How should you see today? For those who do not know God and do not believe he is active in human history all days eventually become "dust." Eventually a life is over and all that is left of that life is a memory in another person's mind. But then those who remember die and then nothing is left of a life at all. This is the "empty way of life" that Peter said Jesus has redeemed us from. (1 Peter 1:18). If you know God then you are known today. This day is not mere "dust" and your life will never become the dust of death. You will live forever because Christ was born into human history. What you think, feel, and do today matters. It matters today and it will matter into eternity. Every day is shaping us; every day is a day that God intends to use for his purposes. Do not see today or any day as an "empty" day. Those days ceased to exist when Christ redeemed you. The day before or behind you right now may seem to be void of eternal meaning but things are often not as they seem. A baby in a manger did not seem to be the pivot point of human history but he was. The angels "saw" it, and proclaimed the truth to the shepherds.

Your days must be seen now in light of that day. Emptiness no longer rules the day, any day. Redemption rules your day if you are in Christ. It is incumbent on you to live this day in your mind, will, and emotions in light of the gospel. You can if you will.

Week 51/Day 1
Read:
Rev. 21:1-5 Then I saw a new heaven and a new earth, for the first heaven and the first earth had passed away, and there was no longer any sea. I saw the Holy City, the new Jerusalem, coming down out of heaven from God, prepared as a bride beautifully dressed for her husband. And I heard a loud voice from the throne saying, "Now the dwelling of God is with men, and he will live with them. They will be his people, and God himself will be with them and be their God. He will wipe every tear from their eyes. There will be no more death or mourning or crying or pain, for the old order of things has passed away." He who was seated on the throne said, "I am making everything new!" Then he said, "Write this down, for these words are trustworthy and true."

Reflect:
Waiting can exacerbate suffering. In fact part of what makes suffering what it is, is the waiting. If we are hurting physically or mentally our pain can be increased by the fact that we are anxious to see it come to an end. If we have a set time frame and if we know when a current challenge will end then it can make the waiting easier. Not easy, but easier. When there is no set time for our suffering to be alleviated, when all we see is another day followed by endless days of trouble...our suffering today increases. Waiting is difficult work. Waiting well is powerful work. How does one wait "well"? Particularly when the waiting is during a painful season of life? The starting point for waiting well is gaining a compelling vision for the power and long-term impact of waiting. Advent Season is a season of waiting and a reminder of the power of waiting well. Generations waited for Christ to come, and he did. Generations have waited for Christ to return, and he will. Now for all who live between the great "waits" it is important to see the value God places on waiting well. If we are going to maximize the benefits of waiting we must capture a compelling vision for the value of waiting. The Scriptures are full of waiting and the powerful ways in which God uses waiting in our lives. Your own life is very likely a living example of the power and beauty of waiting. Have you paid attention to how God has used waiting in the past to shape you? Are you paying attention right now to how God is using a season of waiting to make you more like Christ in character? You will have to wait; it is the nature of being human. God waits as well, but never impatiently or with anxiety. His waiting, like all of his activity is joyful, purposeful and powerful. Notice I said waiting is a form of his activity.

To wait well we must learn to wait actively. We do not wait like a dead thing lying on the ground...powerless to do anything except to lay there. We wait as living children of the living God. We wait empowered by faith and love to move decisively towards God and others. Our waiting must be powered by a vision of hope. "No" we do not know when God will move. "Yes" we do know that he will move. In the meantime our vision of waiting is a passionate, active, loving, faithful vision. Wait actively on God.

Day 2
Read:
Rev. 21:1-5 Then I saw a new heaven and a new earth, for the first heaven and the first earth had passed away, and there was no longer any sea. I saw the Holy City, the new Jerusalem, coming down out of heaven from God, prepared as a bride beautifully dressed for her husband. And I heard a loud voice from the throne saying, "Now the dwelling of God is with men, and he will live with them. They will be his people, and God himself will be with them and be their God. He will wipe every tear from their eyes. There will be no more death or mourning or crying or pain, for the old order of things has passed away." He who was seated on the throne said, "I am making everything new!" Then he said, "Write this down, for these words are trustworthy and true."

Reflect:
What are you waiting for today? Are you waiting for a new job? New child? New relationship? New health prognosis? New season of the year? Waiting is the common fare of human life. We spend brief moments "living" in the moment and the bulk of our lives "living in the future." We wait for something that is not currently true to become true. When we get what we have waited for we don't spend long enjoying the experience, we most often move on in our minds to what is next and next after next. What we wait for in the future shapes who are becoming in the present. What we wait for captures much of our mental capacity and imagination. What captures our minds and imaginations is the most powerful shaping force in our lives. Think about what you think about the most. It is most likely something that is yet to happen. Either something you hope will happen or something you hope will not happen. Now reflect on the fact that what you think about the most shapes your life. Your "inner" self will eventually become your "outer" self. So, can you decide what you will "wait" for? That sounds ridiculous, or course you cannot decide that. The things you wait for are outside the realm of your will; you cannot control them. But is that really the case? By choosing the things you wait for I mean choosing the things that are in the future that you will think about the most.

If you fix your thoughts on things that shape you into a person who is full of angst, or fear, or greed, or insecurity, or discontent...then the things you are waiting for are in fact misshaping you. On the other hand if you fix you're thoughts on things that are good, true, pure, lovely, admirable, excellent, and praiseworthy then you truly being "shaped" by the future. People who are seriously ill or very old think much about death and less about life. They tend to believe, and are often right...that the bulk of their earthly existence is behind them. They "wait" for the life to come. They can do this with dread or with expectancy. If you love the Lord you must, whatever you age or health status...fix your "waiting" on your future life with Jesus. These kinds of waiting thoughts make you into a person who lives more fully and more joyfully and more wisely in the present. Decide today to wait on your future with the Lord. Let that waiting shape your living today.

Day 3
Read:
Rev. 21:1-5 Then I saw a new heaven and a new earth, for the first heaven and the first earth had passed away, and there was no longer any sea. I saw the Holy City, the new Jerusalem, coming down out of heaven from God, prepared as a bride beautifully dressed for her husband. And I heard a loud voice from the throne saying, "Now the dwelling of God is with men, and he will live with them. They will be his people, and God himself will be with them and be their God. He will wipe every tear from their eyes. There will be no more death or mourning or crying or pain, for the old order of things has passed away." He who was seated on the throne said, "I am making everything new!" Then he said, "Write this down, for these words are trustworthy and true."

Reflect:
If you have believed the gospel your future is bright. It is a future void of death, grief, and pain. Your future is an inheritance that cannot be lost or taken because God protects it. However, now for a "little while" you will likely suffer the grief of various trials. These trials are part of God's refinement process that is directly connected to your bright future. "Praise be to the God and Father of our Lord Jesus Christ! In his great mercy he has given us new birth into a living hope through the resurrection of Jesus Christ from the dead, and into an inheritance that can never perish, spoil or fade — kept in heaven for you, who through faith are shielded by God's power until the coming of the salvation that is ready to be revealed in the last time. In this you greatly rejoice, though now for a little while you may have had to suffer grief in all kinds of trials. These have come so that your faith — of greater worth than gold, which perishes even though refined by fire — may be proved genuine and may result in praise, glory and honor when Jesus Christ is revealed. (1 Peter 1:3-7)

Now, about that phrase a "little while." Peter either had a different perspective on time or he was exaggerating. The trials that you are enduring certainly do not feel like a "little while." For some they are life long struggles. Peter was not exaggerating; he did in fact have a different perspective. He had trained his mind to see the current struggle from the perspective of the promised end. It is true that Peter is unique; he had a front row seat to the earthly life of the Lord. It is also true that Peter gained this perspective in the same way that you can. He set his mind on the promises and power of God and over time this shaped his perspective into what it became. He is not making light of present trials he is making much of future glory. Lest you think he was alone in this perspective Paul said much the same thing, "For our light and momentary troubles are achieving for us an eternal glory that far outweighs them all." (2 Cor. 4:17) Paul might seem to be diminishing or even belittling the terrible struggles that people endure but he was not. Like Peter he was making much of the future, he was not denying the weight of the present. Compared to the weight of glory, the present struggles are lightweights. Maybe you are not there yet in your perspective. Don't worry; just keep closing the gap. You can but if you will. It is not easy work to get a great perspective but it is good work. And if you are willing, God is happy to help you.

Day 4
Read:
Rev. 21:1-2Then I saw a new heaven and a new earth, for the first heaven and the first earth had passed away, and there was no longer any sea. I saw the Holy City, the new Jerusalem, coming down out of heaven from God, prepared as a bride beautifully dressed for her husband.

Reflect:
When we wait for a future "when" we don't merely want another time we want other circumstances. People do not just want to see next month, or next year come around if they are unhappy with their current circumstances. They want the circumstances of their lives to change. The future they hope for and wait for is a different life not merely a different time. So we are waiting not merely for "when" but for "what"...what will be different then that will make life better. As followers of Christ we wait primarily for "who" not "when" or "what." We wait for the time when what is true about our lives is that we will live fully in the presence of God. God himself will be with us. He will very directly do away with the things that bring pain and sorrow. He will bring about the new order where all of heaven and earth is remade. Part of preparing for this future now is that we are being trained through present trials and troubles to trust God. There is a theology that is prevalent among Christians that says God is primarily concerned with giving his children abundant "stuff" now.

That is, the focus of growing our faith should be on accumulating wealth and possessions and maintaining physical health, precisely the things that most non-believers value and pursue. This theology shapes the human heart in a direction away from God. Why would a heart that has been taught throughout life to value everything except God suddenly find itself valuing God alone above all else? We are training for eternity now. Eternity for the Christ follower will be full of discovery and adventure but mostly it will be full of the presence of God. We are learning now to love God, to hope in God, to value God above all else. Only when we believe this and pursue it as a compelling vision will what Paul wrote make any sense at all. "Therefore, since we have been justified through faith, we have peace with God through our Lord Jesus Christ, through whom we have gained access by faith into this grace in which we now stand. And we rejoice in the hope of the glory of God. Not only so, but we also rejoice in our sufferings, because we know that suffering produces perseverance; perseverance, character; and character, hope. And hope does not disappoint us, because God has poured out his love into our hearts by the Holy Spirit, whom he has given us." (Romans 5:1-5) Rejoice in suffering not because you love to suffer but because it is part of a compelling vision for your life. You can experience God in fuller ways now and you will experience God in his fullness in the future. Nothing compares to this. Not the accumulation of stuff or the temporary holding on to physical health. In the end you will give up both your stuff and your health. But if you have valued God now the character you have formed will continue on into eternity. This character will not disappoint.

Day 5
Read:
Rev. 21:1-5 Then I saw a new heaven and a new earth, for the first heaven and the first earth had passed away, and there was no longer any sea. I saw the Holy City, the new Jerusalem, coming down out of heaven from God, prepared as a bride beautifully dressed for her husband. And I heard a loud voice from the throne saying, "Now the dwelling of God is with men, and he will live with them. They will be his people, and God himself will be with them and be their God. He will wipe every tear from their eyes. There will be no more death or mourning or crying or pain, for the old order of things has passed away." He who was seated on the throne said, "I am making everything new!" Then he said, "Write this down, for these words are trustworthy and true."

Reflect:
The future is focused on the "new." A new heaven, new earth, new Jerusalem, new "everything." If you like change then you like "new." If you don't like change this may not sound compelling to you. The truth is everyone likes change they like...and everyone dislikes change they don't like. That is a

truism but it reveals the fact that though some people say they like change and others say they dislike change all people like and dislike change at some level. The change that is coming for those who have trusted Christ is "all things made new." This new does not mean totally different. The first time God created the world and people to live in it he declared it "good." The new heavens and new earth will be new but not totally dissimilar to this one. This is important to contemplate so that we will not see the life to come as weird and beyond our ability to even contemplate. How can you look forward to something that you cannot possibly get your mind even partially around? If the future is a blur, a sort of spiritual fog...with vague ideas, mostly from culture not Scripture, of floating around as disembodied spirits then no wonder we rarely think about it with anticipation. What is coming is new...all things made new...but what is coming is fully good and you will like it, you will like it a lot! Paul wrote that what is coming in the future for those who love God is beyond the human mind to comprehend on its on... "However, as it is written: "No eye has seen, no ear has heard, no mind has conceived what God has prepared for those who love him" but God has revealed it to us by his Spirit. The Spirit searches all things, even the deep things of God." (1 Corinthians 2:9-10) But notice the fact that though the human cannot discover through reason or exploration what God alone can reveal has in fact been revealed to us. What we cannot know though unaided reason we can know through God's revelation to us. As we look to Jesus, the Word of God made flesh, we can see glimpses now of the life we are to live then. His was and is a life of complete joy, power, and contentment. He lived a life of ongoing communion with God the Father. We have through the revelation of Jesus and the Scriptures the ability to "conceive" of what God has prepared for those who love him. Now it is important that you give energy and time to these mental concepts (thoughts of what is real) so that they will shape your hearts in the direction of God. What you cannot conceive on your own, you can now see because God has made it known to you.

Week 52/Day 1
Read:
Gal. 5:1-6 It is for freedom that Christ has set us free. Stand firm, then, and do not let yourselves be burdened again by a yoke of slavery. Mark my words! I, Paul, tell you that if you let yourselves be circumcised, Christ will be of no value to you at all. Again I declare to every man who lets himself be circumcised that he is obligated to obey the whole law. You who are trying to be justified by law have been alienated from Christ; you have fallen away from grace. But by faith we eagerly await through the Spirit the righteousness for which we hope. For in Christ Jesus neither circumcision nor uncircumcision has any value. The only thing that counts is faith expressing itself through love.

Reflect:

If you are a follower of Christ you must be careful to not retreat back into an "earning" mode. When people try to earn God's favor they tend to pick and choose how they will do so. The externals, the things that are relatively easy for them to do become their choice of ways to earn God's favor. However if a person really wanted to try and earn relationship with God (an impossible feat) they would have to be perfect in every way. The good news is that Christ has set us free to live in freedom. This sounds redundant. What else would freedom be except to live free? Many people have been set free from a former bondage but do not live in freedom. A prisoner may be out of his cell but in his heart and mind still locked up behind mental and emotional bars. He is free in one sense but not in another, even more important sense. Christians have been set free from earning God's favor, but they must choose to live fully in that freedom. We cannot earn but we can try. When we try to live in an earning posture towards God we are choosing to live in a jail cell. The door to the cell is unlocked and open; we can walk out if we want to. There is no jailer there guarding the door, there is not judge or judgment to sentence us there. If we sit in this cell we do so because we have put ourselves there. As you contemplate a life of closing the gap on faith and love do not turn this opportunity into earning. God offers you a life of his abundance. Jesus said..."The thief comes only to steal and kill and destroy; I have come that they may have life, and have it to the full." (John 10:10) His life of abundance must be "lived in", that is it must be pursued and embraced into our hearts and lives. Since this abundant life is a real thing, not some vaguely religious semi-real thing, we must actually, practically move into it with our wills. The ongoing challenge humans face is to mistake receiving what is offered freely by choice and effort with earning. Love freely offered, whether from another person or from God, requires ongoing action and attitudes to enjoy that love. Do not confuse these actions and efforts with earning they are not the same. The actions are motivated by gratitude and devotion, they are the choices of a person who has been accepted and wants to experience and express this acceptance more fully. The "earner" is trying to be or feel accepted and their actions are driven by insecurity and fear. The actions may look similar but the attitudes and the final effect on the soul are quite different. Reject anything that smacks of earning, earning is an affront to love. Choose actions and attitudes that will move you farther into joy this action is the close friend of love.

Day 2
Read:

Gal. 5:1-6 It is for freedom that Christ has set us free. Stand firm, then, and do not let yourselves be burdened again by a yoke of slavery. Mark my words! I, Paul, tell you that if you let yourselves be circumcised, Christ will be of no value to you at all.

Again I declare to every man who lets himself be circumcised that he is obligated to obey the whole law. You who are trying to be justified by law have been alienated from Christ; you have fallen away from grace. But by faith we eagerly await through the Spirit the righteousness for which we hope. For in Christ Jesus neither circumcision nor uncircumcision has any value. The only thing that counts is faith expressing itself through love.

Reflect:

A great challenge for people who enjoy the blessings of God in their lives is the tendency to not make the connection between God and his blessings. That is they experience the freedom, joy, security and other manifold blessings that come from life in Christ. They experience those things because of God's grace manifest in their lives and because they have made choices to live in that grace. They have sought the Lord in his word and prayer. They have pursued community with others who are like-minded. They have approached the Lord with humility because they have most often seen how powerless they are without him. Then as the grace of God flows in and through their lives they become more "whole and healthy" they begin to rely on themselves more and more. They have come to this place of increased health because of the grace of God operational in their lives but now they are attempting to live their lives on their own power. Uzziah became king at the age of sixteen and reigned for fifty-two years. The nation prospered under his leadership and he was a very popular king. He sought the Lord and relied on him for success and the Lord gave him success. His success, which was tied to his reliance on the Lord led him to begin to trust himself. This is the backstory for the fearful verse found in 2 Chronicles. "His fame spread far and wide, for he was greatly helped until he became powerful. But after Uzziah became powerful, his pride lead to his downfall." (2 Chronicles 26:15,16) James said that "God opposes the proud but give grace to the humble." (James 4:6). Uzziah was the recipient of grace...God's power at work in his life...until he became proud. Then he made God his opponent through his pride. Why would God become the opponent of the proud...indeed why would he not? Would you have God empower people in their attitudes and actions in opposition to him? Pride makes us first opponents of God...we are the ones who take a stand against God when our hearts become pride. Pride is insanity; humility is reality. God lives resolutely in reality, we often do not. Paul understood the need to rely on Christ in both the hard and the good times...do you? "I know what it is to be in need, and I know what it is to have plenty. I have learned the secret of being content in any and every situation, whether well fed or hungry, whether living in plenty or in want. I can do everything through him who gives me strength." (Philippians 4:12-13)

Day 3
Read:
Gal. 5:6 For in Christ Jesus neither circumcision nor uncircumcision has any value. The only thing that counts is faith expressing itself through love.

Reflect:
Paul says that externals, mere religious exercises, have no real value in bringing about or revealing our relationship with Jesus. The only thing that matters is confidence in Christ...revealed in love to others. Our full confidence must be in Christ not in our efforts. This kind of faith will show up in love for others. If "faith" in Christ does not show up in actual love for others then it is not the kind of faith that Paul says actually counts. This "faith expressed in love" theme is common in the Scriptures. Micah said it like this..."He has showed you, O man, what is good. And what does the LORD require of you? To act justly and to love mercy and to walk humbly with your God." (Micah 6:8) John wrote, "For anyone who does not love his brother, whom he has seen, cannot love God, whom he has not seen." (1 John 4:20) Jesus famously said in the great commandment...'"Love the Lord your God with all your heart and with all your soul and with all your mind.' This is the first and greatest commandment. And the second is like it: 'Love your neighbor as yourself.' All the Law and the Prophets hang on these two commandments." (Matthew 22:37-40) Not only is it a common theme it is a core theme. Jesus said that the key evidence of being his apprentice is the way we love one another. "By this all men will know that you are my disciples, if you love one another." (John 13:35) Closing the gap on faith and love are flip sides of the same coin. Growth in faith in Christ will result in growth in love for others and to really love others well will require a life of growing faith in Christ. This is not to say that those who don't love Christ can't love others, they can. But to love others with God's kind of love is only possible for those who are living in God's kind of love. It is unfortunate, to say the least, that many have claimed to have great faith in God and have expressed little love for others. In the first place without love for others there can be no real faith in God, at least not the kind that actually matters to God. In the second place it is unfortunate because it makes faith in God look like a meaningless thing. If a faith relationship with God does not show up in relationships with others then what good is it? In fact, what is it? Is it a real and living thing at all? "In the same way, faith by itself, if it is not accompanied by action, is dead." (James 2:17) James would say it is not a real, living faith. Do not be dismayed, this is not meant to be a rebuke but an encouragement. Our faith can and will result in growing love for others. God will make it happen. If we will set the Lord always before us and if we will make him and his priorities our priorities and if we will do the things that shape our values to conform to his values...then we will see that we are learning to love people more and more. Close the gap on real faith...you will close the gap on real love.

244

Day 4
Read:

Gal. 5:1-6 It is for freedom that Christ has set us free. Stand firm, then, and do not let yourselves be burdened again by a yoke of slavery. Mark my words! I, Paul, tell you that if you let yourselves be circumcised, Christ will be of no value to you at all. Again I declare to every man who lets himself be circumcised that he is obligated to obey the whole law. You who are trying to be justified by law have been alienated from Christ; you have fallen away from grace. But by faith we eagerly await through the Spirit the righteousness for which we hope. For in Christ Jesus neither circumcision nor uncircumcision has any value. The only thing that counts is faith expressing itself through love.

Reflect:

We leak perspective. We have it, we see things clearly...then we don't have it and things become a fog once again. So we need a continual infusion of perspective in order to live with consistent clarity. Time with God and his word bring perspective when that time is more than "putting in time." It is possible to "say some prayers" and read some verses from the Scripture and have your perspective untouched by these things. We must come to God with the intention of "seeing" what we need to see. We need to see ourselves clearly from his perspective. We need to see our circumstances clearly from his perspective. We need to see others clearly from his perspective. This takes time and it takes putting aside a hurried approach to hearing from God. We must learn to be still and listen. There is a cost for this. It will cost us time. It will cost us "productivity" as other things are not being done as we are being still before God. There is a far greater cost for not doing this. We will hurry through life seeing life through a fog. The fog will lift but it might be after we have squandered a good bit, if not all, of our lives. Day by day, and even more often than that we must turn our full attention to God. We must ask him to lift the fog on our perspective. As he does and we begin to see what is important to see we must move resolutely into what God has shown us. With this clarity of sight will we take decisive action? Will we move as he moves and go where he leads? Most often this will not mean to quit jobs, or sell homes but rather to go to others and ask for forgiveness or serve them or simply listen to them. We tend to look for clarity leading to something spectacular, miraculous, and life changing. But what is spectacular, miraculous, and life changing? It is to move towards others in consistent agape love. To love others with "God's kind of love." There is no greater thing to see or do than to see the opportunity to love the people God has placed in your life and to do what love would have you do for and with them. The Bible in a sentence is, "For God so loved the world that he gave his only Son." God loved...God gave. "God is love. Whoever lives in love lives in God, and God in him". (1 John 4:16) Do you want to live in the fullness of God? Love the person God has put in your life today?

Do you want to see where God is moving and join him? Take your eyes off of yourself and see others around you today. It is hard to see what God is doing when our eyes are on ourselves. Lift up your eyes to the Lord. Then he will lift up your eyes to others. Yes you have needs, struggles...important things to be addressed. God will help you there but first you need his perspective. Look to him in faith look to others in love. This is the beginning of 20/20 vision.

Day 5
<u>Read:</u> Gal. 5:6...The only thing that counts is faith expressing itself through love.

<u>Reflect:</u> As another year comes to close and you wake up to a new year what has really changed? A number we arbitrarily assign to "today" has gone from a thirty-one to a one. Likewise a number assigned to the year has increased by one. But what has "actually" changed? Have you changed? How do you measure whether you have? You can measure a year or a day gone by on a calendar. But how do you measure whether you have grown in faith and love? There are ways to see growth but it is hard if not impossible to quantify. The real question is not whether you can measure but whether you need to measure. We measure things in order to see if something is actually happening or not. To see if what we are doing is working. So we get on a scale to see if the number has dropped and therefore our plan for weight loss is effective. But in closing the gap on faith and love we don't really need to measure to know if what we are doing is working. You can measure how many times you prayed or read your Bible. You can keep track of how many times you served others or even how many times you held your tongue and did not speak in anger to others. These are not bad but they also do not measure actual growth in faith and love. They may be effective means to that end but they certainly do not in themselves indicate you are achieving the end. Means are important, they are necessary, and we will not progress without them. Measurement, in terms of closing the gap on faith and love is not so important. If it helps to find ways to track "progress" fine, use them. But you don't confuse your measurements with actual change. Measure in the moment, right now. Is my heart, right now saying, "yes" to the Lord? If not, then repent and return to "yes." If so, rejoice, and live out that "yes." Israel was being trained to trust. The way the Lord did this was not by giving them a map but by leading them day-by-day very directly by a cloud and a pillar of fire. "At the LORD's command the Israelites set out, and at his command they encamped. As long as the cloud stayed over the tabernacle, they remained in camp. When the cloud remained over the tabernacle a long time, the Israelites obeyed the LORD's order and did not set out. Sometimes the cloud was over the tabernacle only a few days; at the LORD's command they would encamp, and then at his command they would set out.

Sometimes the cloud stayed only from evening till morning, and when it lifted in the morning, they set out. Whether by day or by night, whenever the cloud lifted, they set out. Whether the cloud stayed over the tabernacle for two days or a month or a year, the Israelites would remain in camp and not set out; but when it lifted, they would set out."(Numbers 9:18-22) This is how the Lord wants you to measure progress. Are you right now following his lead? Are you living in a state of ready "yes"? If not repent. If so rejoice. Then follow him. Close the gap on faith and love as a life long journey of faith and love.

19919103R00137

Made in the USA
Middletown, DE
08 December 2018